Turns of Thought

Turns of Thought

Teaching Composition as Reflexive Inquiry

Donna Qualley

Boynton/Cook
HEINEMANN
Portsmouth, New Hampshire

Boynton/Cook Publishers, Inc.
A subsidiary of Reed Elsevier Inc.
361 Hanover Street
Portsmouth, NH 03801-3912
Offices and agents throughout the world

The author and publisher wish to thank those who have generously given permission to reprint borrowed material:

A much earlier version of sections of Chapter Five first appeared in Qualley, Donna and Elizabeth Chiseri-Strater. 1994. "Collaboration as Reflexive Dialogue: A Knowing 'Deeper Than Reason.'" *The Journal of Advanced Composition* 14:1 (111–130).

Excerpt from *Transforming Knowledge* by Elizabeth Kamarck Minnich. © 1990 by Elizabeth Kamarck Minnich. Reprinted by permission of Temple University Press.

Library of Congress Cataloging-in-Publication Data
Qualley, Donna
    Turns of thought: teaching composition as reflexive inquiry / Donna Qualley.
        p.   cm.
    Includes bibliographical references and index.
    ISBN 0-86709-418-4
    1. English language—Rhetoric—Study and teaching (Secondary)
    2. English language—Composition and exercises—Study and teaching (Secondary)   3. Reflection (Philosophy)   4. Learning, Psychology of.
    I. Title.
    LB1631.Q83   1997
    808'.042'0712—dc21   97-2906
                                                                       CIP

Editor: *Thomas Newkirk*
Production: *J.B. Tranchemontagne*
Manufacturing: *Louise Richardson*
Cover design: *Mary C. Cronin*

Printed in the United States of America on acid-free paper
00   99   98   97   DA   1   2   3   4   5   6   7   8   9

To
my parents, Helen and John

Contents

Acknowledgments
ix

Introduction
Teaching Composition as Reflexive Inquiry
1

Chapter One
Understanding Reflexivity
8

Chapter Two
Writing and Reflexivity
31

Chapter Three
Reading and Reflexivity
61

Chapter Four
Collaborative Inquiry and Reflexivity
95

Chapter Five
Some Tentatives for a Reflexive Pedagogy
138

References
163

Index
173

Acknowledgments

The means to bring the thoughts in this book to consciousness owes much to the teaching and learning communities that I have been a part of over the last twelve years. Because I want to emphasize the powerful influence the communities themselves have had on my thinking, I have acknowledged individuals who were members of more than one community more than once. I first want to express my thanks to the thirty classes of composition students I have taught and had the privilege of learning from. I am especially grateful to Anna, Avery, Chad, Emily, Kay, Mark, Mindy, Ralph, Rob, Serena, and Susan, whose writing and insights appear in these pages.

I learned to teach composition from and among an extraordinary group of composition scholars, instructors, and writers. This book carries the visible and invisible traces of conversations I have had about writing and the teaching of writing with many people in the English department at the University of New Hampshire, particularly: Bruce Ballanger, Elizabeth Chiseri-Strater, Robert Connors, the late Gary Lindberg, Thomas Newkirk, Donald Murray, Patricia Sullivan, and Barbara Tindall.

I was part of an interdisciplinary Ph.D. program that encouraged me to take risks and constantly work at the boundaries of my knowledge. When I joined those weekly seminar meetings in Don Graves' home in 1985, I gained entry into an ongoing, passionate dialogue about reading and writing, of which this book represents one more contribution. My understanding of the complex relationships between literacy, inquiry, development, culture, and epistemology has deepened because of the many good teachers and colleagues associated with this program: Elizabeth Chiseri-Strater, Ann Diller, Judith Ferrara, Donald Graves, Jane Hansen, Barbara Houston, Ruth Shagoury Hubbard, Andrea Luna, Peg Murray, Lorri Neilsen, Sharon Nodie Oja, Meg Peterson, Brenda Miller Power, JoAnn Portalupi, Pearl Rosenberg, Tom Romano, Tom Shram, Peg Voss, Cyrene Wells, and Carol Wilcox.

When this book was a dissertation, my advisor, Patricia Sullivan, provided a wonderful model of how to actively listen and quietly lead. Her perfectly timed suggestions always enabled me to see what I needed to do and where I needed to go. The members of my committee, Susan Franzosa, Barbara Houston, Thomas Newkirk, and Paula Salvio, all knew exactly how to push my thinking and support my efforts in different and important ways.

I received good advice, along with laughter and friendship, from women in two very special writing groups that I was part of during my decade in New Hampshire. The first group, Elizabeth Chiseri-Strater, Cinthia Gannett, Sherrie Gradin, Pat Sullivan, and Bonnie Sunstein, continue to offer support from afar. During the dissertation stages of this book, a second group, Ann Diller, Barbara Houston, Pearl Rosenberg, and Paula Salvio, emerged to feed, nurture, and challenge me.

At Western Washington University, where I now teach, conversations about writing, reading, literacy, and learning continue in the small interstices of busy lives. I am grateful for the presence of kindred minds like Nancy Johnson, Bill Smith, and Carmen Werder, whose passion and insight fuel and affirm my thinking; I feel fortunate to be a member of a department that values and demonstrates good teaching. I continue to be informed by my students, especially the graduate teaching instructors with whom I have the privilege of creating a new community of composition teachers.

I also want to acknowledge the support and assistance of several individuals who were critical to the success of this project. I have bounced around ideas about collaborative inquiry projects with Elizabeth Chiseri-Strater and Barbara Tindall for more than a decade; together we have demonstrated their power for learning.

Pat Sullivan, friend and mentor, encouraged me to submit my dissertation for the James Berlin award, and, along with Tom Newkirk and Barbara Houston, took time to write a careful recommendation in support of my inquiry.

However, if Tom Newkirk had not actively sought me out, this work probably would have ended life as a dissertation. More than anyone else, he is responsible for ensuring this project became a book. He has provided important advice, insight, encouragement, and editorial assistance at all stages.

Bill Smith carefully read and responded to the first chapter, giving me important feedback (and energizing me) during the late moments of rewriting, and Bruce Goebel kept me reflexive during the final editing stages.

Last and most important, I want to thank members of my family: Chuck Finnigan, my spouse, offered his love, good humor, patience, and technological support through the many layers of this project;

my companion, my foil, my other, Chuck continues to complicate and deepen my perspectives. Even though my parents, John and Helen Qualley, will probably never read this book, I want to dedicate my effort to them as they have always dedicated theirs to me. Finally, I want to acknowledge the important, complex, and at times disconcerting influence of my Grandmother Qualley. From her I learned how reading and writing are processes we can use to try to make sense of our worlds and ourselves. Twenty-five years after her death, I am still using reading and writing to make sense of her legacy to me.

Introduction

Teaching Composition as Reflexive Inquiry

What inquirers are concerned with is no different than what most people are concerned with—understanding. To call the process inquiry in a more formal sense is only to note that at certain times, when the meanings or reasons of an action or expression are unclear, the attempt to understand is undertaken more intensely, carefully, and self consciously.

—John K. Smith, Interpretive
Inquiry: A Practical and
Moral Activity

Revision is the game a writer plays for life . . . Writing and rewriting gives us an opportunity to confront the major issues in our academic, professional, and private lives. It allows us to revise our lives by understanding the world in which we live and our role in it.

—Donald Murray,
The Craft of Revision

I first encountered Donald Murray through his essay, "The Listening Eye: Reflections on the Writing Conference" (1979). The essay had been reprinted in an Australian educational journal that I happened to stumble across in my high school staff room in 1981. In this essay, Murray muses about what it is like to teach writing by conference. As he sits in his office waiting for the thirty-fifth conference of the day to begin, he worries that he is a fraud, that he will be discovered. And yet, as he reflects on how he came to teach writing by listening to his students talk about their writing, he realizes that his students *are* learning because he is able to show them what they have just discovered themselves. I was immediately drawn to the hesitant sense of wonder this teacher seemed to feel as he reflected on and examined his own teaching. By talking about his experience, Murray invited me to look at mine.

A year later I wrote my first piece on teaching, an article that was distributed to high schools in Victoria and New South Wales. What is significant to me about that piece is how much I seemed to be trying to emulate Murray's ethos, the stance of the tentative teacher-learner, filled with uncertainty about what she is doing, yet energized and (boldly and heroically) proceeding nevertheless: "However doubts begin to threaten my elation . . . I continue because I'm more excited by what I'm discovering than discouraged by how it will fit into the system. . . ." (Even my title sounds Murray-esque to me: "My Students Are Teaching Me to Be a Teacher of Writing: The Voice of a High School Teacher!") Murray's essay had given me permission to examine and share what I was noticing in my own classroom—however partial, approximate, and particular my observations were.

Although I have embraced many of Murray's specific ideas on writing and the teaching of writing over the years, the most valuable and convincing aspect of Murray's work for me has always been his example of self-initiated, ongoing inquiry into his own writing process and teaching. His habit of ruminating on what he is doing and his willingness to reexamine his thinking in light of new information gained from his many encounters with others—writers, teachers, students, and his "other self"—have provided me with a valuable model of teaching and learning. Over the years, Murray has shown me the importance of the provisional, the tentative, or what I have come to think of as the learner's stance, a stance that names itself in the here and now, that can explain how it came to be, but remains open to the possibility of further complication and change. Murray claims that he has had "no need for consistency." He has certainly never pretended to adhere to a single formulation—his own or other's—of how writing works, and yet, he has been consistent. His consistency comes in his willingness to admit the possibility of (and to actively seek) better, clearer ways to understand and to teach writing. What I have learned from Donald Murray is a habit of mind that translates into a way of being in the world.

When we teach composition to students or teachers we teach more than a body of knowledge or set of technical skills. According to James Berlin, when we teach writing we are also "tacitly teaching a version of reality . . . We are teaching a way of experiencing the world, a way of ordering and making sense of it" (1982, 766, 776). My intention, in the following pages, is not to argue for my particular version of reality, but rather to model it and reveal how I came to construct it, to gradually render a more complex understanding of the nature, practice, and value of *reflexive inquiry* for learning. By reflexive, I mean the act of turning back to discover, examine, and critique one's claims and assumptions in response to an encounter with another idea, text, person, or culture. By inquiry, I mean "the sustained work" of coming to understand "through a systematic, self-critical process of discovery" (Phelps 1991, 877).

I teach both writing and reading as methods for reflexive inquiry by teaching what I call the essayistic stance, a way of thinking about ideas that is dialogic and reflexive. Along with a number of scholars writing about the essay, I believe that what distinguishes the essay as a genre is not the form in which it appears on the page, but rather, the stance or approach the writer/reader adopts toward his or her subject and/or audience. It is this stance that I try to teach in my composition courses.

Traditionally, the focus in most composition courses has been on teaching students how to link already formulated ideas effectively and *correctly* through reading and writing. Indeed, much of the university community, most of the public, and so many of my students see writing and reading as *only* an application of technical know-how and skill. Listen to Ann, a student in my honors class of first year composition, as she reveals how to construct a five paragraph essay:

> I had the format down . . . as if it were a mathematical equation: I'd insert the data and out came the results. When I plugged my information into the form (introduction concluding in a thesis sentence, body paragraphs—each with a topic sentence, examples and explanation—a clincher, and a conclusion) a great essay was produced (Qualley 1993, 104).

Technical knowledge entails knowing how to apply a rule, code, or formula to a problem. When a task is unfamiliar or complex, it may also require making some variation of procedure (reflection-in-action and reflection-on-action as Donald Schon's work with skilled practitioners suggests (Schön 1983). Obviously then, the more knowledge and experience one acquires, the more one's technical expertise should develop. And so, much schooling is organized around the assumption that if we simply provide students with knowledge and an opportunity to practice using it, it will be enough. But I don't think it is. Not today. Not for the kind of boundary-shifting world in which we find ourselves living.

I don't think composition studies can limit its practice simply to teaching methods of composing, of putting preformulated ideas together in acceptable or standard forms, without also teaching students how to examine the implications of their compositions. The explanations writers and readers construct to make sense of their subjects, and the genres they use to connect their ideas together matter. Ideas and methods have consequences. On intellectual, practical, and ethical grounds, the reflexive practice of essayistic writing and essayistic reading offers a desirable method for enacting composition's dual responsibility. Robert Atwan recently noted in an interview in *Poets and Writers Magazine*, that "what essays give you is a mind at work. If you don't feel the presence of a mind at work, then you're just getting prefabricated assertions" (Hirsch 1995, 37). As a teacher, I don't want students to simply deliver "prefabricated assertions" in neat, linear, rhetorical arrangements on the page. When students engage with texts—their own and others—I want them to become critically aware of the presence of their own minds at work.

Here is part of another student's reflective course commentary that offers a glimpse of a mind engaged in the process of understanding her world. To frame her semester's work, Jean draws on a recent collaborative research experience in which she and another student attempted to come to grips with the case of Hedda Nussbaum, an abused woman accused of child neglect. She writes:

> I was continually reshaping my ideas and trying to see Hedda's situation from a new perspective. I have truly learned that I need time to combine my feelings, opinions and past experiences with the facts to come to some type of conclusion. This thinking and rethinking process, which I never clearly understood before this class, has carried over into my personal and social life. Now when I have a disagreement with someone, I find myself holding off on making a decision or starting a fight or debate. I would rather go to my room and think. I try to see the situation from the other person's point of view, see where the other person is coming from in order to understand his or her reactions and reasoning . . . Understanding how I think is important because it helps me to better understand myself and why I feel the way I do about certain subjects and how my past experiences play an enormous role in shaping my personal thoughts.

This is what Jean teaches me: Jean is learning to compose an understanding. Understanding complex situations takes time. Not only does it take time for Jean to grasp a "new perspective," that is, the "reactions and reasoning" of an other, it takes time for her to discover her own thoughts. To arrive at this understanding, Jean connects her subjectivity, her "feelings, opinions and past experiences," to the objective "facts" at hand. This process is recursive; it involves "continually reshaping," "thinking," and "rethinking." Jean has let me know that the kind of learning she has experienced in her composition course has repercussions for her life beyond the immediate classroom. What has transferred is not a form of composition, but rather composing in its largest sense: a way of making sense of, connecting, and responding to situations, texts, and ideas that is open, provisional, and dialogic. Jean is not engaged in a finite dialogue designed to produce consensus and agreement, but rather in an ongoing, reflexive, and ethical dialogue of inquiry that serves to continually illuminate and enlarge her understanding of others and herself.

In a culture increasingly fractured and polarized by competing discourses, we need a method that will allow us to continually reflect on our own positions in light of our ongoing transactions with others. Reflexivity involves a commitment to both attending to what we believe and examining how we came to hold those beliefs *while we are engaged in trying to make sense of an other*. As such, reflexive inquiry may offer one of the most powerful means we have to understand and bridge, without effacing, the differences that too often divide us. Paul Connolly suggested years ago that "a course in essay writing is more importantly a course in living . . . In the process of composition, it is men and women who grow composed" (1981, 4). Indeed, when the process of composition includes the habit of reflexive inquiry, then we begin to see more clearly how writing and reading the word, the world, and the self are always in continual dialectical interplay.

In the following pages, I have also tried to show how my understanding of writing and reading as methods for reflexive inquiry has developed and continues to evolve. Like Jean, I am a learner who is used to monitoring her own understanding. Like Murray, I am a teacher whose understanding of epistemological matters is tempered by my experiences in the classroom. It's hard for me to think about knowledge without also thinking about the means for learning and acquiring it. When I suggest that writing and reading can be used as vehicles for reflexive inquiry, and that reflexive inquiry can deepen and complicate students' understanding of their subject and themselves, I do so always with a specific pedagogical context in mind.

Ideally, I assume students are writing on topics about which they have some knowledge and interest (or topics that they have been allowed to gain knowledge and interest), but not so much expertise that they have no inclination to inquire further. I assume students have time to explore their subjects, to talk about their ideas with others, to write multiple drafts, to read, change their minds, revise, or start over without fear of failure or penalty. I assume that teachers are actively engaged in these processes as well by introducing other voices and perspectives in the form of readings or through conferences and class discussion so that students will learn to view their thoughts and beliefs from these other positions. I assume the composition course offers an ongoing opportunity for students to revisit and rework their earlier papers from their current positions of knowledge and understanding. By the same token, when I claim that reading texts openly, tentatively, dialogically, and reflexively can deepen students' understanding, I mean it to be understood that this assumption holds true only *if students are shown how to read this way.* And here, I mean true in a pedagogical sense. Truth, like understanding, like the processes of reading and writing themselves, is always context specific and always acquired by degree. So, yes, essayistic reading and writing can complicate students' understandings—more or less. And the composition course can provide an excellent site for learning how to use reading and writing to engage in this kind of intellectual and ethical inquiry—more or less. The rest of this book describes and demonstrates this method for teaching and learning in which both teachers and students continually attempt to move beyond the bounds of their current understanding by making repeated, dialogic excursions into the realm of the other, and then spiraling back once again to confront their own provisional insights.

Like both Jean and Murray, I haven't arrived at my current understanding of reflexivity quickly or directly. It is only when I turn back and become reflexive myself that I come to realize the extent to which my ideas continue to be made and remade over time. In the next chapter, I offer a fuller sense of what reflexivity is by engaging in my own reflexive inquiry. This essayistic journey through specific moments in my intellectual and lived history demonstrates how understanding is gradually shaped and complicated though many dialogic encounters with others. I invite readers to experience a similar process as they read, and to watch their sense of my subject build and gradually deepen, hopefully gaining both clarity and complexity.

In subsequent chapters I focus on individual students' efforts to engage in a similar process of inquiry between self and other in their writing and reading. In Chapter Two, I begin with a brief discussion of the relationship between writing, thinking, and learning, and then introduce my notion of the essayistic stance. I describe and illustrate the features of essayistic writing by examining the papers of composition students. I continue developing an understanding of the essayistic stance in Chapter Three by focusing more specifically on reading and reflexivity. After illustrating and examining my students' efforts to engage reflexively with different texts, their own and others, I turn back to reconsider my own attempts to read these student texts fairly and openly. In Chapter Four, I further complicate and clarify the relationship between reflexivity, dialogue, and learning by presenting a detailed reading of the dynamics between three students involved in a long-term collaborative inquiry project. Chapter Five examines some of the practical, epistemological, and ethical features of a reflexive pedagogy. I conclude by once again turning back to examine my own assumptions and readings of my students' work.

Chapter One

Understanding Reflexivity

I am going to do what I can to show you how I arrived at this opinion . . . I am going to develop in your presence as fully and freely as I can the train of thought that led me to think this . . . At any rate when a subject is highly controversial . . . one cannot hope to tell the truth. One can only show how one came to hold whatever opinion one does hold. One can only give one's audience the chance of drawing their own conclusions as they observe the limitations, the prejudices, the idiosyncrasies of the speaker. . . .
—Virginia Woolf,
A Room of One's Own

At the age of 22, I went to Australia to teach high school for fifteen months; I stayed nine years. I packed my suitcase with my suburban, midwestern values (tempered by a 1960's philosophy), and headed to the Land Down Under with a state university certified, guaranteed-to-work-anywhere-in-the-world, objective theory of education. Every new teacher faces a bit of a culture shock when she enters her first classroom, but nothing prepared me (not even the *National Geographics* I had so carefully studied) for living or teaching in the small town of Moe, Victoria. I realized that if I wanted to help my students become better readers, writers, and thinkers, I would need to understand their everyday culture, history, lives, and values. I didn't realize how learning more about them would also mean learning more about me.

I had lived in Australia for five months, when one day I drove to the lumber yard in Moe to purchase some molding and kitchen faucets. It was just after New Years. When I arrived, I found the place closed for the rest of the month. I then drove to the hardware store, which had plumbing supplies, but not the correct ones. The sales clerk said that he could order the taps, but they would not arrive until the first of February, since most of their suppliers were closed between Christmas and the end of January. I was stunned. I couldn't understand why these businesses didn't stagger their employees' vacations over the year. Didn't they realize that if they kept their businesses open, the company would make more money?

The sales person seemed to read my thoughts. He looked at me and shrugged. "This isn't America, mate," he said, "we're not all bloody capitalists here." But I wasn't a capitalist, was I? Surely it was just good business to want to make as much money as possible.

At first I thought these practices were part of the laid-back, "no worries mate she'll be right" attitude that seemed to dominate Australian work philosophy. Even the high school had a twenty-minute recess every morning and an hour break for lunch. During these breaks, while the rest of the staff chatted and drank tea in the social room, I often took the opportunity to grade a few more papers or to organize myself for my next class. I learned later that my fellow teachers thought I was being rude or showing off. "Kissing up" they called this behavior. I called my behavior "work hard and you'll succeed." As a new teacher, I couldn't keep up with everything I thought I needed to do. But what seemed to me to be a normal (and noble) way to compensate for my lack of experience was considered aberrant behavior by my Australian colleagues. It had never occurred to me that the work ethic that was so much a part of my own country was not a universally ingrained truth. Nor had it occurred to me how much I actually subscribed to it. But Australia had been (un)settled by convicts, not Puritans. Australians did not see work as a direct route to goodness.

The sociologist Alfred Schutz's (1971) concept of "the stranger" is helpful in explaining my revelation about capitalism. Schutz suggests that the person trying to enter a new social environment tends to interpret the new environment with the automatic but unconscious "scheme of reference" of his or her home culture. But he or she soon finds out that this ready-made approach is inadequate. Like most travelers, I had entered a new culture wearing the automatic but unconscious lenses provided by my home country. But my viewing of Australian work practices through my middle-class, American frames led to a situation that didn't make sense: Why wouldn't Australians want to make money?

My first response, to simply conclude that Australians had poor business practices, didn't help me understand them any better.

According to Schutz, "the discovery that things in his new sur-
roundings look quite different from what he expected them to be at
home is frequently the first shock to the stranger's confidence in the
validity of his habitual 'thinking as usual'" (35). If I really wanted
to *understand* Australian culture, and not simply judge it according
to my American biases, I would have to call up and make the im-
plicit and unconscious assumptions I had acquired in my home
country explicit. I would have to become *reflexive,* although I didn't
know this at the time.

I first encountered the notion of reflexive thinking and the concept of the stranger ten years ago while reading Douglas Barnes'
book, *From Communication to Curriculum* (1975). Barnes asks if
engaging in "the stranger" experience might be connected to the
development of "hypothetical and reflexive forms of thinking," and
if protecting students from having the stranger experience "might
delay their movement toward reflexive thinking" (103–104). Although I wasn't sure exactly what Barnes meant by reflexive thinking—I didn't know if it was another term for Piaget's formal
operations or simply the British spelling of reflective—I was immediately attracted to the metaphor of the stranger experience. At that
time, I was concerned about my composition students' reluctance to
interrupt the flow of their reading by thinking and writing about
what they were reading. In a one-page response paper to Barnes'
book that I wrote in 1987, I said:

> The stranger metaphor works for me. It explains that disconcert-
> ing feeling of being "between," the feeling perhaps first experi-
> enced in adolescence when supposedly formal operations develop
> . . . By choosing not to reinterpret old knowledge in light of new
> experience, people avoid encountering the "other voices" that
> might interrupt the (limited) homogenous flow of their lives. They
> can remain in a sea of shallow provincialism or worse, evangeli-
> cal born-againism. Does this mean that people who find them-
> selves constantly "between" are more reflexive thinkers? Is it okay,
> though, if we never get out of between?

The "between" is a term I lifted from a science fiction series by
Anne McCaffrey. Between is a transitional space of nothingness and
sensory deprivation "between here and there" (1978, 743). In McCaffrey's books, dragons have the ability to take their human riders to
other places and times by going "between." As difficult and taxing as
going between is for human beings, it is necessary for connecting life
in the dragon riders' world. I seized the term to describe those moments when my students' sense of the subjects they were writing
about became so murky, tangled, or confused they temporarily lost

their bearings. My students didn't like these moments of uncertainty when they became strangers to themselves and their own purposes and intentions, and would often try to avoid them. I, on the other hand, always had the opposite problem; I seemed to dwell in the between. When I voiced these last two questions in my response to Barnes, I was thinking about my own difficulties in coming to closure. I wondered if this behavior was simply a personal quirk or if my resistance to closure might have some redeeming intellectual value.

My sense of the between has been deepened by Victor Turner's rich notion of liminality. Although the liminal, or threshold, stages of rituals and rites of passage have been likened to "a no-man's-land betwixt and *between*" (my emphasis; Turner 1986, 41), Turner describes liminality as "the subjunctive mood of culture, a mood of maybe, might be, as if, hypothesis, fantasy, conjecture, desire . . . " (42). Rather than a cold space of nothingness and sensory deprivation, he reveals liminality to be a rich storehouse of possibility, a generative space of "fructile chaos" (42). Barbara Myerhoff and Deena Metzger, drawing on Turner's work, note that "liminality is the great moment of teachability . . . an opportunity is provided not only for psychic and emotional reorganization but for theoretical and philosophical enlightenment as well" (1980, 106). The liminal space of between invites reflexive thinking.

Reflexivity, Reflection, and Metacognition

Reflexivity is not simply the British spelling for reflection. As I understand it now, reflexivity is a response triggered by a dialectical engagement with the other—an other idea, theory, person, culture, text, or even an other part of one's self, e.g., a past life. By dialectical, I mean an engagement that is ongoing and recursive as opposed to a single, momentary encounter. In the process of trying to understand an other, our own beliefs and assumptions are disclosed, and these assumptions, themselves, can become objects of examination and critique.

Reflexivity is not the same thing as reflection, although they are often part of the same recursive and hermeneutical process. When we reflect, we fix our thoughts on a subject; we carefully consider it, meditate upon it. Self-reflection assumes that individuals can access the contents of their own mind *independently of others*. Reflexivity, on the other hand, does not originate in the self but always occurs in response to a person's critical engagement with an "other." Unlike reflection, which is a unidirectional thought process, reflexivity is a bidirectional, contrastive response. The encounter with an other results in new information or perspectives which we must hold up to our current conception of things. The juxtaposition of two different representations often reveals their ill fit. In order to make sense, we are compelled to identify and examine our own underlying assumptions. Once we actually articulate these tacit beliefs, they themselves become open to reflection, critique, and perhaps, transformation. My conclusion that Australian business practices were different (and, in my opinion, not as sensible) as American business practices was a simple reflection: I simply accessed my current understanding of the work ethic and applied it to the Australian situation without identifying or examining the constructs or assumptions that had given rise to these beliefs. It was only when my engagement with the other compelled me to examine my own assumptions about the work ethic that I became reflexive. When the salesperson identified me as an American, and therefore, capitalist, I became conscious of the implication of my words.

Although similar, reflexivity is not exactly the same as metacognition. Metacognition, the conscious monitoring of one's cognitive activities, is a term that came into use in the 1970s when a more exact (i.e., scientifically measurable) term was sought to describe the inner workings of the mind, one that would replace the more nebulous concept of introspection. Karen Kitchner (1983) argues that metacognition, as it is conceived by most psychologists, is fine for dealing with simple, routine situations, but it is insufficient for describing the complex processes adults use to deal with problems involving conflicting assumptions and beliefs and that require them to negotiate multiple solutions and realities. She notes that problems that don't come with already known solutions require that people draw on their "epistemic beliefs" to deal with them. Kitchner's work on the development of "reflective judgement" provided me with my first indication of a relationship between an individual's philosophy of knowledge, learning, and reflexivity.

It would seem that an individual's epistemic assumptions would most certainly be involved when understanding requires more than the addition of new information, when understanding might necessitate a rethinking of one's core constructs. Reading theorist Frank Smith (1978), helped me understand why. He makes a distinction between the processes of learning and comprehension. For Smith, learning involves a modification of what's currently in our head as a result of our encounters in the world. At its simplest level of modification, learning might mean adding to what we already know. But learning can also involve deepening, complicating, challenging, or transforming what we currently understand. For the latter two forms of learning to occur, I believe learners must first become reflexive and undergo a process of *unlearning*, the gradual revision of previous understandings. Comprehension, on the other hand, simply means the ability to connect or relate what's already in our head to what we encounter in the world. Now, if what's in our head is sufficient to understand what we find out there, no modification is necessary and no learning takes place. So, in my example from Australia, the ideas in my head were not sufficient for helping me to make sense of Australian business practices. The only way I could comprehend this situation was to conclude that Australians were lazy or simply business remedials; either conclusion made learning according to Smith's definition unlikely. Smith's theory also helps explain one of the most prevalent responses my students make to the texts they read (both their peers' and other's): "You can relate to it." I now see this response as a comment on the comprehensibility of the text or situation. When students make this comment, they seem to be suggesting that they can already relate the theory in their heads to what they see in the text/world. Thus, no further effort and no learning is required. If our encounters with differing others do not also compel us to examine our own prior theories and assumptions, our interpretations risk simply being self-confirming. In other words, we will only comprehend what we already know. And if we only understand what we already know, how will we ever learn anything new?

I believe the most educative experiences—in Dewey's sense, the ones that deepen or transform thinking and lead to learning and further inquiry—are reflexive as well as reflective. The line between these processes is shaky, however, especially when the "other" is an individual's "other self" or past life. For example, when Donald Murray talks about the conversation between the writer and the writer's "other self" is he being reflective or reflexive? I might tentatively suggest that reflection is adequate for monitoring our conscious beliefs, but that reflexivity is needed to call up our unconscious, epistemic beliefs.

In the introduction to *A Crack in the Mirror* (Ruby 1982), Barbara Myerhoff and Jay Ruby argue that a critical awareness of one's reflections is part of the condition for true reflexivity. Reflection refers to "a kind of thinking about ourselves, showing ourselves to ourselves, but without the requirement of explicit awareness of the implications of our display. Without the acute understanding, the detachment from the process in which one is engaged, reflexivity does not occur" (3). Anthropologist Barbara Babcock (1980) uses Narcissus in Greek mythology, who falls in love with his own reflection, to describe the difference between reflection and reflexivity:

> Narcissus's tragedy then is that he is not narcissistic enough, or rather he does not reflect long enough to effect a transformation. He is reflective, but he is not reflexive—that is he is conscious of himself as an other, but he is not conscious of being self-conscious of himself as an other, and hence, not able to detach himself from, understand, survive or even laugh at this initial experience of alienation (2).

Reflexivity complicates our understanding and efforts to know by making us self-conscious, cognizant of our role in the production of knowledge. I might suggest that it is precisely reflexivity's capacity for altered consciousness that can lull us into believing that "ignorance is bliss." If we could simply know without ramification to our past and present beliefs or to our present or future actions, if we were not implicated in any way, gaining knowledge would indeed be a safe, neutral, straightforward activity. But of course it is not. Although reflexive awareness is not a sufficient condition for emancipation or action, according to philosopher Elizabeth Minnich, it is, perhaps, a necessary condition:

> [T]hinking reflexively is one of the grounds of human freedom, in part because it reveals to us that we are both subject and object of our own knowing, of our culture, of our world. We are not just products, objects of our world, nor are we just subjects existing in a void. We are free subjects whose freedom is conditioned—not determined—by a world not of our making but in many ways open to the effects of our actions (1990, 189).

The Process of Reflexivity and Reflexivity of Process

For as long as I can remember, I have been more afraid of becoming set in my ways or being stuck in one place (physically or mentally) than I have been of drifting, of never finding a home. The idea that I couldn't move, change, grow, or seek new ground if I wanted to, if I needed to, was unthinkable to me. I have always seen this feeling as the result of the odd coupling between the philosophy I was born into: the work ethic and the American Dream, and the philosophy I came of age in—a 1960's suspicion of commitment and distrust of the status quo. Both my Puritan self and my 1960's self feared becoming too comfortable or complacent because such a state would either make me lazy or make me set in my ways. And both my Puritan self and my 1960's self each naively believed it had the freedom and the power to avoid, stave off, and rise above its own conditioning.

I grew up in a family that accepted (by which I mean did not think to question) rules and authority. If critical thinking meant wrestling with difficult questions, my parents might tackle the occasional quiz in *Reader's Digest*, but for them, all the hard questions had been pinned down; the answers were very clear.[1] There were no public spaces in my house for children to openly speak their minds, to disagree, or contend. And so I moved my speaking life inside, first in books, and later in letters and journals.

My Grandmother Qualley was instrumental in fostering my independence and showing me the way to my interior self through reading and writing. While I was growing up, she came to stay with us for a few months each year. I greeted these visits with mixed feelings: I looked forward to fresh-baked bread, homemade tapioca pudding, and our weekly trips to the library; at the same time, I knew it meant tiptoeing on cat feet, lest my actions meet her oppressive gaze—or worse, call up a rapid deluge of criticism from her sharp tongue: "Take those shoes off!" or "Stop that noise!" Even our "good time racket" made her crotchety. Grandmother Qualley was not a children's grandma. She attributed her sore eyes, arthritis, and high blood pressure to the nervous tension she felt when she was around us children for too long a time. But for children who expressed a grown-up interest about the secrets contained in books, she had a great deal of time.

I can remember when she brought home *Little House on the Prairie* by Laura Ingalls Wilder from the local library for me to read. Perhaps she sensed in me a kindred spirit, one easily drawn to frontier fiction about rugged individualism. She greatly admired the pioneer women for their strength and courage. (She loved reading Grandpa Smith's diary from the 1890s.) In her own diary, she wrote, "I always have a feeling of nostalgia for a life I never knew, but always seemed so desirable." Life seemed so simple then, even if it was hard. But Grandma Qualley believed a hard life made for strong people. "It's a great life," she would say, "if you don't weaken." And as she would not tolerate softness in herself, she would not accept it in anyone else: independence and self-reliance—this was the true meaning of America. "Let those laugh who wish!" she arrogantly proclaimed, "I belong to those who wrested this nation from the wilderness and I am proud of it!"

My Grandmother traced her lineage to the Mayflower—and beyond. To William the Conqueror, she told us: "I want my children to be proud of their blood as I am. My blood is pure New England—over 300 years of it." She kept meticulous records, recording dates and genealogies, worrying that no one else would keep up the family archives when she was gone. She was a Daughter of the American

Revolution, a DAR in good standing. (She had the papers to prove it, papers she would set aside for me in the hope I would follow her.) She was very smart, my mother told me. But Grandma's intelligence revealed her exasperation with things she couldn't control or appropriate. More often than not, she just sounded mean and ornery to me.

When my Grandmother's moods dipped and chafed bottom, she sat, an open book in her lap, with empty eyes in a state that my father as a boy had described as "the stares." "I am the last of my own folks," she would say. "I'm not interesting to anyone but myself. . . ." She visited the doctor hoping for some magical elixir (it was the fifties). Instead, she would come home with an assortment of green pills, atropine from belladonna, and whatever else the doctor thought might calm her. These elixirs worked for a while; then she would return for more. "The children make me so nervous," she would tell the doctor. Finally he advised her to stop taking things so personally. But she would take his words to heart and become more miserable than ever, saying "I am just an ungrateful old lady. I should pull myself up by my bootstraps."

The 90th Psalm was my Grandmother Qualley's favorite: "So teach us to number our days that we may get a heart of wisdom." I am struck by the phrase "heart of wisdom." Perhaps my Grandmother wanted to unite head and heart, but didn't know how. Instead, the mind berated the heart for feeling as it did: "Sometimes I think too much about how I feel . . . my task for the time I have left is to be as little 'old-age difficult' as possible . . . but it is impossible for me to hold my tongue . . . then I spend days regretting it." Grandma read numerous psychology books in an effort to understand her moods. "What makes folks go down and wallow in the bottom once and about so often?" she wondered. She always went for the authority of books, the salve of the self-reliant.

To me, Grandma was a critic; in her earlier life she might have been a critical thinker; that is, before her self-imposed rigor turned into dogma and narcissism. She had a marvelous capacity for detecting imperfection, error, and heresy in everything and everyone, including (and especially) herself. She could always see a way to "improve" our lives. And yet, Grandma herself could not tolerate change: "I have moved so much all my life—too much. I am like a cat contented in my own garret . . . even the scratches on the wall mean something because you know how they got there . . . Oh for a sense of security . . . to just know you aren't facing change, eternal change all the time." And if she wasn't open to change, she couldn't learn from others. Grandma never traveled in another country (literally or figuratively), and she never stopped to consider the implications of her thoughts and actions. Grandma was introspective and self-reflective, but not reflexive. Reflection does not require the presence of an other. One can reflect all by oneself.

As I recollect my Grandmother Qualley, I think it is reflexivity that separates the critical thinker from the critic, and distinguishes the skeptic from the cynic. Critics and cynics do not see the need to identify or examine the assumptions that form the basis of their critique. They are simply the agents of that critique, never the subjects. The genuine critical thinker is reflexive, self-critical as well as critical, something my grandmother was not.

After I shared an early draft of this chapter with students in a graduate seminar (one that I was not teaching), Leah, a first year master's student, asked why I had included the section about my grandmother. I explained that I had hoped that the story of my grandmother would reveal the kind of critical intelligence that may be reflective and introspective, but is so self-absorbed that it lacks the ethical component, the attention to the other, that would make it reflexive. Leah pointed to where my grandmother had written, "I belong to those who wrested the nation from the wilderness and I am proud of it," and said,

"But your grandmother was a colonizer!"

Leah was a passionate and knowledgable student of postcolonial literature. However, not being immersed in that particular discourse, colonizer was not a term I would have naturally used myself. Writing more essayistically than academically, I thought I had implicitly revealed my grandmother's arrogance and appropriative nature. Apparently not. Leah felt that I should have specifically named my grandmother's behavior.

I began to wonder. Had I been so focused on teasing out the differences between critics and critical thinkers and reflection and reflexivity that I overlooked or ignored the colonial attitudes my grandmother exhibited?

My grandmother's racism and classicism are easily detected with today's vigilant divining rods. But I find myself still hesitant to call her colonizer. The word itself is saturated with such significance today that it too easily eclipses her complexity and my conflicting emotions about her. I never once saw Grandma pause to consider the implications of her words or actions toward another (although her diaries suggest that she might have regretted her tongue when it lashed out to those close to her). The way she talked about "wresting the country" from the Native Americans was the way she talked (down) to and about everyone as far as I could tell. My mother always felt that Grandmother thought she (my mother) wasn't smart enough and her Kentucky roots weren't sophisticated enough for my father. As a child, I referred to her as my "mean grandma" to distinguish her from my other grandmother. Nonetheless, I was fascinated by and drawn to her literacy. She was the only member of my family who read. She had a mind filled with historical bric-a-brac—a fascinating jumble of places and dates: Gettysburg, 1066, Little Big Horn; Grandpa Smith was born in 1818, the same year as Queen Victoria. And like a yard sale junkie, I scavenged for odd bits and interesting stuff that I had no immediate use for, but nevertheless felt compelled to collect. My grandmother was quick with labels and judgments, and I don't want to consciously adopt her methods here. But now when I listen to the sound of my voice, I sometimes hear my grandma's self-righteous tones, a didactic and accusatory mode of discourse issuing from my lips, and I wonder exactly what it is I have collected from her.

I became a teacher, or the reason I gave for becoming a teacher, was because I believed the schools stunted students' growth by not encouraging them to search for their true potential. In a paper written for one of my first education courses in 1971, I worried about the loss of individuality in education. Interestingly, my suggestions then were not all that different than what they are now: I argued that teachers should "develop a tolerance for ambiguity and irresolution," that they "not force students to make a decision too quickly," and that "new and applicable ideas must not be condemned too soon." No wonder I would find the tentatives of process theories and pedagogies so attractive a decade later.

What I thought were my isolated and unique concerns, ideas that showed I had escaped the conservative influence of my own education and culture, were probably evidence to the contrary. As an undergraduate student in the early 1970s, I was being shaped by the political and ideological currents of the time. In his recent book, *Fragments of Rationality*, Lester Faigley notes that a number of popular critiques of American education emerged during the fifties and sixties (spurred on by the fear of communism) that pointed to growing concerns that our schools were "based on conformity and order rather than individualism and creativity" (1992, 56). My concerns about education and schooling now seem to be simply the concrete manifestation of this larger cultural suspicion.

In a paper I wrote in 1974 for an undergraduate humanistic psychology class, I suggested that all people needed to make their dreams and goals become "a reality" was "a desire to work and a courage and willingness to experiment." I wrote that an individual's ability to "change was hampered by a lack of awareness, lack of desire, and just plain old apathy and reluctance to change, especially if people are comfortable in their present conditions or if they fear they are losing a sentimental tradition." At any rate, I naively assumed that individuals could always change themselves and their worlds. Faigley suggests that my belief that I was capable of knowing and critiquing my world—and changing it—reflects the:

> postmodern, free individual of consumer capitalism: one who can change identities at will because identities are acquired by what one consumes. The conception of the free individual is at the foundation of dominant American ideology because it promises to empower individuals through their choice of consumer goods and thus justifies the existing social order. Because the individual is said to be free to choose her or his 'lifestyle,' politics, religion, and occupation, as well as which brand of soap to use, the poor are alleged to choose to be poor (16–17).

I wrote that "happiness is a state of mind that we control. We can decide to make ourselves miserable and let things bother us or we can decide to be happy and perceive ourselves as being so." In other words, we can just say no to misery or yes to happiness—it has nothing to do with the situation that precipitates our reactions. Work hard, have a positive attitude, and you'll succeed. At twenty-one, a year before I went to Australia, I see that I had absorbed a lot of my grandmother's "I'll do it myself, others be damned" notion of agency.

I'd like to be able to say that I have rid myself of all my bourgeois and ready-made notions in the last twenty years. But that would not be true, possible, or even desirable. I'm still not sure how one can be a teacher and not believe that in spite of everything, individuals do have some power to pull themselves up by their bootstraps and change. Otherwise, why bother with education? Instead, what I'm trying to show here is how my early thinking has contributed to and been reinvented in my present ideas.

Process theory legitimated the beliefs I already had. When I returned to graduate school in 1984, I entered the field of composition studies swept along behind "The Winds of Change: Thomas Kuhn and the Revolution in the Teaching of Writing," Maxine Hairston's influential 1982 essay, which proclaimed that a paradigm shift from product to process had occurred in the teaching and researching of writing. I didn't need too much convincing. Process theory confirmed my negative assumptions about the fixed, the static, and the inevitable, and sanctioned a way of being in the world that I was already being. There was nothing radical in my embracing of process. In a response paper I wrote to John Dewey's *Experience and Education* in 1987, I noted that for most systems to operate efficiently, harmony and balance were essential, but not so for education. I went so far as to suggest that education only occurs when the learner is slightly out of sync and off-center:

> [C]ontinual modulation . . . allows for insight, for learning to occur . . . Just as the learner reaches for an answer that will bring her near center, another question must be ready to move her away from this stasis . . . Knock the individual too far from center and she is left flailing in confusion. Keep her too close to center, she stagnates and education stops. Plato spoke of the soul being constantly in motion. Vygotsky noted the speed, velocity, and optimal distance from center—the proximal zone—in which this movement takes place. Dewey sees the shape and continuity of motion: the "active quest" to learn is a continuous spiral . . . Process is another word for movement.

Ironically, my belief in the necessity of ongoing inquiry and movement in itself might appear dangerously constant from what I have implied thus far. However, this conviction has undergone and (as I hope the following pages will demonstrate) continues to undergo reflexive scrutiny. I see that I eventually qualified this understanding of the importance of continual process and change with ideas from the developmental psychologist, Robert Kegan, when, five years later, I wrote:

> Kegan helps me to see that movement "from center" is not simple, continuous, or linear. His notion of "balances" suggests that individuals must return to center; it's only "stasis" if they return to the *same* center. Our job as teachers may be to either (1) nudge students away from center or (2) help our students who are already "out there" return to different centers.

In *The Evolving Self* (1982), Robert Kegan offers a model that envisions development as a lifelong tension between autonomy and community. Each developmental position represents a temporary balance or resolution, an "evolutionary truce . . . between the yearnings for inclusion and distinctness. Each balance resolves the tension in a different way . . . [I]t is because each of these temporary balances is slightly imbalanced that each *is* temporary" (108). This idea is similar to William James' notion of "flights and perches" and Dewey's belief that inquiry leads to a "consummation" rather than "cessation." Kegan's theory that development is not all process and movement, but also includes periods of rest, helped me begin to re-think my fear of staying put as well as my hesitation for being in perpetual motion; it enabled me to see the importance of living in an idea long enough to be able to understand it. Kegan began to ex-plain why it makes a difference whether you experience a place as a tourist for three weeks or a resident for nine years.

If process theory initially helped to loosen many people from their fixed traditions, postmodern theory seems to have ensured that they will stay adrift. Quoting from David Harvey's *The Condition of Postmodernity* (1989), Lester Faigley writes that "postmodernism swims, even wallows, in the fragmentary and the chaotic currents of change as if that is all there is" (1992, 4). But maybe that is not all there is.

Judith Kegan Gardiner (1993) offers a thorough critique of the "subject-in-process." Just as Robert Kegan's model depicts develop-ment as alternating periods of evolutionary movement with periods of "evolutionary truce," Gardiner writes: "That people change is a fact. But that does not mean they must always be in the process of chang-ing or afraid of any fixation or attachment" (309). She observes that the

> emphasis on process . . . depends on an implied opposition of pro-cess to product in which process is validated as active and chang-ing as opposed to a static and reified commodity . . . and so reinforces the connotation that "process" is inherently progres-sive. This connotation rests on the belief that change is always for the best since the status quo is assumed to be a total oppressive system (305).

Furthermore, Gardiner notes that process doesn't necessarily imply progressive transformation from one state to another, but can mean endless repetition designed to delay progress and avoid substantive change or decisive action: "If the continual overthrow of everything is the only goal, then one doesn't need to figure out what our spe-cific problems are or what institutional transformations might solve them" (313).

So while process theory may have often lacked a critical reflex-ivity, the spiraling turns of postmodernism might be criticized for being hyperreflexive. Reflexivity—the turning back on oneself—in-terrupts the flow of change long enough for us to examine it. By the same token, unceasingly turning back on ourselves just about guar-antees that we won't get anywhere. How could I ensure that a pro-cess of change would be reflexive without being hyperreflexive? In hindsight, I see my solution was to reconceive process as dialecti-cal, as bidirectional, rather than unidirectional.

In a paper I wrote in 1990 called "From Dialogue to Dialectic," I reenvisioned education, not as a linear process that separates individuals from their former selves, but as a dialectical process that allows students to "mediate oppositions" and explore connections between abstract ideas and lived worlds by going *between*. I wrote:

> As teachers, the best thing we can do for our students is accustom them to this flux and flow, and encourage them into the uncertain and beckoning spaces of "between." Through dialogue with themselves and with others, our students can learn to negotiate their way onto firmer ground. And once there, we must ensure that the dialogue continues as all of us, teachers and students, reexamine our positions.

The problem with such a theory is that many students try to arrive without having travelled through this dialectical process first. They attempt to bypass the messiness and uncertainty of between, and like the six blind men of Indostan, remain blind to other perspectives as well as their own positioning:

> It was six blind men of Indostan
> To learning much inclined,
> Who went to see the elephant
> (Though all of them were blind),
> That each by observation
> Might satisfy his mind . . .

In this poem, John Godfrey Saxe explains how the six blind men of Indostan each touch a different part of an elephant's body, the leg, trunk, tail, torso, ear, and tusk, and each, on the basis of his individual observation, reaches a different conclusion. The elephant, it seems, is like a tree, a snake, a rope, a wall, a fan, and a spear. The poem ends with each blind man arguing for his version of the elephant:

> And so these men of Indostan
> Disputed loud and long,
> Each in his own opinion
> Exceedingly stiff and strong,
> Though each was partly in the right,
> And all were in the wrong.

My students often read this poem as confirmation of their relativism that "everyone is entitled to their own opinion" or that "there is no such thing as objective reality." When I first read this poem many years ago, I saw it as a parody of the scientific method. Empiricism was not infallible, and generalizing the whole on the basis of the parts sometimes can lead to humorous distortion and senseless argument.

As a teacher, however, I have come to understand that parts and approximations are usually all we have to construct an understanding or make a judgment about our subject of inquiry. Rarely are we ever positioned to see the elephant in its entirety or complexity during our first, isolated encounter with it, but rarely are we taught to acknowledge the limits of our initial perspectives. Nor are our courses set up to allow students or teachers time to linger, chat, or return later for another look. Our schools are designed for covering the elephant, not uncovering it. The rush to closure abbreviates thinking and curtails further inquiry. And the pressure students sometimes feel to name the elephant (so they can quickly move on to the next subject) replaces any desire for learning about it. My students, like these learned blind men "each in his own opinion exceedingly stiff and strong," are often more focused on persuading others as to the correctness of their conclusions, rather than exploring the tensions in their different perspectives and really understanding the elephant, the subject at hand. And so, this parable now seems to speak of politics and power as much as it does epistemology. This objectivist way of knowing is not only cognitively inadequate, it seems adversarial and ethically bereft as well. As Parker Palmer notes, "Once the objectivist has 'the facts,' no listening is required, no other points of view are needed. The facts are, after all, the facts. All that remains is to bring others into conformity with objective 'truth'" (1983, 68).

A few years ago, when I was trying to formulate a definition of critical thinking, I wrote that "thinking critically involves the ability to step outside of one position, not only for the purpose of entering and understanding and assessing another position, but also for the purpose of seeing the original on a new or fuller way." By this definition, these six blind men of Indostan, like my Grandmother Qualley, are not critical thinkers, and they certainly are not learners for they can not step outside of their own limited perspective. They are not interested in understanding or making sense. But if I may borrow from Elizabeth Minnich, making sense captures a kind of intellectual and ethical relationship between knowers and knowledge that is both open and critical. Minnich writes in the opening chapter of *Transforming Knowledge* (1990),

> I realized that the praise I sought . . . was "This makes sense. Of course. It really is obvious, isn't it." *That* was what I wanted, not to be "right, but to simply be part of a common effort to make sense. Making sense meant that I had found and spoken *with* what people were thinking in a way that made even new thoughts their own. That is the kind of thinking, the kind of relationship—political and moral as well as intellectual—in which I believe (6).

Suppose these blind men had operated under a different set of rules, one that didn't require them to be right but to "be part of a common effort to make sense." What if these blind men had seen their first conclusions as tentative, partial, approximate, and open to further examination? What if they had engaged in dialogue with each other and with themselves? Would they have succeeded in making sense and deepening their understanding of the elephant? Rather than bombarding each other with their findings, what if they had examined their own location and then attempted to explain how they had arrived at their conclusions? Perhaps then their discussion would have been, in philosopher Ann Seller's words, more "epistemologically effective and less politically coercive" (1988, 177). Allowing for multiple subjective (and reflexive) perspectives, rather than precluding the possibility of knowledge, might have pushed the blind men closer to realizing the elephant in all its true wall/snake/spear/rope/fan/tree complexity.

Finally, what if our scientists had done as psychoanalyst and feminist critic Jessica Benjamin (1988) suggests and adopted:

> some of the quality Keats demanded for poetry—negative capability[?] The theoretical equivalent of that ability to face mystery and uncertainty "without any irritable reaching after fact and reason" would be the effort to understand the contradictions of fact and reason without any irritable *reaching after one side at the expense of the other* (my emphasis, 10).

In the next three chapters, I will show how such a pedagogy might work to develop more complex forms of understanding with composition students. But before I turn to a more lengthy and focused examination of my students' work, I want to briefly look at the role subjectivity plays in both understanding (the elephant) as well as our own assumptions. As Parker Palmer notes, "The knower who advances most rapidly toward the heart of truth is one who not only asks 'What is out there?' in each encounter with the world, but one who asks 'What does this encounter reveal about me?' " (1983, 60).

The Importance of Subjectivity

According to Jay Ruby, interest in reflexivity in research is connected to "the restoration of subjectivity as a serious attitude, a basis for gaining knowledge and evaluating it, a ground for making decisions and taking action" (1982, 7). As a teacher, I have always intuitively understood that my subjectivity was important because I've known there could be no such thing as a teacher-proof method. Teachers need to combine their subjective experience with the objective facts at hand to achieve what Louise Phelps (after Aristotle) calls "practical wisdom" (1991). The process of adapting theory to fit the needs of individual students in specific contexts requires judgment. And judgment, of course, requires subjectivity. What is a judgment call, after all, but an acknowledgment that understanding will not come from the objective facts of the situation alone; a human agent is needed to make sense of the facts. Like the ethnographer, the teacher's subjectivity is "an instrument of observation and interpretation" (Holzman 1993, 2).

Students also need to learn to use their subjectivity as an instrument of interpretation. Irene Papoulis (1993) echoes some of my own feelings as a teacher when she writes: "I am dismayed by the infectiousness of the notion that to think well in a discipline one must put aside one's subjective reactions to academic material" (133). Students do need to take their subjectivity into account to "think well in a discipline," if thinking well means constructing one's own thoughtful understanding of the subject matter. But like any instrument of interpretation, our subjectivity is capable of seeing some things but not others. That is why this subjectivity needs to be a reflexive subjectivity.

The following essay illustrates just how a student draws on his subjectivity to deepen his sense of an academic subject as well as his own experience. In this essay, which is both an example and a discussion of how subjectivity and objectivity work together, Chad combines knowledge learned from his major, social philosophy, with the personal circumstances of his own life to form a more complex understanding of what education means.

Chad's Essay: "Head and Heart"

"Head and Heart," Chad's ten page essay, begins with the sentence, "I started attending college so I could get a better job." But he tells us that after he was in school, "I saw that the real reason I was there was to feed a starved intellect, lift a sagging ego, and find my heart." Chad explains that growing up with an abusive father taught him some unique survival strategies:

> When the violence was upon us I would use my intellect to put a buffer between me and it . . . When your father tells you that you are a piece of crap, only not so nicely, you have to say the right things in response so the verbal attack will not escalate into a beating . . . It was safe to live inside my head. Since I defended myself daily, the intensity of thought combined with having to constantly

analyze the situation led to a mind that could handle such inten-
sity and [one that] would often overanalyze . . . My survival came
from a quick response that came from my head.

The emotional bracketing of his own subjectivity that he learned to
do as a child led him to major in philosophy. Chad notes that at first
he sought refuge in safe abstractions because of the abstract way he
had learned to relate to the world growing up.

> As a child, I heard words used in church like love, forgiveness and
> father. In my home the meanings of these were different. At home
> father meant pain. In church father meant love. The only way to
> rectify my perception of the world when the language applied to
> the actions did not correspond to the language and actions of out-
> side sources was through abstractions.

Chad's education, however, provides him with another way to use
his ability to theorize and abstract. "I use education to find and create meaning in my world. To do this, I have to apply the concepts to
my life." Instead of separating him from the circumstances of his
life, he finds that he can now use his thinking to reconnect him to
life—a realization my grandmother probably never made.

Echoing Parker Palmer's belief that "the shape of our knowledge
becomes the shape of our living" (1983, 21), Chad observes that
"how we relate to the world is determined by how we think about
the world." Because he has discovered how the events and circum-
stance of his own life have contributed to the way he thinks and
feels about his world, he begins to see that the ideas in the texts that
he reads are not simply abstractions, but might also represent the
accumulation of meaning from the author's lived experience.

> When I read a text I try to see how the author thinks and feels
> about his or her world. The words the author gives me are alive
> with the accumulation of meaning inherited from other authors
> and his or her contributions to life.

Chad's terms for the dialectical interplay between objectivity
and subjectivity are "head and heart." He doesn't forsake his objectivity. He doesn't replace reason with feeling, or theory with experience; rather he shows how head and heart must work together and
why theory needs to be grounded, lived, felt, experienced. The activities of "writing, talking to another person, rereading, and thinking are ways to clarify my thoughts. They help me to understand my
heart through my head and my head through my heart."

Theory is necessary because it is "a way to uncover or rediscover
our hearts." At the same time, theory can shield Chad from his

heart. As a child of an abusive father, he learned to distance himself from his heart, and he admits, "I've found that when my heart is too heavy with grief or sorrow . . . I use my intellect to hide away, much like I did as a child." The only difference is now he is aware of the effect of his actions on himself and on others:

> [When] I let my head control my actions I . . . usually project my low self-esteem onto others by talking down to them or by shutting them off in conversation. But when I use my head and heart together, I can put myself in their place and empathize with them.

For Chad then, "the separation of head and heart can't be allowed." Objective knowledge (in Chad's words, abstraction, theory, concept, intellectualization) is necessary but insufficient for his understanding and for his (moral and political) being in the world of others. As Palmer notes, "[t]he way we interact with the world in knowing it becomes the way we interact with the world as we live in it. . . . [O]ur epistemology is quietly transformed into our ethic" (1983, 21).

Lorraine Code: Taking Subjectivity into Account

In her book, *What Can She Know* (1991) and her essay, "Taking Subjectivity into Account" (1993), feminist philosopher Lorraine Code argues that "knowledge is, necessarily and inescapably, the product of an intermingling of subjective and objective elements" (1991, 30). Code's assumptions about knowledge not only mirror what Chad has discovered in his essay, I believe they also describe the ways many (reading and writing) teachers think about understanding and learning. In this chapter, I have tried to show how my understanding of reflexivity is also a product of an intermingling of subjective and objective elements. I should clarify at the outset, that Code's conception of knowing seems more in keeping with my notion of understanding. For many people, knowing and understanding are interchangeable terms. People talk about specific kinds of knowing and knowers, e.g., women's ways of knowing or teacher knowing. I have opted to describe the product generated by knowers in response to themselves and their worlds as understanding. The process I see is also one of understanding or making sense. When I say that subjectivity is important for making sense, readers need to bear in mind I am making a distinction between knowing and understanding. To *know* Plato's concept of the dialectic may not require subjectivity. I believe that to *understand* what this knowledge means does. To understand or make sense, a knower must be actively engaged in constructing meaning for him or herself. For the most part,

I have tried to not use the term knowing or conflate it with understanding or learning. However, here, in discussing Code's work, I use her terms.

I remember once when I approached my undergraduate physics teacher for help, he said: "Good God girl! The facts are right there in the book." But they were not in my book. I couldn't see them, although my professor, operating under the same paradigm as the six blind men, seemed to think that the facts of physics p were there for any subject-knower s to discern. Traditionally, Code explains, epistemologists have used (objective) knowledge of everyday objects (things that can be known by perception and observation from a distance) as the paradigm case of knowing. In theory, a knower should be able to fill the role of s and still discern the same facts p. The knower's subjectivity is not at issue. In practice, subjectivity *is* at issue. As teachers know, learning and knowledge making for many of us are not so clean and simple. Lorraine Code notes that while the facts may be "*there*, present for analysis . . . [they] may mean different things to different people, affect some people profoundly and others not at all" (1991, 45–46). For Code, then, facts are both subjective and objective: "[O]bjectivity *requires* taking subjectivity into account" (1993, 32). She reminds us that the circumstances of knowers, e.g., their historical, cultural, geographical, and political location, their creativity, motivation, and passions, must all be considered.

Code maintains that the ways in which we come to know human beings have at least as much claim to being the Rosetta stone of epistemological analysis as does the way we come to know inanimate objects. Her reasons are instructive for those of us engaged in the human arts and sciences. The kind of knowledge necessary for knowing people requires more than objective perception of the facts. As Code notes, "we can know all the facts about someone" and still we "would not know her as the person she is. No more can knowing all the facts about oneself, past and present, guarantee self knowledge (1991, 40). I would argue that in the same way, I can know all the facts about physics and still not understand physics. The six blind men can know the facts of the elephant and still not see the elephant. Chad can use his head to abstract or intellectualize, but as he says, his understanding is not complete.

Code also observes that knowledge of other people develops over time and this kind of knowledge "admits of degrees in ways knowing that the book is [the color] red does not" (1991, 37). This conception of knowledge fits with my understanding of teaching and learning. Knowledge of my subject—reading and writing—is not an all or nothing knowledge. It accrues gradually through instruction, experience, and reflection on that experience. And like knowledge of people, knowledge of reading and writing is never final or complete. It requires constant learning and revision (which is one of the reasons, for example, Donald Murray says he continues to write—writing is a subject one never masters). Likewise, knowing people, "precisely because of the fluctuations and contradictions of subjectivity, is an ongoing, communicative, interpretive process. It can never be fixed or complete: any fixity that one might claim . . . is at best a fixity in flux" (1991, 38). In other words, we can never say we know another person with the same degree of certainty that we can know the book is red.

Acquiring knowledge of other people (like acquiring knowledge of the self) is a slow, tentative process and is "open to negotiation between knower and 'known', where the 'subject' and 'object' positions are always, in principle, exchangeable" (Code 1991, 38). Thus, we can see how knowing becomes a bidirectional process in which both knower and known are implicated. As Code notes, even "knowing other people peripherally cannot be unresponsive, emotionless, neutral" (1991, 51). In addition, this kind of interpretive, dialogic, never-complete approach to the getting of knowledge seems to offer "a safeguard against dogmatism and rigidity" (1991, 38).

By examining what is involved in the process of knowing other people, we begin to understand why Code argues that "subjectivity has always to be taken into account in making and assessing knowledge claims of any complexity" (1993, 39). Specifically, the knower's subjectivity needs to be "a situated, self-critical, socially produced subjectivity, yet one that can intervene in and be accountable for its positioning" (1991, 82). It also needs to be a reflexive subjectivity, because reflexivity provides a way for knowers to monitor and analyze their own subjectivity. Furthermore, if the knower plays a self-critical role in the making of knowledge, as Code suggests, then it would seem cognitive agency also entails some kind of ethical responsibility. As Code notes, "knowing well is a matter of both moral-political and of epistemic concern" (1991, 72).

Code's theories of knowledge supply an epistemological rationale for what both writers and teachers seem to have realized intuitively (but more than likely have learned from experience): the student/writer/reader's subjectivity is needed to see the elephant, to translate knowledge and fact into meaning and understanding. This process is always provisional and is never a straightforward or neutral endeavor. As ethnographer Alan Peshkin notes, ignoring subjectivity doesn't make you a "value-free participant observer, merely an empty headed one" (1988b, 280). I don't want my students or myself to be empty-headed depositories of Freirian banking theories of education, or arrogant, blind, and distanced observers. As human agents, we need to be aware of how we are making sense.

Notes

1. I refer only to the family I perceived while growing up. Like many women, my mother has become more radical (although she would not use that term to describe herself) and more outspoken with age.

Chapter Two

Writing and Reflexivity

[A]n act of composition constitutes one of the most important forms of nonviolent individual empowerment in late twentieth-century America; the essay is the most egalitarian form of literature we have.
—Donald McQuade,
Composition and
Literary Studies

An essay is an invesitgation of a subject, but not its possession; it probes a reality with a succession of hesitant contacts.
—Marcel Tetel, *Montaigne*

Many claims have been made about the relationship between writing, thinking, and learning. Writing has been said to support, enable, or transform the thinking of individuals. In their book, *How Writing Shapes Thinking* (1987), Langer and Applebee study the ways writing improved the thinking and learning of secondary school students. They find that while writing does indeed assist learning, "different kinds of writing activities lead students to focus on different kinds of information, think about that information in different ways, and in turn, to take quantitatively and qualitatively different kinds of knowledge away from their writing experiences" (135). Short answer responses and extended, analytical forms of writing (as opposed to note taking, comprehension questions, or summaries) seem to increase students' knowledge of the

31

topic under consideration and encourage students to reconceptualize the information and integrate it with their own knowledge. Analytic writing enables students to manipulate a smaller amount of information in more ways, process it in more depth, and remember it for a longer period of time. Other kinds of writing lead to a more superficial understanding of a larger body of information. In addition, Langer and Applebee's work suggest that writing has a greater effect on learning when the subject is more complex. When the information to be studied or manipulated is familiar or well understood, writing appears to contribute little if anything to learning.

Langer and Applebee's quantitative study, which focused mostly on students' ability to recall and use topic knowledge and construct a gist from their reading, seems more concerned with comprehension than learning. If we recall Frank Smith's definitions, comprehension—the ability to relate what's already in our head to what we find in the world—may or may not occur as a result of learning. If what's already in our head is sufficient to understand what we encounter in the world, no modification is necessary and no learning occurs. But if we have to modify what's in our heads before we can make sense of our encounters with the world or as a result of our encounters in the world, learning does occur. Langer and Applebee do not distinguish between comprehension and learning, nor do they specify what they mean by learning. Learning might simply entail adding to what individuals already know; it might mean complicating or deepening what they know; it might mean transforming what they already know; or it might mean identifying or articulating what's in their heads—what it is that they know that they didn't know they knew.

Because Langer and Applebee's study was confined to examining assigned writing about specific, teacher-selected subject matter (e.g., economic expansion in the early twentieth century), it does not provide a sense of how interest might affect the writing-thinking relation. As Frank Smith reminds us, we do not usually think well about material we find boring, tedious, or purposeless. We do not think well about material that we have only engaged superficially. Being asked to write about such information compounds the tedium (or the confusion). However, Smith notes that both reading and writing can "promote thought—provided that what is read is worth thinking about [to the reader] and that writing is used for extending the imagination of the writer" (1990, 128).[1]

Meg Peterson-Gonzalez's research examining the writing of peace corps volunteers complicates Langer and Applebee's findings by suggesting that it is not simply the writing task or the kind of writing that contributes to what we learn; it is also a matter of the individual's personal and cultural ways of apprehending the world. In Chapter One, I suggested that we are more likely to become reflexive through dialectical encounters with others and that such encounters can potentially result in learning, i.e., significant modification of the theories in our heads. Peterson-Gonzalez's work supports this contention, but it also reveals the extent to which individuals may work to resist this modification.

Writing to Learn: An Example from the Peace Corps

In her dissertation, *Vivencias: Writing as a Way into a New Language and Culture* (1991), Peterson-Gonzalez examines how writing contributes to the cross-cultural transition process of four peace corps volunteers to the Dominican Republic. In their training classes each week, the volunteers are required to write a "lle" (pronounced zhay) in Spanish, usually on a topic of their choice. In some ways, the lle is similar to a personal essay. Peterson-Gonzalez describes the lle as an account of a "life-learning experience" (vivencia) that holds significance for the writer or an experience that changes the writer in some important way. Although the lle has a prescribed form consisting of five parts, the "essential elements of the lle are the experience itself and the reflection on that experience to create meaning" (15).

Peterson-Gonzalez suggests that an individual's literacy, which she defines as his or her "way of knowing about the world, of learning, of adapting [himself or herself] to new circumstances," (336) determines the manner and degree to which the person is able to integrate into the new culture. All of the volunteers (Peterson-Gonzalez included) use their literacy in various ways to "try to contain this new world and make it more familiar, to act upon it, to reflect upon it, to understand it, to present [them]selves to it, and to try to control the emotional stress of the transformation [they] were going through (337). However, the volunteers also "had characteristic ways of using literacy which were in part a product of [their] personal and cultural history as literate persons and in part [their] reaction to suddenly being thrown in a totally unfamiliar environment" (337). What is more, the volunteers seem to approach the writing of the lle in ways that mirror their approach to the new culture (347).

Even though the lle is an analytic genre where informants can write about what is interesting to them, and even though they are writing about complex material, because the informants also have to actively manipulate the language and their ideas, it is not simply the writing task, but also the ways the informants interpret the task that contribute to their learning. No one is able to grasp the concept of the lle right away, and one volunteer—the same volunteer who resists or limits her integration into the new culture—never does. Rather than modify the theory in her head to fit her new circumstances, Leanne, a fifty-year-old, fundamentalist Christian from the midwest, modifies what she finds in the new culture to fit the theory she has in her head. Leanne reconceives the lle as a story or account with a Christian moral or universal truth attached to it. She does not use the lle to construct meaning in Spanish or to try to understand her experience in the new culture. Instead, she focuses on technical correctness, limiting herself to using only the words and forms she knows. As Peterson-Gonzalez notes, Leanne did not "allow the lle to become authentic, precisely because of its potential for catalyzing cultural and linguistic transition" (372). However, "[t]hose who were able to use the lle in more personal ways seemed to integrate better into the Dominican community" (370).

Personal ways refers to the volunteers' capacity for using the lle as a vehicle for reflecting on and making sense of their experiences. For most of them, it appears true that "the road to a clearer understanding of one's own thoughts is travelled on paper" (Gage 1986, 24). Three of the volunteers use the lle in personal yet different ways.

Gerald uses the lle to determine what an experience means and to draw a lesson from his experience. The lesson, or the significance of the experience, only becomes clear to him in the actual writing. Marie uses the lle like a journal; it is a place for her to make sense of her emotional experience and "to work out personal issues" (375). Like Gerald, she discovers her meaning as she writes. The process of writing is what is most important for her. Maggie, on the other hand, has a better indication of what she will say about the experience before she writes. She uses her lle to extend and craft her thinking. For these three volunteers, writing becomes a way for them to deepen their understanding of the new culture and enlarge their understanding of their native culture and themselves. Writing the lle thus provides the occasion for reflexive or bidirectional learning. As John Gage notes, "the serious attempt to compose one's thoughts in writing is what can lead one to the very important discovery not only of *what* to think, but *why* . . . This is the most significant sense in which writing is a way of learning" (1986, 25).

Writing for Discovery: Generating Earned Insights

As three of the Peace Corps volunteers demonstrated, and many writers, academics, and students will attest, writing (like teaching) can be a useful medium for making ideas, beliefs, and assumptions more fully manifest—not only to another audience but also to oneself. In the process of trying to articulate an idea for another, we can inadvertently discover new meaning, significance, or depth in that idea ourselves. I believe that the notion of writing for discovery, which Donald Murray, Peter Elbow, and others have written extensively about, is in many respects a reflexive process.

Writing for discovery is very much connected to reading for discovery and involves what Donald Murray (1982) described many years ago as a process of "internal revision." Once writers have produced a text, they "read to discover where their content, form, language, and voice have taken them" (Murray 77). The written text becomes a medium for discovery. Writers look "through the word—or beyond or behind the word—for the information the word will symbolize . . . [They] discover what they have to say by relating pieces of specific information to other bits of information and use words to symbolize and connect that information" (Murray 79).

This process of internal revision can yield what Thomas Newkirk (1989) has coined "earned insights." I comprehend an earned insight to be a kind of understanding whose essential truth is only realized or more fully grasped as it is made manifest through the individual's experience and contemplation of that experience. Earned insights may be contrasted with what I call ready-made conclusions. When a parent tells a child not to touch the stove because it is hot, the child is expected to accept this already formulated truth based on the parent's knowledge and experience. However, if the child touches the stove and experiences the heat for herself, she earns her knowledge and comes to understand the truth of the parent's request in a different, personalized (and sometimes painful) way; it is a truth now confirmed by her own experience. Obviously, we would not need or want to have to earn every bit of knowledge we own. For example, I am quite willing to accept ready-made conclusions about what my car needs and how my computer works. I am thankful that I do not have to earn my insights.

Gerald, one of the Peace Corp volunteers in Peterson-Gonzalez's study, provides another example of an earned insight. A few weeks into his training, Gerald writes an lle about how he has come to understand his teacher's point that Spanish *es diferente*. In the lle,

Gerald writes, "I understood that I was not thinking correctly. Spanish had a different set of rules. This recognition has made learning Spanish much easier" (Peterson-Gonzalez 130). However, in the course of discussing his lle with Peterson-Gonzalez, he commenced a process of internal revision. Gerald looks "through the word—or beyond or behind the word" and, drawing on his own experience in the Dominican Republic, realizes that *es diferente* can also be applied to cultures as well as languages: "[E]ach culture has evolved within its own traditions and 'seems logical within a certain paradigm.' Behavior in different cultures *es diferente* and difficult to interpret, especially when 90% of the clues you have in the United States, including language, are missing" (130). Gerald has earned this insight. His experience has not only confirmed the truth of his teacher's statement, it has also allowed him to extend or apply this truth about language to culture.

Like Leanne, the volunteer who only wrote lle that confirmed her world view, many student writers have only learned to use writing as a medium to communicate ready-made conclusions. They have not experienced or been taught the generative capabilities of writing. When writers already understand the significance of what they write before they begin to write, or when writers simply attach a generic point or meaning to some event or experience, they are not writing to discover or earn their insights. However, when writers use their writing to think through their encounters with new ideas or reflect on past experiences, it seems likely that they may begin to formulate new understandings.

Much of the text I have written here—indeed, much of the text I will write—is the result of internal revision. Working with an abundance of information (and abundance needs to be emphasized; the pump must be primed for water to flow. Discoveries do not appear *ex nihilo*), I write by juxtaposing one idea with another idea and then reading what I have written to find out what it means or what it suggests. In the process of trying to explain the idea of writing for discovery to my readers and myself, I have made a connection between the concept of internal revision and the notion of earned insight. Of course, I wouldn't have thought to do this if I hadn't already had this information (from my research and experience) available to begin with. Putting these two ideas side by side on the page has enabled me to flesh out a fuller description of writing for discovery, and I find that my own understanding of both internal revision and earned insight has deepened. Thus, I come to see that writing to discover entails more than writing to find out what I think about a given topic: it also involves making these kinds of unanticipated insights. Written texts, however, do not usually reveal their writers' personal epiphanies. Certainly these discoveries are not visible in most academic texts or works of fiction. They would not be discernible in this text if I had not deliberately chosen to expose them by moving from straight exposition into *essaying*.

Perhaps then, one way that the process of writing contributes to thinking is through its capacity to generate earned insights. It is important to note, however, that working on any piece of writing for an extended period of time has the potential to assist the writer in coming to know something in a different or more complicated way. Immersion and experience play a role here. Seasoned, well-practiced writers (novelists, poets, nonfiction writers) or scholars who use writing regularly in their work (scholarly or philosophical articles or essays) are also more likely to discover new meaning through writing no matter what they write because of their stance and approach to inquiry. For less-practiced writers or for persons not used to the rigors of long-distance thinking, learning to write exploratory essays (on topics these writers find engaging) might be a particularly useful practice for enabling them to make connections and generate earned insights through writing.

Before I discuss more fully what I consider to be the qualities of personal essay writing that make it a useful vehicle for inquiry, let me offer an example of a student essay that I think depicts writing that *earns* rather than simply carries its own insights. This was the final version of a paper that Susan, a student in my upper level composition class a few years ago, had worked on intermittently throughout the semester.

Susan's Essay: "What's In a Name?"

In her essay, Susan writes about trying to decide whether or not she should take the name of her mother's new husband who wishes to adopt her and her twin brother. She and her brother, Rich, are both twenty-one years old and, as she observes, "being adopted seems out of the ordinary at this age . . . [I]f we were younger . . . adoption would not seem like such a peculiar thing to do." Nonetheless, Susan has been leaning toward taking her stepfather's name: "We have grown together as a family, full of loving, caring and sharing . . . Our acceptance of his name would mean a great deal to him and make him very proud."

Her choice is complicated by the fact that Rich does not wish to change his name. Because they are twins, they feel they should have the same name. As Susan begins to examine their reasons for their choices, she realizes that she and her brother are each looking at this decision from a gendered perspective: "We are both playing the roles that society has dictated," she determines.

Susan tells us that Rich is faced with deciding whether to adhere to the tradition "that the male(s) are responsible for carrying on the family name throughout the generations." She writes:

> My brother is torn between accepting the name Barton at the expense of terminating the continuation of our family name, Johnson, given to us by our natural father. There is, among men, a sense of loyalty to their fathers in this respect. If they were to give up that name for any reason, it would be as if they were betraying their father. I know that Rich feels this as well . . . I remember him distinctly saying, "How would you feel? It would be like a slap in the face to Dad."

But Susan is not so sure. "How could we possibly speculate or know what our father would think without being able to ask him?" For Rich, however, not only would giving up his last name be an insult to his father, it would take away his own identity as a person:

> My brother also feels that his name is what gives him his identity and serves as the backbone of his existence. The name Johnson is his birth right . . . His name is a means with which others will associate with him, with how they will treat him, what they will think of him. How he is accepted by society, determined by his particular name, will indirectly shape the person he becomes. If he were to change his name, the new name would not be a true indication of the person that he is. He would be a person with another name.

Susan wonders, though, if names actually "give us a particular identity, [or] is it what's inside that really counts, or is it a combination of the two?" And it is upon this point—the relationship between one's name and one's identity—that their differences of opinion hinge:

> I believe that one's sense of being and identity comes from within. A name to me is simply a convenience . . . there seems to be too much emphasis on the importance that names carry as indicators of our identities, over and above the importance of realizing the person that lies inside. A name is more like a shell that covers us to represent who we are to the outside world, but that name gives no real representation of the thoughts, ideals, and emotions that make each of us a unique person.

Here, Susan makes a provisional discovery, an earned insight, that emerges through her close examination of the subject. Up until this moment, she has been reflective; now she also becomes reflexive. She begins to contemplate the reasons for her beliefs:

> My own thoughts have been shaped primarily because of the person I am . . . I cannot deny that the person I have become has been a consequence of how I have been raised by my parents, the small town I grew up in and because I am female. I find that I am not socially aggressive, always trying to be different, the one to stand out in a crowd. I don't make a conscious effort to go against the trends in society. I don't feel I have a reason to . . . I don't consider myself a weak person . . . I am old fashioned. I believe in the [traditional] roles of men and women . . . women over the years have not been expected or conditioned, as men have been, to carry on a family name, but rather to accept a new one . . . I am content with accepting a new family name. I will become Susan Barton . . . it is simply the right thing to do for myself.

As Susan begins to articulate why the decision to change her name doesn't create the same conflict for her that it does for her brother, she realizes that each of them, in acting out these traditional, gendered roles, are doing so out of a sense "of loyalty to our father and to his family before him."

> I feel the person my father helped me to become, the identity and the self that I have, lies deep within me. It was not my father's name that has helped make me who I am. It was his soul and the love that he gave . . . That is what I will carry on for the rest of my life.

For Susan, then, accepting a new name (something she plans to do when she gets married) is what her own father would have wanted. She is honoring his values by subscribing to them. It is not the name that is important, but his beliefs that she plans to "carry on for the rest of my life."

Writing this essay has not caused Susan to alter her perspective. She has, however, developed a deeper understanding of why she has come to the decision that she has. What makes Susan's conclusion an earned insight and not a ready-made conclusion is that these traditional beliefs have not been unconsciously accepted; their truth has now been consciously justified by Susan's contemplation of her experience. She has articulated her tacit beliefs and is now more aware of why she holds these beliefs. As readers, we may not agree with Susan's conclusions, or we may feel that she has curtailed her inquiry too soon; nonetheless, we should now *understand* her conclusions. As Newkirk notes, the writer's earned insights are conclusions that often win a reader's respect and understanding, not because they are "startling truths but because of the speculation and the examination of experience that went into them . . . [we] are moved by them because we have had access to the process of their formulation" (1989, 22).

Susan's inquiry has deepened her understanding without actually involving consciousness raising in the most transformative sense. The practice of feminist consciousness raising does involve reflexivity, but here, the woman is often responding to a hostile other. Susan's twin is not a hostile other, although he does become strange when she discovers their different perspectives about the name change. Susan doesn't exactly come to define herself in new ways; nonetheless, she does come to understand her situation differently.

What is important here is the nature of Susan's inquiry. As the teacher, I have witnessed how Susan's ideas have evolved from her prior drafts. I also know that the insights generated in an essay are provisional. As Tetel states in his discussion of Montaigne's writing, "An essay is worth more than the resolution because the passage, the traveling of the mind, surpasses taking a position, since any position is inherently tentative and bound to be supplanted by others" (1990, 2). I have learned from my own experience as a writer and a teacher that often the thinking does not end when the paper does. Susan notes in her concluding paragraph that "this decision has forced me to look at myself as a female in society." Although Susan may have curtailed her inquiry at this point of "temporary illumination" (Good 1988), my hope and expectation as a teacher are that writing this essay has not only helped her to reach a more complex awareness of the factors influencing her decision to keep her name, but that the process of writing this essay has provided Susan with a method for thinking that she can use to see where she stands in relation to many subjects.

The Personal Essay as a Vehicle for Making Sense

When I teach students to write personal essays, I am not just teaching a way of writing but also a way of learning. It is this way of learning or making sense, this method of inquiry, that I hope transfers to students' other courses in the university (and life). While I am certainly interested in obtaining clear, forceful writing, writing that is well developed and detailed, writing that communicates its intentions to readers, I also seek to provide students with a way of understanding and critiquing information and ideas. The personal essay can be a useful vehicle for helping students to make sense of things and engage in authentic learning. Authentic learning—learning that deepens and expands our understanding of both our subject and ourselves—is reflexive.

Reflexivity involves a commitment to attending to what we believe, think, and feel while examining how we came to hold those beliefs, thoughts, and feelings. This kind of monitoring and self-awareness seems critical for enabling us to grasp new ideas and information without ourselves being appropriated in the process. Such a process does not mean, however, that we are resistant to change or transformation. Arguing for a feminist concept of integrity, Victoria Davion (1991) notes that many students arrive in her contemporary moral issues class with "firm beliefs about the issues . . . but without ever having examined how they came to have those beliefs and whether they wish to keep or change them." Her goal is to help students "see that their beliefs about issues reflect deeper commitments and deeper principles." Davion contends that people "are not born with integrity and those who develop it must choose at some point to do so" (185). Since knowledge of one's own beliefs and the principles that underlie them are a necessary condition for having integrity, Davion suggests that the development of integrity can only commence when individuals start to inquire into the origins of their beliefs and actively begin to monitor these beliefs.

Davion does not see the examination of one's own beliefs as being tied to an individual's verbal proficiency; nonetheless, I believe that in a specific pedagogical context (of the kind I outlined in Chapter One), writing, especially essayistic writing, can greatly assist this process by making one's beliefs visible, explicit, and thus open to examination. Kurt Spellmeyer (1989) notes that the essay takes "the writer's situatedness" as its central concern (270). How the writer understands her subject is grounded in her "presuppositions" and beliefs about the subject. In Susan's essay, we see how her decision to take her stepfather's name rests on her beliefs about women's roles in our culture. However, it wasn't until she was involved in the process of writing and rewriting that she came to realize how she was situated (what her beliefs were) and that gender, in particular, was one of the reasons she was situated differently than her twin brother.

In suggesting that the personal essay can provide the occasion for reflexive thought, I need to make the point that the writer herself (recall Leanne) and the topic she's writing about, rather than the kind of writing, are the more important variables here. On the one hand, I believe the propensity to adopt a reflexive stance is context dependent and subject specific. Just as we are not always able or inclined to think critically about every new situation that confronts us, it is difficult, perhaps impossible, for us to be reflexive about unconscious, deeply ingrained aspects of ourselves. And yet, reflexivity may also represent a habit of mind that individuals have learned to use to help them make sense of new situations. Recall Chad's story in Chapter One. He suggested that his ability to deal with abstractions in college was a thinking habit he had developed in childhood as a survival strategy.

Drawing on the work of John McPeck, Frank Smith (1990) says that as long as individuals "know enough," they are "always capable of critical thinking." At the same time, Smith also implies that critical thinking "is a disposition . . . a tendency to behave in particular ways on particular occasions . . . Critical thinking is an attitude, a frame of mind" (103). Just as many philosophers seem to be able to translate every situation into a series of propositional if/then statements, I am exploring the possibility that the personal essay might offer a method for thinking about or approaching a variety of new situations. The personal essay with its bidirectional focus on both the topic and the writer's apprehension of the topic might offer a useful vehicle for engaging in reflexive thought.

I have somewhat reluctantly chosen the term personal essay to distinguish it from thesis-driven, expository writing. The descriptor personal implies writing for and about the self. For many people, personal seems to suggest self-absorption, narcissism, or even the taint of (capitalist) individualism. However, when I use the term personal to describe the essay, I intend it to mean not only writing for and about the self, but also to include writing about a subject other than the self that is examined in relation to the self. What makes such writing personal is the visible and active, self-interested presence (subjectivity) of the writer within the piece. It is important to note that although essays are often written for the self and about the self, they are eventually intended for a wider audience. Even though Montaigne professed a "domestic and private" goal in writing his essays, he himself oversaw their publication in three books (Tetel 1990). The personal essay, despite its self-interest, is still a public form of writing.

Other forms of personal writing, such as the journal or diary, which are written primarily for the self and not intended for other readers, are often reflective; however, such writing lacks the requirement of the other that would ensure the bidirectional movement of thought. Despite claims that the personal essay and journal share similar ancestors (e.g., see Heath 1987; 1990; Gannett 1992; Spellmeyer 1989), the personal essay and the journal differ in both function and form in important ways: Journals are usually not intended to be read by others, and as John Gage notes, "the possibility of being *read* creates responsibilities that thinking alone can neglect" (1986, 25).

For the most part, journal writing does not have as its goal the "creation of consummatory, aesthetic experience" (Graham 1991, 65), something that Dewey felt was necessary for full self-realization. Nonetheless, the journal can sometimes serve as an other within. As Barbara Myerhoff and Deena Metzger (1980) suggest, the journal can be a "means by which subjects make themselves known to themselves" (104). My point here is to suggest that any reflexivity afforded by journal writing probably has more to do with the disposition of the journalist than any inherent requirement in the journal form itself.

On the other hand, the personal essay, at least in theory, embodies a "perennial dialectic" (Kauffmann, 1989) between an other and an I. And while always analytical, the personal essay is more often used for purposes of exploration rather than justification. In suggesting that the essay is always an analytical form, I mean to distinguish it from straight description or narration on the one hand, and linear, premise-claim chains of reasoning on the other. The essayist explores her subject, both rendering and examining it, in order to (tentatively) understand it. Unlike narrative or argument, the essay frequently depicts the writer's process of thinking, of coming to a new understanding rather than simply presenting the conclusion or product of thought. As Molly Haskell observed, "what seduces us in an essay has less to do with the subject itself than with the writer's way of curling up with a subject and rubbing it like Aladdin's lamp until it takes on shadings and lights of the writer's imprint and sensibility" (1989, 10).

Haskell's metaphoric comment about the essay suggests a way of learning, of apprehending knowledge, that I hope my students will experience during their stay at the university. This kind of learning involves the student getting close enough to a subject so that the subject becomes part of her or him. Such a view of learning means conceiving the purpose of education in something other than strictly utilitarian or vocational terms. As Chad, the student whose essay we looked at in the last chapter, put it, going to the university means using "education to find and create meaning in my world." Of course, finding and creating meaning in our worlds is an ongoing process. I believe the personal essay, the essay that is frequently taught in first-year English courses, can be used in many subject areas as a vehicle for making sense: for finding and creating meaning, for deepening understanding of subject matter, and for generating earned insights. And while it is true, as Kurt Spellmeyer notes, that "no genre will automatically empower student writers," the personal essay (with pedagogical assistance) seems "uniquely conducive to dialogue in all areas of knowledge" (1990, 338). And dialogue is an important precursor to reflexivity.

As many theorists have pointed out, *essay* is both noun and verb. It can mean an attempt or a trial, or to attempt, to try; it can mean an assay, a sifting through and weighing out; or to assay, to sift through and weigh out. While I am more concerned with the essay as a verb (a method and process) than as a noun (a form and a product), I see these two aspects as intimately connected. It seems to me that in learning how to write an essay and in trying to figure out what distinguishes an essay from other forms of prose writing, students also learn to essay. In the same way, learning to essay assists students with their writing of essays.

In attempting to define the qualities that mark the essay as a particular form or genre, many professional writers and scholars conclude that the quality that best distinguishes the essay is its versatility and refusal to be rigidly categorized. It is an open form that is continually being remade by its practitioners. Often the essay is divided into formal and informal types following the distinct styles of Bacon and Montaigne. John McCarthy argues that Bacon and Montaigne should be viewed as two sides of the same coin, rather than different coins: "The commonality of Montaigne and Bacon lies in their use of the printed word to promote critical and independent thought. Both were skeptics, both sought free expression of their personal views, both rejected rigid rationalistic systems" (1989, 43). Their differences lie in their attitudes toward their intended audiences and approaches to their subject: "one proceeds intuitively, deductively, the other rationally and inductively" (43). And so a few theorists have begun to intimate that perhaps the form is not what distinguishes the essay as a genre, but rather what characterizes the essay is the stance and approach the writer adopts toward her subject and/or audience. McCarthy suggests that it is the writer's way of thinking about an idea that determines whether a piece of writing is essayistic (58). It is this way of thinking about ideas that concern me here.

Essayism is a way of thinking about or responding to texts or situations that is characterized by tentativeness and openness. The essayist's attitude toward her subject is skeptical but playful and "fundamentally experimental, inquisitive" (McCarthy 41). McCarthy further suggests that we define essayism "in terms of the author's *and reader's* receptive postures" (my emphasis, 315). This is an intriguing idea for it suggests that essayism is a response that may be determined either by the writer's approach to her subject or the reader's way of receiving or interpreting the subject. According to McCarthy:

> True essayism reflects a multiplicity of perspectives presented in an engaging form designed to awaken and maintain reader interest, even after the piece of writing has been 'completed' . . . [E]ven when the essay is finished, it is not complete. If a so-called essay is not marked by a discursive, open-ended quality . . . we should think twice about labelling it essayistic (58).

Is this open-endedness a quality of the writer's text, the writer's attitude toward his or her subject, a perception of the reader, or all of the above? If essayism is a way of approaching texts that is open and tentative, it would seem that it is indeed a posture that could be adopted by either writer or reader (or perhaps in the best possible circumstances, both together). I will explore the reader's role in this process more thoroughly in the next chapter, but for now I want to concentrate on the essay writer/thinker/learner.

Recchio (1989) has pointed out that the writing of either overly formal (objective) responses to texts or strictly personal (subjective) responses to texts allows students to resist genuine dialogic engagement with their subjects and serious reflexive engagement with themselves. The student writer of the objective report, "skeptical about the authority of self," relinquishes her subjectivity and yields to the authority of the other. The writer of the personal narrative all too often ignores the other and reduces "the complex to an anecdote" and "privilege[s] the authority of experience" (276). On the other hand, the writer of essays (ideally) attempts to weave objective knowledge and subjective experience together in mutually informing and enriching ways. As Kurt Spellmeyer (1989) suggests, "students who learn to use writing as a way of thinking dialogically achieve in the process a heightened awareness of their situation, an awareness which allows them to overcome past misunderstandings without at the same time disowning the past" (271). The following paper, written by a student in my freshman composition course, reveals one student's movement away from writing that communicates ready-made convictions to writing that becomes more tentative, more essayistic, and begins to earn its own insights, achieving in the process, I would argue, a more "heightened awareness of the situation."

Like many freshman students, Mindy does not initially approach the idea she is writing about essayistically. She writes only to demonstrate her knowledge and understanding, not to deepen her understanding. In order for Mindy to learn to essay, she must unlearn and reexamine her initial assumptions. It takes several drafts and conferences with her peers and me for her to learn how to adopt an essayistic stance toward her subject.

Mindy's Essay: "'Patients' Is a Virtue"

Mindy's first two drafts of her paper are characterized by certainty. Good student that she is, she has developed her thesis prior to writing her paper. Her thesis is this: The elderly receive substandard care in nursing homes because of the quality of people working there. Her first draft attempts to support this thesis by focusing on the attitude and behavior of Lucille, a nursing assistant who trains her. Lucille "was aloof, sauntering into each patient's room with a look of disgust on her wrinkled face, complaining with each step." When Noel, a patient, asks Lucille about breakfast,

> Lucille chanted back, "Shut up, Noel. You're the grossest thing in here!" I was dumbfounded . . . I looked at her and she sensed my bewilderment. She quickly explained to me that once I got to know Noel, I would speak to him that way too. I made no comment but thought to myself, I don't speak to *anyone* that way, never mind a feeble old man who knows more about the world than I do.

After Mindy has worked at the nursing home for awhile, she begins to notice that the home is filled with many Lucilles, and she wonders "where in the world these people came from." She decides that the nursing home "doesn't pay its employees enough to hire 'respectable people' . . . Filling out an easy application and a quick interview got someone hired as simply as if they were applying to Burger King." But now, Mindy assures us, "steps are being taken to attract a different 'type' of person to become certified nursing assistant[s]." A four-month training program that "costs $800.00" and requires "that one must pass a written and practical state exam" has become mandatory. Mindy believes that "this will definitely weed out those who are actually serious about helping the elderly from those who simply need a job."

In a reflective commentary written at the end of the semester, Mindy admitted that when she began writing this paper she knew what she wanted to say: "I began with one basic thought. I was emphatic that Lucille was cruel. She was in the wrong profession because the job required caring, loving patient people . . . My focus was to write an essay about the abuse Lucille aimed toward the elderly." Mindy had a point that she wanted to make; in this case, though, her already formulated thesis (the preconceived theory in her head) was preventing her from essaying, from learning and inquiring further into her topic. As Elizabeth Hardwick cautions, "A well-filled mind itself makes the composition of essays more thorny rather than more smooth . . . There is seldom absolute true assertion unless one is unaware" (1986, 45). In an early conference, I asked

Mindy to tell me more about Lucille, hoping that she might begin to complicate her assessment of the people who worked in the nursing home. She did. In her commentary, she shares the questions that led to her next draft:

> My mind started reeling. Do I think Lucille first started out as sincere and caring as I? Would I be like Lucille if I worked there for fifteen years? Do I think it has something to do with the nature and demands of the job? Could the administration be at fault for the way the residents are treated?

By imagining the younger Lucille as herself and by projecting herself into a future Lucille, she makes Lucille and the staff at the nursing home less alien, less other, and takes a first step in establishing what Kurt Spellmeyer calls "a common ground." Seeing herself in the other and finding the other within herself allows for the possibility of dialogue. Such a dialogue is capable of generating a more complicated, less assured, and less simplified understanding of Lucille, but it also offers a reflexive boon for Mindy. Earlier, she had wondered where people like Lucille had come from, as if Lucilles were born, not made. Now her questions begin to reveal her growing awareness that perhaps people don't come whole; they are at least partially constructed—as she herself will be—by the circumstances in which they live and work. Her final draft is both more tentative and more complex. Rather than simply impose a single interpretation on Lucille, Mindy begins to view Lucille from multiple perspectives. When she introduces us to Lucille in the fourth draft, Mindy provides additional information that enables readers to begin to construct a more complex understanding of Lucille. Mindy hints at other explanations for Lucille's bad temper beyond the "type of person she is."

> "Great. Who called in sick today? I'm so tired of working short," Lucille grunts. She rolls her distressed eyes. They have large dark circles under them. Her mouth is turned down in a frown. It is a rare occasion when Lucille smiles, and I wonder if she is not only tired of working short, but tired of working. She has been a nursing assistant for the past fifteen years.

Lucille and Mindy make their way to Noel's room. Now, however, when Lucille speaks roughly to Noel, we see her actions in the context of the demands of the job:

> "Where's my breakfast?"
> "Shut up Noel! You're the grossest thing in here." Lucille yells. I hate when she speaks to him like that. Her face is wrinkled

and filled with disgust. I hope that maybe Noel thinks she is jok-
ing with him. Who am I kidding? Just because he's old doesn't
mean he's stupid.

"You're breakfast will be here soon, Noel. You'll just have to
be patient." I try not to sound rushed, but we still have thirty-four
people to wake before the breakfast trays can be passed out.

Mindy then takes us through the rest of her morning rounds, and in
each room we get to experience her ongoing conflict between wanting to provide quality care and needing to provide for a large number of people:

> I decide to take care of Henry . . . Parkinson's disease has over-
> taken him and he has a hard time doing things for himself because
> of his trembling . . . As I am finishing, he asks me to shave his face
> for him. I can tell it hasn't been done in a week.
>
> "I asked the girl yesterday to do it for me but she said she
> didn't have time. Imagine that!" he stutters.
>
> I don't have time either. He doesn't like the electric razor, so I
> have to use the plastic one with the dull blade. I am getting ner-
> vous. I have to hurry but I don't want to cut his face . . . Slow
> down, I tell myself, but I know that's impossible . . . .

Later, as Mindy attends to her unresponsive charges in the ward
the staff refer to as the "loony bin," she begins to imagine herself in
"Bermuda or Hawaii or even Hampton Beach." She worries that if
she loses her ability to daydream that she "may lose [her] own sani-
ty." Reflecting on her own tenuous situation enables her to see Lucille less absolutely: "I wonder if that [losing her ability to
daydream] is what happened to Lucille. Maybe she has just become
hardened, no longer capable of showing emotion." Instead of cast-
ing normative judgments or imposing ready-made conclusions on
Lucille's behavior, she now attempts to understand it. She has relin-
quished certainty to embark on an inquiry that will earn her a more
complicated insight, an insight, however, that will reveal her own
complicity. Later, as Mindy gets more and more behind, she is told:

> "Just get in there. Do what you have to do and leave."
>
> She is right. I don't want to admit it, but she is exactly right.
> Lucille, with her constant bickering, incessant complaints, and
> never ending grievances, speaks for us all. I feel guilty when I
> think some of the same things that she verbalizes. I wonder if I
> would be like Lucille if I worked here for 15 years. I'd like to think
> that I wouldn't, but I'll never find out. I can't deal with the way
> this place is run for that long.

Mindy has already caught herself thinking what Lucille openly ver-
balizes. Yet, rather than continue to face the difficulty of the job, a

job that has already begun to affect her, Mindy knows that she will leave: She knows that she can leave. It is the knowledge that she could become like Lucille—indeed, that she may already have started the process of transformation—which enables her to see that, perhaps, fifteen years ago, Lucille may have once been very much like her. She has just discovered "where these people come from."

When Mindy began writing this paper, she did not comprehend Lucille because she could not relate to her. Lucille was an other. Only when Mindy finds a way to connect her own experience of working in the nursing home to Lucille's behavior, does she begin to modify the theory in her head and use writing to engage in learning. At the close of her paper and the close of the day's shift, Mindy remembers that she hasn't visited with one of the patients whom she had promised to see, but reasons: "she always naps at this time and I don't want to disturb her. Besides the elevator is on its way up. I'll see her tomorrow." We are left wondering at what point rationality begins to merge into rationalization, as Mindy stands "zombie-like" waiting for her "escape."

In her commentary on this draft, Mindy says that she now realizes there are many factors that might explain Lucille's behavior. She is more aware that the situation is complex and that her current understanding is provisional.

> I now place the blame on the nursing home administration rather than on Lucille. And who knows, if I were to investigate why the nursing home operates as it does, maybe I would find that the blame I place on them also involves multidimensional dilemmas. I suppose nobody has a single, definitive answer to any of life's complications.

In writing this essay (or in learning to write this essay), Mindy is also learning a method of inquiry. A final essayistic comment reveals her willingness to open up her own conclusions to further scrutiny—an examination that seems aimed at complicating the pedagogy of over-zealous English teachers: "I only wonder if they really are legitimate complications or if the human race, unconsciously, creates the multifaceted complications surrounding most every issue in our lives." Indeed!

Douglas Hunt (1990) notes that "essayists have been drawn to subjects where the facts do not speak for themselves, but must be measured against some personal frame of reference" (1). Both Mindy and Susan, whose essay we looked at earlier, measure the facts of the situations they are writing about against their own personal frames of reference. But what Hunt's statement does not reveal is that an essayist's "frame of reference" is not always something that the essayist is consciously aware of prior to her encounter with her subject. It is through the essayist's open and dialogical engagement with the other that she comes to identify, enlarge, and at times, challenge her own perspectives. Not only do essayists measure the "facts of the situation" against "some personal frame of reference," as we saw with Mindy's later drafts, they also measure their "frame of reference" against the "facts of the situation." If we recall Frank Smith's definition of learning and comprehension, we might say that the practice of essayism can enable individuals to modify the theories in their head so they can relate to or understand what they see in the world.

To gain a better sense of how important identifying and examining our own frames of reference are for enlarging our understanding, I now turn to the last draft of a paper in which the student does not approach the situation he is writing about essayistically; he does not use the paper as an opportunity to probe his own perspectives; nor does he acknowledge how his frame of reference works to shape his interpretation. This writer's inability or refusal to examine his own assumptions and how he came to hold these assumptions prevents him from viewing this situation from multiple perspectives and limits his ability to engage essayistically with his subject. After four drafts, this paper remains virtually unchanged in both content and surface structure.

Ralph's Essay, "Who Wears the Pants": Take One

Ralph's paper describes the effects of his friend Steve's romantic relationship on Ralph and their male friends. Ralph said he chose to write about this topic because he had not completely resolved how he felt, but as the following description of Steve's relationship makes clear, there is little doubt as to where Ralph stands:

> Steve couldn't do this; Steve couldn't do that. He couldn't go here; he couldn't go there. And all because she said so. If God were a woman, she would've been named Sheila. How does she think she can control him like that? Does she even realize what she's doing? She has taken a really nice, outgoing guy and turned him into silly putty. Steve used to "cut loose" with us whenever we had a big night lined up, but sadly, that's a thing of the past. He simply has too much trouble convincing Sheila that "the guys" are entitled to a night by themselves once in a while. So now instead of confronting Sheila when they have a conflict of interest, he keeps his mouth shut and, as a result, we never see him. I always thought the male was supposed to wear the pants in a relationship. Boy, was I wrong. Sheila doesn't wear the pants in the relationship; she

wears the pants, shirt, shoes, socks, boxers and suspenders. Poor Steve is butt naked and not sure what to do about it.

The question Ralph really seems to be asking is, Who *should* wear the pants in a relationship? The answer, the foregone conclusion, is "the male." As Ralph sees it, Steve doesn't spend time with "the guys" anymore because he is no longer the same old Steve, that "really nice, outgoing guy." Now, Steve "doesn't drink, tell wild stories, or get a little rowdy." Now, Steve is "silly putty." The reason for this metamorphosis of character is Sheila, who has taken to wearing the pants in their relationship, leaving Steve defenseless and "butt naked." She has bewitched Steve, and he "simply seems to have lost his confidence [and] assertiveness. . . . We never see him anymore, at least not without her. I hate that."

Not only does Ralph hate the fact that he doesn't get to spend as much time with his friend Steve, he also sees this situation as unjust: "What she's doing is not only unfair to Steve, but it's unfair to us also. Because of her, we hardly get to see Steve, and that's not right." It's as if a moral code has been broken.

For Ralph, Sheila—the woman—is an other, a foreign being who doesn't seem to operate in the same (moral, logical, sensible) manner as he and supposedly other normal males (males not under the influence of a woman?). Not only does he not comprehend why Steve appears to be "afraid to stand up to her," he doesn't understand her. For instance, he has noticed that since Sheila began dating Steve she seems to have "almost abandoned her girlfriends . . . . No one told her to 'dump' her friends . . . . Steve didn't dump us, thank God." His explanation for such "irrational behavior" is that perhaps "she is insecure or just plain lonely without him." But for the most part, Ralph remains utterly confused: "Why Sheila can't see that she's crowding him absolutely mystifies me. Perhaps that is just the way some women are . . . ."

Here, then, is part of his difficulty: Unlike Mindy, Ralph can find no common ground, no way to connect his experience to Sheila (or Steve for that matter). When he attempts to measure the facts of the situation against his own personal frame of reference, he comes up mystified: women are different; that's "just the way they are." And in this case the differences are threatening: he feels compelled not to examine his own perspective but to privilege it, to argue for its superiority. After all, he is doing this for Steve's own good, which, as he sees it, is the right thing to do.

> As good a friend as Steve is, I always have trouble talking with him about Sheila because while I want to be honest, I don't want to

condemn her. . . . I'm always afraid I'll get Steve mad. Maybe that's
what we need to do, though. Get him good and pissed by talking
about the negatives of their relationship so he actually wants to
confront her in order to bring about a change. It may sound like we
are sticking our noses where they don't belong, but Steve is a good
friend, so we have all the right to involve ourselves to a certain
extent.

Ralph feels that he and his friends have an obligation to Steve. Loyalty and longevity of friendship gives them the right to interfere.
After all, they "have known Steve since kindergarten." Even though
Steve's behavior with Sheila makes them "so mad at Steve that we
don't want him anywhere near us," that's "not right" either: "We've
got to stick beside Steve through thick and thin because we've been
friends for too long to let anything come between us."

In writing this paper, I do not believe Ralph comprehends or
learns. He cannot relate to Sheila or Steve, nor is he able to modify
his own perspective so he can begin to make sense of this situation.
In fact, he seems unaware of his perspective. Writing has not
brought him any closer to understanding what his own beliefs are or
what principles might underlie these beliefs. Like Leanne, the peace
corps volunteer in Peterson-Gonzalez's study, Ralph seems to be
modifying the world to fit the theory already in his head, a theory
that is unconscious but pervasive.

It is interesting to note that Ralph wrote this paper in a special
section of an upper level composition class that focused on exploring how gender affects the way people think. Students in this class
had read the literature describing connected and separate ways of
knowing and various articles that examined the relational needs of
males and females. I encouraged students to draw from their reading to inform their revisions of their papers. Instead of using the literature to complicate his understanding, however, Ralph seems to
have found a way to make it support his current world view. The
inclusion of the following paragraph in his final draft constitutes
Ralph's total rethinking of his topic:

> Maybe women just have the tendency to gear into a relationship
> more than guys. Women traditionally "define" or "see" themselves
> through their relationships, so perhaps that is why they involve
> themselves so thoroughly. On the other hand it is believed that
> men "define" themselves apart from their relationships, which
> means that their friends and other "outside" variables still bear
> great importance.

Because he takes relationship to mean specifically male-female relationship, Ralph merely uses these ideas to further confirm what to

him already seems very clear. Sheila needs a male (Steve) to define her sense of herself, and, thus, she abandons all her female friends; Steve doesn't need Sheila to know who he is as an individual, and therefore, he doesn't need to dump his male friends. Instead of using these theories to open a window to the other, a reflexive window that might also shed light onto his discomfort with this situation, Ralph remains firmlys but unconsciously entrenched in his position and no closer to understanding the actions of his friend. To Ralph, Steve seems dangerously on the verge of going "native," of losing his real (unified and coherent) self to the other, and Ralph feels duty bound to try to pull him back, to "get him good and pissed by talking about the negatives of their relationship," and to return him to his senses (which, interestingly, also happen to be Ralph's senses).

Essayism is a close relative of process in that it is as concerned with understanding the thinking that leads to the thought as it is with the thought itself. Thomas Harrison suggests that an essay "give[s] shape to a process preceding conviction . . . and records the hermeneutical situation in which such decisions arise" (1992, 4). He notes that a conviction is a decision that has already been made. The essay, on the other hand, seeks to capture the mind in the process of reaching a decision, of coming to know or understand something. As such, it offers wonderful pedagogical possibilities. If we can understand how our students come to the conclusions they do, we will be in a better position to know how we need to respond as teachers. More importantly, if students write about how they reached the conclusions they did, they may discover underlying causes, reasons, and principles that they can examine further. Both Susan and Mindy concentrate on the process preceding their conviction in their essays: In "What's in a Name?" Susan "records the hermeneutical situation" that gave rise to her decision to change her name. Mindy does the same: By taking readers with her on her daily rounds in the nursing home, she allows them to experience the situation as she experiences it, a situation that they come to understand will probably result in her leaving or risk becoming more like the other workers. However, Ralph does not show us how he came to his conclusions about Steve and Sheila. Instead, he presents his already formulated (and formulaic?) convictions and tries to argue for them. As far as we can see, there has been no dialectical encounter with his topic (much less any reflexive engagement with his own assumptions). Not only do his arguments not convince, his stance makes it harder for readers to read his paper essayistically, in an open, dialogic manner. Because we have little reason to believe that

Ralph's conclusions are provisional, we are more likely to adopt an agonistic stance in response. I will return to this issue of reading in the next chapter.

I have examined student papers like Ralph's (papers that boldly parade their black and white perspectives) through many theoretical lenses over the years and yet, interestingly, I now realize that my pedagogical response has been similar no matter what my current theoretical stance is. It does not seem to make a difference whether I examine students' writing from a developmental, feminist, or ideological frame. My sense of how I should respond as a teacher has remained the same: I realize the need to provide some kind of situation that poses a counter-discourse (or, in my current language, that allows for a "dialectical encounter with an other"), which might expose a student's previously unquestioned assumptions. In a sense, I am also seeking to model a process I hope students will learn to perform for themselves: the habit of reexamining their ideas through the lens and frame of an other. As we can see with Ralph, such a strategy does not always work. And yet, as the next paper suggests, we must look closely at our students' writing or we may miss the bare beginnings of more complicated thinking trying to emerge.

Mark's Essay: "The Reality of Life"

Mindy took several drafts, but her writing became more essayistic over the course of half a semester. Ralph's paper never did. An important shift in thinking seems to occur when (or if) students move from writing ready-made conclusions to writing for earned insights; however, learning to write essays can be frustrating to students who do not enjoy "feeling around the contours of shapes that may never become wholly visible . . . To those for whom solutions have not as yet become problems, who live under clear moral skies . . . the essay in its essential incertitude can have little point" (Danto 1990, 22). Mark, a student in my freshman English class, provides a good example of such a person. At the end of the semester, when asked to submit a piece of writing from one of his courses that best revealed what kind of thinker he was, he submitted a computer program:

> With this program that I have written, you input data into the computer and the computer will give you the answer. I think that this says something about me as a thinker and a learner. I prefer to deal with everything in black and white. I feel that there is a right answer and a wrong answer to every question. There can be no middle ground. The computer operates in the same way. If you

have not entered the proper data, a computer is not going to give you an answer half way between right and wrong. The computer will reject your input until you do it correctly. I think that I function in much the same way as the computer.

For a good portion of the semester, Mark worked on a paper that dealt with a life-threatening accident that occurred when he was four years old. He severed all the veins and arteries in his hand when he put it through a glass door. The doctors didn't know whether he would live, and if he did, whether he would regain the use of his hand. Mark tells us that he was "motivated from the inside" and he "never gave up," a trait he attributes to his "stubbornness of nature." He says he has "been a very determined person since then . . . I never know when to quit." The point he wants to communicate is that people never know what they have until they come close to losing it. If you are stubbornly persistent and work hard, you'll succeed in overcoming adversity and reaching your goals, and if by chance you don't succeed, you can rest easy knowing that you tried and knowing that you deserved to make it. His thesis reflects part of the ready-made mythology of our culture about work and success, and Mark accepted it wholly and uncritically.

I should pause for a moment here to consider just how much Mark sounds like the twenty-five-year-younger me I described briefly in the previous chapter, the person who wrote that all "we needed to make our goals a reality was a desire to work and courage and willingness to experiment," the person who only discovered that the work ethic wasn't a universally ingrained truth when she was confronted with the otherness of Australian culture. I didn't make this connection at the time I was Mark's teacher. Like Mindy, who finds an earlier Lucille in herself during and after her repeated forays and excursions into her text, this discovery of an earlier me in Mark has come through my dialogic textual (re)encounter with his work. Making this connection helps me to better comprehend Mark, or "relate to him," as my students say. At the same time, Mark is an other, and this encounter is unsettling. Have I completely missed the point? I wonder. Developmentally, perhaps both Mark and I seem to have come to rest in a similar position, one that believes in the power and autonomy of the individual to overcome his or her situation. And yet, I realize that the cultural context in which we each reside is different. I was perched at a point when the cultural wheel seemed to be spiraling toward more creativity and less conformity, and so my belief in the individual's capacity for growth and change, as I mentioned in the last chapter, simply mirrored some of the currents of the time. Mark's assumptions need to be viewed against the backdrop of a culture that is now attempting to shed the excesses of the 1960s and ground itself in more certainty and stability. Tentatively, I might suggest that in this milieu, what I have been calling the ready-made truth can appear on the surface less reactionary and anti-intellectual. Nonetheless, as I mentioned earlier, my job as an educator is to attempt to complicate students' understandings by providing a counter discourse (something that didn't happen for me until I went to Australia).

As poet, Richard Hugo notes, "One mark of a beginner is his impulse to push language around to make it accommodate what he has already conceived to be the truth, or in some cases, what he has already conceived to be the form" (1979, 4). Sometimes a semester is simply not long enough (and, as I have recently discovered, a quarter most certainly is not) for us to witness the effects that our counter discourses have on our students' thinking and writing. A term is not long enough for some students to move from writing whose only purpose is to communicate ready-made truths in grammatically correct sentences to writing that first discovers and then interrogates its own assumptions. However, if we look closely at our students' drafts, and if we listen to what our students have to say about their writing, we may begin to discern evidence that learning is taking place. The writing may appear less certain and self-assured, less seamless, possibly inconsistent, and even contradictory at times. Although Mark's final draft of the term does not yet demonstrate an essayistic stance, there are clues in the writing that suggest he is beginning to poke around the edges of his tightly constructed theories. In one part of his draft, he says:

> If you are as stubborn as I am, you are more likely to work hard and accomplish a goal. Yet, if you are so stubborn in your attempt at that goal that you neglect the possibility of failure, you are no longer focused. You can gain a lot if you are a stubborn, relentless person, but you also stand to lose quite a bit because of your stubbornness.

For the first time during the process of writing this paper, Mark admits that being stubborn and relentless contains both positive and negative qualities. Too much stubbornness can cause a person to become unfocused in his or her quest for success, and that might lead to the "the possibility of failure." Later in the paper, however, after telling us about his failure to make the all state team as a senior (despite his hard work and the fact that he "deserved to make it"), he adds, "I am just a person who does not know when to give up. I guess that would make me either stubborn or stupid. I have found that there is a very fine line between the two." Here, then, is another hint of grey emerging through the black and white canvas of Mark's world view. And yet, I wonder: Does Mark actually believe that there is a fine line between stubbornness and stupidity? Or is he merely giving the teacher what she wants in this draft by attempting to respond to questions that I have raised during our conferences on previous drafts?

Earlier, I had asked Mark if hard work always leads to success and if failure always means that a person hasn't worked hard enough. Could he imagine a situation where it might be wise for a person to admit that more hard work would be counter productive? Mark writes:

> I believe that most people have adversities to overcome in life. For some, it is a physical handicap, or for others, it could be the geographic location of where they live and its effects on their lives. Some people feel limited to a certain social position because of the way they were raised. I realize that quitting or not trying at all could be the easiest thing to do at times. If everyone gave up and no one ever tried nothing would ever get done.

It is hard for Mark to imagine a situation where it might be in the best interests of a person *not* to work hard to meet a goal or overcome a problem. As far as Mark is concerned, everyone has "adversities," and he makes no distinction between kind or degree of adversity. Quitting only leads to a situation where "nothing would ever get done." And yet, a few sentences later, he appears to contradict himself when he adds: "The ability to know when to quit is a positive quality of an individual. One does not always succeed at everything one attempts. It is important to work hard and learn from our experiences . . . ." Although Mark does not reveal how he has arrived at this new conclusion, he now acknowledges that people will not always succeed (despite their hard work), and so it is good to know when to quit. It may appear that Mark is finally beginning to examine and complicate his earlier assumptions. However, a closer examination reveals that Mark has simply replaced one ready-made truth (work hard and you'll succeed) with another (it is okay to not succeed as long as you work hard enough to learn from the experience). Quitting is okay if a person learns something. It is still important to work hard, however, because "on any occasion there is the chance that everything will work out."

In his final draft, Mark hasn't actually modified the theory in his head as a result of his encounters on the page, but he has added to it. The resulting mix is messy, and, yet, the contradictions in his paper may be an indication that Mark is beginning to complicate his thinking, although he has not become reflexive. His response has not yet become bidirectional. For students like Mark who admit they are more comfortable in a world of certainty, reflexivity—the identification and examination of unarticulated assumptions and motives—is difficult. When confronted with new ideas, black and white thinkers seem to have two options: they can either adopt the new ideas wholly and uncritically or reject them outright as not-fitting. The reason I believe Mark's paper reveals a movement toward a more essayistic stance is that Mark has not chosen either of these options. Instead, he tries to incorporate a new idea (that quitting can have a positive side and stubbornness may have a negative side) into his current belief structure by simply adding to what is already there. On this occasion he cannot implement the only strategy for learning that he knows—replace a wrong idea with a right idea— because he is not convinced his old idea is wrong and this new idea is right. For now, he is left with little alternative other than to include both ideas regardless of their ill fit.

In offering my readings of these student papers, I too have measured (and continue to measure) their work against my own subjective and multiple (personal, professional, theoretical, and cultural) frames of reference. My perspective is interested and situated, born of who I am, my practical experience with students, and my theoretical meanderings with texts. Of course these readings are subjective. How could they be otherwise? As I suggested in the previous chapter, the teacher's subjectivity is an important instrument of observation and interpretation. And yet, as with all tools, the subjective instrument is capable of seeing some things and not others; it has its limitations, and these limitations need to be reflexively uncovered, recognized, and understood. In the next chapter, I talk about essayistic reading and teachers' reading student texts.

Making Connections

Essayism may not be the discovery of new ideas as much as it is the "creative discovery of new rational relations" between phenomena (Harrison 1992, 15). It involves the ability to make connections, as Steven Jay Gould observes:

> My talent is making connections. That's why I am an essayist. . . .
> I can sit down on just about any subject and think of twenty things
> that relate to it and they are not hokey connections . . . . It took me
> *years* to realize that was a skill. I could never understand why ev-
> erybody just didn't *do* that . . . . Most people *don't* do it. They just
> don't see the connections (Shekerjian 1990, 5).

To be able to make connections or discover "new rational relations" between ideas, experiences, and texts, students need to approach their subjects of study openly, tentatively, and most importantly, they need to engage them more than once. Students need to know that their first encounters with texts (their own or others), are just that—first encounters. They are exploratory forays. We do not usually become reflexive in a first encounter with an other.

The kind of essayistic approach to ideas I talk about in this chapter and the next two chapters requires that individuals learn to adopt a stance of suspended closure, and this stance necessitates a pedagogy that allows time for inquiry, dialogue, and revision. Practically speaking, I believe this translates into a course in which students write fewer different papers and read fewer different texts; instead, they experience multiple cycles of (re)writing, (re)reading, and discussion for each paper and each text. Students would be encouraged to revisit their earlier work, reexamining (and revising) it in light of understanding they have gained from their current work. I think one reason many students never learn "to see the connections" (and examine them) is because they haven't been given the opportunity to immerse in any one idea long enough to do so. As we shall see more clearly in the next chapter, making connections is an important first step for making sense.

Notes

1. In his book *To Think* Frank Smith (1990) suggests that the activities of thinking, remembering, comprehending (understanding), learning, and imagining take place simultaneously; they are all part of the same mental function, indistinguishable from one another and occurring all the time. For Smith, however, "imagination is the dynamo of the brain, the source of all our intellectual energy and creativeness" (54). Smith argues that as long as our imagination is in charge, we think, remember, understand, and learn easily and effectively. However, when something overrides the imagination's control, "the brain loses its integrity (in both senses of the word), [and] it is thrown out of gear and every facet of thinking is shattered" (54). When Smith speaks then of the capacity of writing for "extending the imagination of the writer," he means that writing works to extend thinking and learning.

Chapter Three

Reading and Reflexivity

> *We reach an understanding with our object and appropriate it into our own self-understanding when we have learned from it and taken account of its views in formulating and refining our position. This kind of consensus represents a "fusion of horizons" in a two-fold sense: on the one hand, we understand the object from the point of view of our assumptions and situation; on the other, our final perspective reflects the education we have received through our encounter with the object.*
> —Georgia Warnke,
> *Gadamer: Hermeneutics,*
> *Tradition, and Reason*

In the last chapter I intimated that essayism is a stance, a way of openly and reflexively approaching and negotiating ideas that could be initiated by readers and writers. In this chapter I want to further explore the essayistic stance from the reader's perspective. My emphasis is on a specific kind of dialogic and reflexive reading that is not primarily literary or aesthetic (although it is not precluded from also being literary or aesthetic). I am talking about reading as a form of inquiry.

In a piece written over ten years ago for *The New York Times Book Review*, Harold Brodkey suggested that reading is a "most dangerous game." Reading puts the reader at risk, and if "the reader is not at risk, he is not reading" (1985, 44). Reading is risky business because it "leads to personal metamorphosis, sometimes irreversible, sometimes temporary . . . A good book leads to alterations in one's sensibility and often becomes a premise in one's beliefs" (44). This dangerous, transformative capacity of reading is possible because of the intimacy involved, "the prolonged (or intense) exposure of one mind to another" (1). Brodkey is referring to a kind of literary (highbrow) reading here, and yet, what he says about "cultured" reading applies equally well (maybe better) to the kind of dialogic and reflexive reading I have in mind when I think of reading essayistically.

Brodkey's description of reading as an intimate and long term encounter with an other begins to sound much like the ethnographer's extended foray into the field. In each situation, during the dialectical process of trying to comprehend or understand an other, one's own beliefs and assumptions are disclosed, and may themselves become the object of interpretation, critique, and even metamorphosis. It is this *risk* of alteration to one's view of the world that makes this kind of reading dangerous, but also valuable. If the reader is not at risk, his or her current understanding and (self-)awareness remain safely immune to further complication or illumination.

The kind of essayistic, ethnographic venture I am talking about here—really, a form of hermeneutic inquiry into texts—is not a way of reading (or writing) that many students have experienced before coming to college, but I believe it's a way of reading students need to learn. However, to engage oneself in risky reading, notes John McCarthy, one "must be disposed to intellectual exertion and the times are not always favorable to that disposition" (1989, 56). Indeed! Evidence for the anti-intellectual preferences of today's reading public abounds. When I first began to draft this chapter during the week of December 6, 1993, Rush Limbaugh's *See, I Told You So* and Howard Stern's *Private Parts* competed for the top of the *New York Times* nonfiction best seller list. And now, two and a half years later, during the week of July 21, 1996, a glance at the best seller list reveals two books about the O.J. Simpson murder trial, *Outrage* and *In Contempt*. They are joined by basketball personality Dennis Rodman's autobiography, *Bad As I Wanna Be*. No doubt all these books put the reader at risk, but certainly not in the ways Brodkey, McCarthy, and other theorists have in mind.

To read essayistically means to approach a text with the conscious intention of engaging in genuine dialogue with its ideas, a dialogue that may put the reader at risk because it can easily become a reflexive dialogue. This notion of risky and reflexive reading takes us back to Frank Smith's concepts of comprehension and learning. I understand Brodkey to mean that comprehension—the ability to relate what's already in our head to what we encounter in a text—does not constitute reading, at least not in terms of Brodkey's normative ideal, but rather, reading that puts the reader at risk involves learning, the modification (or risk of modification) of what's in our head as a result of our encounters with a text. Both Brodkey and Smith see risk and modification as always leading to something better, which is obviously a debatable contention, as we shall see. However, to my way of thinking, this better would be a more complicated understanding.

To write essayistically, it is helpful if one can read essayistically. And yet, one does not have to be writing an essay or reading an essay to be writing and reading essayistically. It is possible to read any kind of text essayistically in this dialogic, reflexive manner. In essayistic reading and writing, readers and writers put themselves at risk by opening themselves to the multiple and contrasting perspectives of others. At the same time, however, they reflexively monitor their own beliefs and reactions to the process, lest they: (1) lose their own sense of being and integrity by inadvertently "going native" and succumbing to the persuasiveness of being born again wholly, fully, and uncritically in the new position; (2) attempt to objectify, dominate, or deny the autonomy of the other. For example, in the previous chapter, Susan and Mark risk the first danger: the uncritical acceptance of the culture's ready-made beliefs. Susan is in danger of following the custom of women who change their names simply because "it is the thing to do." Mark seems to succumb unconsciously to the myth of "work hard and you'll succeed." Mindy and Ralph, on the other hand, risk the second danger, objectifying the other. Mindy's first drafts make no attempt to try to understand Lucille's perspective, but when she scrutinizes her own reactions to the conditions at the nursing home, she comes to see Lucille in a more complex way. Ralph does not examine his perspective about male and female relationships; he privileges it, precluding any possibility of dialogue with Steve and Sheila that would enable him to understand their positions. Readers need to be both the subject and object of their reading (they read themselves as they read the text), which ensures that their encounter with ideas will be dialogic and bidirectional rather than unidirectional. Essayistic reading is a sophisticated process that requires some degree of agency and confidence. Otherwise, readers cannot easily open themselves to another or withstand their own critical examination.

My conception of what it means to read essayistically shares many characteristics with the kinds of reading that David Bartholomae and Anthony Petrosky advocate in *Facts, Artifacts, and Counterfacts* (1986) and in their anthology, *Ways of Reading* (1987; 1990; 1993; 1995). Their work has been instrumental in contributing to my thinking and to my teaching of reading composition students. We all seem to view reading as an ongoing and reflexive transaction between readers and texts, and we teach reading as a method of intellectual inquiry.

Bartholomae and Petrosky's methods of reading were specifically designed to afford basic writing students "access to the language and methods of the academy" (1986, 9). I think essayistic reading may have a wider application in that it is an approach that may be used by all students to read academic texts, their peer's texts, or their own developing drafts. It may also be used by teachers reading students' texts. Perhaps another distinction I would make between their practice of "strong, aggressive, labor-intensive reading" (1993, 5), and what I am calling essayistic reading is one of approach and stance. Whereas I have characterized essayistic reading and writing as open and tentative, Bartholomae and Petrosky present reading and writing as "a struggle" in which a student has "to appropriate or be appropriated by a specialized discourse" (1986, 8). Needless to say, this image of appropriation is not the image I want to have of the ethnographer seeking entry to a new culture. One reason I prefer an essayistic approach to texts is that it suggests the possibility of a "both/and" stance. Bartholomae and Petrosky's "appropriate or be appropriated" methods feel uncomfortably agonistic and either/or. However, I realize that "both/and" is a sophisticated stance that students may only begin to assume after having traveled through many "either/or" positions. It may be that Bartholomae and Petrosky's approach can provide a necessary corrective to the "banking method of education" that is typical of much high school instruction.

Rhonda Leathers Dively (1993) offers a similar reading pedagogy that she has used to encourage students to explore and interrogate their unexamined religious beliefs. She asks her students to read texts that show how their authors have *earned* their religious insights through intellectual engagement with their beliefs, rather than simply adopting somebody else's ready-made conclusions wholesale in born-again fashion. Dively argues that:

> To facilitate the interrogation [of their beliefs] we should encourage students to theorize about their own subjectivity as the product of multiple interpellations rendered by various discourse affiliations. By doing so we can help broaden or complicate their understanding of themselves . . . Once students reach this level of self-awareness, they will be better prepared to address the complexity and conflict in their own writing about religious experiences and a host of other issues (101).

In the rest of the chapter, I will attempt to flesh out a deeper sense of my concept of essayistic reading by discussing students' responses to the texts they are reading and their reflections on the texts they themselves have written. Finally, by examining my own (teacher's) reading of students' texts, I hope to further reveal the complexities in this process.

Essayistic Reading: Open, Dialogic, Reflexive, and Tentative

Ostensibly, in the minds of many of our students and a great portion of the public the purpose of a college education is to learn information that will cause a person to become educated. Most people, both inside and outside the university, assume that much of this education will occur through the reading of texts. However, many texts that students will encounter at the university can not be easily understood if students merely attempt to absorb, memorize, or summarize their contents. (Texts should not be confused with textbooks, which, for the most part, can be absorbed, memorized, and summarized.) Some texts must be read actively and reflexively if students are to make sense of them. For these texts, students need to stake their claim to understanding them by first remaking these texts within the context of their own ideas and experiences.

Hermeneutic theory suggests that understanding is rooted in preunderstanding, which is to say that what we can understand is determined by what we already understand. Or, to put it in Frank Smith's terms, what we can learn is determined by what and how we already comprehend or perceive the world. This idea has been used to support theories of how knowledge is acquired in many fields (including the pedagogical dictum, "begin where the student is at"). In literary theory, it forms the rationale for such different arguments as E. D. Hirsch's theory of cultural literacy and Stanley Fish's notion of the interpretive community. To make sense of (or to understand or interpret) a particular text, readers (individually or as members of a particular group) draw upon their tacit knowledge (Polanyi) as well as their more explicit theories and hypotheses about how the world works. However, readers may not be aware of the kinds of preunderstandings they bring to a text. It is during the process of reading, or "through the dialogical encounter with the otherness of text," that both the text's meaning and the reader's "foremeanings and prejudgments" are simultaneously disclosed and themselves become open to interpretation and reflection. A hermeneutic account of reading "is reflexive because as it discloses the text, it concurrently discloses the interpretive standpoints of the inquirer" (DiCenso 1990, 148).

Because understanding is thus conditioned or constrained by readers' preunderstandings or "prejudices," a text can never be fully absorbed or disclosed by any one reader or any one reading. In the following excerpt from an end of the semester reflection on her work, Liz, an upper level composition student, uses Paulo Freire's theories to describe how to read Paulo Freire's text dialogically and reflexively:

> [Freire's] type of writing requires the reader to think more in-depth than most writing demands. The reader must go away and come back to the writing as often as necessary in order to bring his own information to it, such as personal experience. This will help in ultimately understanding the work. A person with a banking education would not be able to handle such material . . . because according to Freire, this type of person has no thoughts [of his own] and therefore no ability to think creatively . . . (Qualley 1993, 111).

Liz makes the important point that understanding a complex text like Paulo Freire's *Pedagogy of the Oppressed* involves multiple readings. Readers have to "go away and come back to the writing as often as necessary . . . ." Understanding does not magically emerge full-blown during a first or solitary encounter with a text; rather, understanding is an ongoing process, occurring gradually by degrees. This kind of reading is dialogic or conversational. In Liz's words, the reader "must bring his own information to [the text] such as personal experience." In Bakhtin's words, the ideas and language of others only "become 'one's own' when the speaker [reader] populates it with his own intention, his own accent . . . adapting it to his own semantic and expressive intention" (1981, 293). Only when a person populates the ideas of others with his or her own knowledge and experience does the "externally authoritative" word become "internally persuasive." Bakhtin says at this point the individual becomes author of his or her own perspective. I would say it is at this point that the individual reaches a new level of understanding, one that has been enlarged, complicated, or transformed. In order to engage in this kind of reading, students need to rid themselves of the myth that good readers read quickly and only need to read the text once; teachers need to allow time for this reading conversation to unfold.

To read essayistically, then, the reader's judgments must remain tentative, open to the possibility of elaboration, modification, or revision through further dialogue and ongoing reflection on the text and/or other's reactions to the text. Tentative, however, does not mean nonconclusive. Listen once again to Jean, the student I spoke about in the Introduction, as she reflects on her learning:

> I always felt I had to make a final decision, [but] I never really had the chance to think through my thoughts. This became most obvious to me when I worked through my feelings about Hedda Nussbaum and the question of her culpability . . . Through my reseeing of the events of Hedda's life and her psychological state at the time, *I was able to come closer to a conclusion, though this conclusion is not really final since my thoughts are in a constant state of reshaping by my experiences and my environment.* (Emphasis added)

In order to learn to read essayistically, some students may also need to unlearn a critical approach to reading that many of them have only recently come to adopt (or mimic). Here, the text is seen as an antagonist that students must confront, master, and critique. In this kind of reading, students often prematurely pronounce judgment and thus, close themselves off to further inquiry. In her end of the semester reflection, Carla alludes to the limitations of this method of reading that speaks with too much certainty too quickly.

> Another thing I've learned to do when reading is not to jump to conclusions. In "The Feminization of Love," I disagreed with Cancion's sentence: "It is especially striking how the differences between men's and women's styles of love reinforce men's power over women." As soon as I read that sentence I thought, How can she say that? She must be a wimp with an obnoxious, overbearing Italian macho man for a husband. I immediately defamed her before I read on. It clouded an open mind, and I carried around a bias for the remainder of the reading.

Many students adopt this hypercritical and closed stance in reaction to their prior uncritical methods of reading, where they would read only to imbibe information, or as one student said, "I read to get absorbed in the characters so I can escape life." Students switch from simply absorbing "authoritative discourse" or the "otherness of text" to immediately confronting, even attacking, this otherness (shoot first and ask questions later). This move can be a temporary, developmental overswing on the part of the student learner who is simply trying to move away from accepting the authority of texts unquestionably. Both approaches, though—uncritical acceptance or offensive attack—are antithetical to the spirit of essayism. In the first approach, the self surrenders to the other; in the second, the other is assimilated by the self. Neither approach is dialogic or reflexive.

Wayne Booth observed that the truly "critical mind does not know in advance which side it will come out on" (qtd. in Gage 1986, 22). By comparison, the truly essayistic mind will more than likely not come out firmly on a "side" at all; rather it will come out with a more complex understanding of all the sides, including (hopefully) its own. The following discussion of one student's response to Paulo Freire's chapter,"The Banking Concept of Education," suggests how essayistic reading can complicate and extend a reader's understanding of a text and herself.

Kay's Response: "I Sometimes Look at the World As Being Separate From Me"

Kay was a first-semester student in my freshman English course. Her encounter with Paulo Freire's text occurred about two-thirds of the way through the semester when she was becoming more comfortable with the rituals of my class. The reading ritual involved a process where students would read and mark a text for lines and passages they found interesting, significant, or confusing. They would then discuss the passages they had marked with other students in small groups. After rereading the text, students examined their ideas further by writing informal responses several pages in length. In these written responses, students might elect to elaborate on their initial response; they might examine their own experiences and beliefs that led them to see the text in a certain way; they might compare their reactions to other group members and try to account for the various interpretations; they might make connections between this text and other texts they had read. I responded with written comments on their papers. Students could elect to continue this dialogue by writing additional responses throughout the semester.

Prior to reading Freire's chapter, the class had read, responded to, and discussed essays by Jane Tompkins, Richard Rodriguez, Richard Wright, Joyce Carol Oates, and Walker Percy.[1] None of these texts, though, prepared them for Freire's difficult, abstract language. Like many students, Kay's first encounter with Paulo Freire's chapter about the banking concept of education from *Pedagogy of the Oppressed* left her with a feeling that she "could not quite grasp." However, after a field trip to see the Boston Symphony she returns to the text and writes in the margin, "I sometimes look at the world as being separate from me." In her response, Kay notes that "Freire's chapter finally made sense to me because of a child on a Boston sidewalk." She goes on:

> We came by an older man who was rattling a cup and saying, "Change please. Change please . . ." But we all walked by consoling any guilt we had by thinking that he wanted the money to buy alcohol or drugs. However, directly after him, a little boy rattled the change in his cup . . . My heart dropped as he said, "Change please, Ma'am?" Yet we all walked by . . .

Kay's encounter with this child is important because it provides the concrete experience she needs for gaining access into Freire's abstractions and difficult discourse. It also provides her with a perspective, a place to position herself, so that she can begin a dialogue with Freire's ideas. If she is first grounded in her own experience, then she is more likely to be able to locate herself in Freire's text without being swallowed by it in the process. In David Bartholomae's terms, Kay's experience affords her the opportunity to "speak." But this utterance will evolve into a reflexive dialogue as Kay begins to use Freire's ideas to examine and "complicate" her prior knowledge and experience with "the homeless."

> I have seen homeless people before, yet, as Freire stated, I passively accepted pieces "from the world outside [my] mind." I lived in "ivory tower isolation." I knew all the statistics of the homeless. I saw them on television and read about them in newspapers and books, yet never linked my "fragmented view[s] of reality" together. I did not realize that homeless people were human like myself . . . "Man is merely in the world, not *with* the world or *with* others; man is a spectator, not a recreator . . ." In a way the problem of the homeless was background material . . . At least until I looked into that little boy's eyes, then it became part of my conscious experience. . . .

Kay's way of integrating Freire's words into her own text suggests that she is neither passively absorbing his ideas, nor is she imposing her views onto his text. Rather, she is engaged in a process of trying to understand both Freire's essay and her own experience. Understanding in Gadamer's sense always means coming to see something in a new way or "understanding differently." Essayistic reading is a process of understanding that begins when a reader makes a connection with the text. Once a link has been established, readers can travel back and forth along that link, simultaneously reading the text and reading the self, furthering their inquiry into both realms. Kay will use her subjective experience to examine and assess the truth of Freire's claims, as well as her own understanding of these claims. This process of understanding begins when she "rewrites" Freire's text into her own language by replacing the generic, nameless "student" of Freire's text with herself:

> Freire says that as a student, I was oppressed and my mind was "filled" with "contents which [were] detached from reality." He also said that the "teacher talks about reality as if it were motionless, static, compartmentalized, and predictable." Freire blames the education system and the teachers for my false perception of the reality of the homeless. . . .

By putting Freire's ideas into a familiar framework (her own experience), she is in a better position to test their credibility and determine if she comprehends them by seeing how closely his theories (or the objective facts of the situation) "fit" her world view (her subjective frame of reference).

> I remember specifically writing down the numbers of the homeless in the United States and how [these numbers] have changed throughout the years. Then I memorized the numbers in preparation for my test, ready to spit them back to my teacher.

What Freire says about students in general seems to be "true" of Kay's experience in particular. As a student, she too is "filled" with "content which is detached from reality." It's at this point of comprehension that many students would (prematurely) curtail their inquiry. They end their encounter with text before they can use the relationship they have established to begin a reflexive dialogue, one that could deepen their perspectives. However, Kay does not stop her inquiry here. The next part of her response begins to suggest why this kind of reading is risky. Kay realizes that not only are the teachers and educational system responsible for the "objectification of the homeless," *so too is she*:

> Freire would say that the statistics [on the homeless] were too "critically objective" and that I should look at the statistics subjectively as something that can be changed. He would also remind me that the reality of the homeless was "formed by men's actions" and thus, I, a human, could in part be blamed for the homeless. He would say that I need more "critical intervention" with the homeless to understand the reality of homeless humans and how they affect the world. *Then and only then, might I say, "I sometimes look at the world as being part of me."* (my emphasis)

Kay's understanding of Freire's text centers on her realization that as long as she views the world (the other) as something outside of her, separate, "different," cut off from her "consciousness," she contributes to the "objectification" of such "problems" as the homeless. It is important to see how this kind of reading is a bidirectional process. Kay populates Freire's text with her experience of the homeless child, but, as we have seen, her understanding and experience of the homeless have also been complicated and illuminated by Freire's theories.

Essayistic reading is risky because it has the capacity to alter consciousness, and once individuals become (self-)aware, they cannot easily or simply go back to the way they were. Anthropologists Barbara Myerhoff and Jay Ruby explain:

> We can not return to our former easy terms with a world that carried on quite well without our administrations. We may find ourselves like Humpty-Dumpty, shattered wrecks unable to recapture a smooth, seamless innocence, or like the paralyzed centipede who never walked again once he was able to consider the difficulty in manipulating all those legs. [However,] once we take account of our role in our own productions, we may be led into new possibilities that compensate for the loss (1982, 2).

Fortunately, Kay's reading of Freire does not leave her "paralyzed" or a "shattered wreck," but energized as she is led into seeing "new possibilities." In their end of the semester reflections, I asked that students select passages and ideas from one or more of the texts we had read or their responses to these texts to help them theorize about themselves as readers, writers, thinkers, and learners. Kay uses the insight she has gained about the importance of "seeing the world as part of herself" to make new connections with some of these texts. I should note here that often it is the proximity of experiences that determine the kinds of links students establish with texts. One reason that Kay makes a connection between Freire and the homeless was that these two events coincided in time. Therefore, the way teachers sequence or group particular texts and assignments in a composition course may in part determine the kinds of connections students are likely to make. Of course, it also helps if the course is designed as a spiral so that recursiveness is embedded in the structure. If students are not encouraged to revisit earlier work in light of understanding gained from later work, proximity is less of a factor in understanding.

Perhaps displaying a bit of the epiphany of the newly aware, Kay notes that, like Richard Rodriguez, her past education was based on "imitation" and "regurgitating what the teacher says." Then, drawing from Walker Percy's essay, "The Loss of the Creature," she continues:

> I must salvage the meaning that I get from my education, not what my whole educational package says I must learn . . . . I am surprised, for example, when my psychology teacher speaks of the same parasympathetic nervous system that my zoology teacher

spoke of . . . I have trouble connecting what I learn to real life . . . I feel as if I am cheating myself of an education . . . .

Kay's understanding is reminiscent of Chad's, who also sought to connect his education to his life. Kay wants to see the world represented by her education as a part of her life, not separate. She doesn't want to cheat herself of an education like Richard Rodriguez, the scholarship boy, or Marya, the character in Joyce Carol Oates' fictional excerpt, "Theft" who always worries about her grades. Kay writes:

> As Freire in "The Banking Concept of Education" said, "Man is merely in the world, not with the world or with others; man is a spectator, not a recreator." Rodriguez and Marya are spectators separated from others. They believe the only important thing in life is their structured and predictable education . . . I must learn from each experience by not only taking advantage of it, but by reflecting, questioning and relating that experience to other experiences.

Kay is learning to read these texts essayistically. She is reading as an inquirer, open to new possibilities and ready to reexamine her own assumptions and experiences in light of her encounters with the ideas of others. She does not master the texts in any all-encompassing sense (nor does she need to); instead she uses the ideas contained in these texts as theories to complicate and enlarge her understanding of her own experience. And it is her subjective experience that makes the abstract ideas of these texts accessible in the first place.

To begin a dialogue with these texts, Kay has had to find some point of commonality. Even though our aim as educators may be for students to eventually understand others (texts, persons, cultures, etc.) on the other's terms (as much as that is possible), to this point, as I have already shown, individuals need to first establish a "common ground" between the other and themselves. To establish a common ground, the individual frequently first attempts to understand the other in terms of some feature of the individual's own experience. According to Reed Way Dasenbrock, philosopher Donald Davidson's concept of "interpretive charity" suggests that when we encounter "something to interpret, we interpret so as to maximize agreement, so as to credit the other speaker or the writer with beliefs as much like our own as possible" (1991, 13). It may seem that interpretive charity implies we are tied to our beliefs and ways of seeing, that we are prisoners of our specific "interpretive communities" (as Stanley Fish might argue),[2] or stuck in a hermeneutic circle; that is, we can only understand what we already understand. In Dasenbrock's reading of Davidson, however, we can only begin the process of interpretation by assuming commonality and agreement (interpretive charity) "precisely because that enables us to find and make sense of disagreement" (1991, 13). In the process of trying to understand an other we may start to question and modify our own beliefs. When we discover the "anomalous," things that don't quite fit our "prior theories," we may be forced to construct what Davidson calls "'a passing theory,' a modified version of the prior theory adjusted to fit what we have learned about the other" (qtd. in Dasenbrock 1991, 13). Thus Kay, in response to her engagement with Freire's text, questions and alters her prior theory about education as a process in which one is cut off, separated from the facts one is learning about. She develops a passing theory in which she herself is implicated in the process of learning. Whether this passing theory is simply temporary, constructed for the occasion of reading this text, or if it becomes a more permanent part of Kay's philosophy remains to be seen.

I do not think the process of understanding can commence if one can only see the other as being fundamentally different, because there would be no way (or even any incentive) to begin a conversation. When the fundamentally different other is a text, students will often make comments such as "I couldn't get into it," or "It was boring." (Translation: This text is not like me and I am not like this text; I have no interest in reading it, and I have made no attempt to try to comprehend what this text had to say.) Obviously, the claim that we first must attempt to understand an other as we understand ourselves seems to go against much of what our postmodern sensibilities tell us about respecting difference and maintaining the integrity of the other. In fact, Iris Young (1986) and Gregory Clark (1994) argue just the opposite point when they both propose a concept of community based on difference. According to Clark, such a community works not by "identifying one's self with another, but by measuring and considering the consequences of the distance that divides self from another" (69). What Clark proposes may be the eventual aim, the endpoint of the process, but I don't believe it is the way to commence trying to understand differing others.

Nonetheless, at the same time, if we are to learn—that is, if we are to modify the theory in our head as a result of our encounters with others—our interpretations cannot be simply self-confirming. Our encounters with others should lead us to critically examine and reflect on our prior theories and assumptions; otherwise we can only comprehend what we already know and understand. We can not learn anything new.

Rob's Response: Interpretive Charity Run Amok

In her discussion of Gadamer's hermeneutical philosophy, Georgia Warnke (1987) asks, "Is there a difference between a situated perspective that illuminates the meaning of an object and one that distorts it?" (75). I believe a perspective that distorts the meaning would be a perspective that did not take the other or the text into account at all. As Lorraine Code (1991) notes, taking subjectivity into account should not "entail abandoning objectivity" (41). Each is needed to constrain the other. To illustrate how interpretive charity can run amok if unchecked by dialogue with others and a reflexive monitoring of one's own "prejudices," let me briefly contrast Kay's response to Freire's text with another freshman student's response. In comparing Kay's and Rob's written responses, I am not comparing Kay and Rob themselves as students. I am trying to illustrate the differences between a response that shows evidence of essayistic reading and one that does not (yet).

When Rob announces at the outset of his first response that anyone who reads Freire's essay "can sit down and interpret it anyway they desire," I already suspect that an authentic and (self-)critical dialogue is not likely to be forthcoming. If each reader is ascribed carte blanche to interpret text, then reading becomes a *purely* subjective activity, and any dialogue that could enlarge the reader's understanding becomes superfluous. Rob's way into this text is to connect Freire's teacher-student partnership with the brother-pledge relationship in his fraternity: "My own personal evaluation [of the essay] drives me toward my experience pledging Theta Chi." Here is the proximity factor operating once again. Just as Kay used her encounter with the homeless child to help her make sense of Freire's text, Rob seems to be using what is in the forefront of his mind to help him connect to Freire's text. However, as we will see, Rob seems to be more concerned with trying to make sense of the brotherhood than engaging with Freire's text. Although I want to encourage students to use their reading to help them make sense of their present situations, I don't want students to end their reading excursions with a purely idiosyncratic understanding.

Rob explains that the "whole idea behind the fraternity atmosphere breeds manhood. Its whole purpose is to produce better men through relationships with your fellow man." (I can't help but wonder to what extent Freire's use of "men" and the masculine pronoun throughout his essay has contributed to Rob's interpretation.) Just as the teacher and student are coinvestigators in liberatory education,

Rob notes that "in the same way that the brotherhood teaches the pledgehood, the pledges teach the brothers . . . Through the pledge process, we expand the ideals of the fraternity giving it another dimension." And just as Freire's problem-posing teacher "presents the material to the students for their consideration, and reconsiders his earlier considerations as the students express their own," Rob explains that both the brothers and pledges benefit from "the understanding and utilization of the democratic process in meetings." Rob appears to "maximize agreement," to use Davidson's terms, between the text and his own world view when he turns Freire's revolutionary liberatory method into a manifestation of the (American) democratic process (the same process, of course, that is exhibited by the fraternity).

> With a grand total of fifty-nine active brothers and twenty-four pledges, innumerable ideas arise in these meetings, bringing out different dimensions on how to best operate the fraternity. In no way do the brothers' suggestions outweigh the pledges. True, a majority rule does come into effect, but not before every idea has been torn apart, embraced, criticized, and then finally voted on. Through this type of dialogue, the knowledge that best suits the fraternity is brought out.

Rob's concept of democratic dialogue—a rule designed to let everybody have their say—is vastly different from Freire's transformative notion of a dialogue that leads to critical understanding. For Rob, the dialogue in fraternity meetings seems to be more like a procedure that allows people to gain access to the floor so they can air their views and argue for what they *already* think. Even though Rob says every idea is "embraced," the real aim is consensus. Unlike Kay, Rob is not engaged in an authentic dialogue with Freire's text or with his own experience of the fraternity; he is merely using one to comprehend, or *relate* to the other. When Freire writes, "The pursuit of full humanity, however, cannot be carried out in isolation or individualism but only in fellowship and solidarity," Rob responds: "This quote pretty much sums up the fraternity . . . . The fraternity does indeed provide a unique opportunity for individual personal development but it is still superseded by the concept of brotherhood." Rob is arguing for a particular version of reality, not exploring one.

Interpretive charity runs amok because Rob's inquiry has ended prematurely; he maximizes agreement without also looking for points of disagreement, for instance, the ways in which Freire's text does not "sum up the fraternity." At this point, I should emphasize that students may not ever go beyond simply relating to a text on the basis of their own experience without the intervention of a teacher or peer. The fact that Rob curtails his inquiry prematurely may be the fault of a pedagogy (or teacher) that does not nudge him hard enough to continue. Learning to examine the differences between positions is a critical habit that, as I have already suggested, has to be taught rather than simply acquired. As Bartholomae and Petrosky note, "reading against the grain" is more difficult than "reading with the grain" precisely because it involves traveling against the text's natural currents (1993, 12). And it is particularly hard to read against the grain of one's own perspective.

And so, while a reader's subjectivities and prejudices are what makes understanding possible, the reader must always be open to the possibility that his or her prior theory will be changed or challenged. This is what Brodkey means by risk. This is what Smith means by learning. In this reading, Rob has achieved a kind of partial comprehension because he has been able to relate his ideas about the fraternity to specific ideas in the text. Since he is still trapped inside the shadow of his own gaze, however, he does not learn from Freire's theories or manage to complicate his own understanding about the fraternity. Without reflexivity, the critical examination of his own perspective, he cannot discern the differences between Freire's philosophy and his fraternity. For example, I notice Rob doesn't consider his privileged pledge status in the fraternity in light of Freire's observation that "the oppressed, who by identifying with charismatic leaders, come to feel that they themselves are active and effective" *when they are not.* It is the distinctions rather than the similarities that expand understanding. In answer to Warnke's question, Rob's "situated perspective" distorts rather than illuminates because he doesn't complete the process. Like the blind men of Indostan, he only touches the elephant; he never sees it fully.

In the next example, we will see how Chad uses his subjectivity to illuminate the meaning of both Alice Walker's essay, "In Search of Our Mother's Gardens," and his own experience by attending to differences as well as similarities.

Chad's Essay: "Prompted By Alice"

In the "Head and Heart" essay that we looked at in Chapter One, Chad explains that when he reads, he tries to understand "how the author thinks and feels about his or her world." But to begin to understand Alice Walker's essay, Chad must first find a way to connect his own experience of being white and male with the experience of being black and female in this culture. Obviously, this is no easy task.

Early in his paper, Chad writes that like the African-American women in Walker's essay, he too was oppressed: "In my family I was treated like a second-rate person. From an early age I was told I was dumb and stupid, then pushed to the side. I felt as if I didn't have the right to exist." Without knowing the particulars, this point of comparison might seem presumptuous at the very least. Even knowing that Chad did, in fact, grow up with an abusive, alcoholic father, a reader might still feel uneasy with this comparison because it seems as if the black women's oppression is about to "get disappeared" or meliorated before it can be comprehended. Unlike Rob, however, at the same time that he is seeking common ground, Chad is continually monitoring the differences between his experience and the experience of the African-American women. He is careful to note at different points in his response that similarity does not constitute sameness:

- My oppression was different than the blacks. I am white and male, which allows me greater access to the opportunities of our culture. . . .

- I was tracked into the lower level with the blacks who couldn't write or speak correctly. We were the kids who would never go to college. But I was different from them. I was white . . . .

- I got into college where the upper class were. I had to work hard to fight my low self-esteem all the way. But I didn't have to fight prejudice. I stepped in with the whites and was one of them . . . .

- When I lived in North Carolina, the unemployment lines were filled with what whites called "lazy blacks." I never heard anyone call me lazy and white when I was in the same unemployment lines. . . .

Chad's purpose, however, is not to compare his oppression with the oppression of the African-American women in Walker's essay. Instead, what interests him is the idea of the "spirit," the "notion of song," that Walker talks about:

> Unlike the women in Walker's story, my sex and skin color did not block me from the tools to express my creativity or my spirituality. But like them, I was blocked. For a long time my spirit was held captive by others and then by my own oppression. Rarely was I able to develop myself or explore and express my spirituality. But it was there. . . .

But Chad doesn't know how his own spirit was maintained as he was growing up or how he knew (without knowing) his spirituality was there. What kept the notion of song alive in him, a white male? If Chad can begin to grasp how the African-American women kept their spirits alive despite the brutality of their lives, then maybe he can begin to understand his own experience of oppression. Tentatively, Chad explores what it would be like to be an African-American woman and attempts to open himself to the experience of the "other" in a way that Rob was not able to do in his response to Freire's text:

> I wonder what it would be like if I were a black woman? In the run down shacks of North Carolina, I'd fit in. There would be plenty of blacks there. I'd properly bear several children that I couldn't support. Then I'd teach them to respect themselves and send them out to a world where they would receive little respect. Painted on a door of a small store in North Carolina, I read "No blacks or dogs." What would my children think of themselves if they were to read this . . . . But what about in New England? I wouldn't live in a shack, but I also wouldn't be able to go to a store without people looking at me as if I were out of place . . . . In and among thousands of whites, I'd stick out.

As Chad thinks about the effects of discrimination on African-American women, his dialectical foray into the realm of the other turns reflexive as he is confronted with a sobering reminder of his own privilege. In the next sentence he adds, "but as a white male I'd blend in." To understand the experience of African-American women, not only does Chad attempt to cross racial boundaries, he must also consider gender distinctions. He continues his exploratory dialogue:

> What would the white men think of me? I've heard from many men they would like to sleep with a black woman. If I were a black woman among men who wanted to sleep with me because I was black, how would that feel? Would I feel like an item, like on a menu? I'd be a commodity like Walker's grandmother. Maybe the men would talk to me as if I were special—no, probably different. I'd feel out of place . . . Would my spirit be strong enough for me to find my place instead of having to be where and what they thought I should be?

Returning to his own situation, Chad notes that his own spirit "hasn't always been strong enough to find its own place." Although Chad is white and male, he has experienced both sexual abuse and class oppression. As he considers his own experience, he comes to see that like the African-American women, his "spirit" and "drive to be," was kept alive. And yet he knows his circumstances are different. So, given the privileges afforded his race and sex, what has kept his spirit alive?

> I learned long ago that if I want[ed] anything I had to bow to the powerful males. I felt as if I were in the wrong world . . . . My spirit

waited much like Walker's spirit waited . . . . Walker's mother and mother's mother kept alive what was most important, the notion of song, or as I see it, the drive to be. Somehow my drive was never taken. Through beatings, rape (by a white male) and prolonged alcohol usage my spirit was kept alive; broken, at times, but never lost. *In those ways, I'm like the black woman. But I'm different in that I'm a white male and I don't know what kept my spirit alive* (emphasis added).

Chad's oppression is less visible and overt than the kinds of discrimination experienced by African-American women. But it is this distinction that, interestingly, enables him to begin to understand what all forms of oppression have in common—the loss of self and agency. At this point, the horizons separating Chad's experience and the experience of the African-American women begin to fuse, or at least momentarily blur.

Can anyone see that I am? I'm lost without knowing how to be found. I'm dead. I'm black and female in a white-male's world. But I'm really white and male. No one calls me nigger or (fill in one of many degrading names our culture has for women) so I'm supposed to know who and where I am. I'm supposed to take jobs of power and know I desire them. I'm not supposed to question my own right to exist. But I do. My oppression often left me without any self. I would become whatever someone wanted me to be, at work and in bed. Do I sound like a black woman? Do I sound like a white male?

With a dramatic shift of voice in his final paragraphs, Chad looks through or past difference to focus on what might be termed the common life force, the spirit that fights to exist within every human:

Did you have to fight your self-oppression? Maybe the fight helped keep us alive. Maybe whatever this thing spirit is kept us alive. Take my body and my children. Take my ability to sing. But you can't take me. I remember and soon so will you. So say this thing named spirit, named Walker, named black, named white, named male, named female, named life.

I would argue that Chad has earned this insight. He has engaged in a process of essayistic reading that has earned him a deeper understanding of both Walker's essay and his own experience. He has not attempted to arrive without first having traveled through intellectual liminality. Often, students will first try to erase racial, class, and gender differences by saying things like, "Hey, we're all human beings here." Unlike Mark, the student in the last chapter, who wrote that "everyone has adversities to overcome" without distinguishing between these adversities, Chad has not tried to deny difference. Nor has he diminished the reality of the other by focusing exclusively on his own subjective experience. Instead he has brought his experience (subjectivity) into dialogue with Walker's text (the objective facts at hand).

Like Kay's reading of Freire's text, Mindy's essay about the nursing home, and Susan's essay about changing her name, Chad's essayistic reading of Walker's text doesn't really produce a conclusion with which we should agree or disagree; his reading has produced an understanding, a way of looking at Walker's essay (as well as his own experience) that we too might want to consider or think about ourselves. At least we might want to if we ourselves are reading essayistically.

So far I have looked at students' written responses to their reading of other people's texts. Now I want to consider essayistic reading when a student is reading and responding to her own written texts.

Anna's Reflection: Education as "Consciousness of Consciousness"

Although I ask students to examine their writing and writing process in written metacommentaries for each paper they produce,[3] I want to direct my comments in this section to students' responses to the body of texts they have constructed over time, in this case, a semester's composition course. At the end of each semester, I ask my students to read all of their papers and reading responses as they might a single text. The purpose of such a request is overtly reflective: I want students to examine their own work for patterns or themes and to theorize about what these patterns (or lack of patterns) suggest about them as readers, writers, thinkers, and learners. I am particularly interested in the ways the students will use the ideas gained from their reading to frame and talk about their earlier papers and insights. This assignment is similar to what I did in Chapter One when I used my own texts and experiences to demonstrate how understanding of an idea, like reflexivity, develops gradually over time. In a composition course, students frequently are not aware what they are learning or that they are learning at all. They have no sense of themselves developing as readers and writers. This assignment often surprises them.

As Anna, a first-semester freshman student, reviews her work, she writes, "I can see examples of where I have developed into an active reader, a conscious writer, a perpetual thinker, and a connecting learner." Her twelve-page reflection traces the development of her understanding of what it means to be educated. She frames this retrospective reading of her papers and reading responses with ideas gained from the essays she has read, especially Paulo Freire's chapter, "The Banking Concept of Education." For instance, after rereading her first paper of the course, a case study of herself as a reader and writer, through the perspective provided by Freire, she notes:

> I was beginning to become aware of my actions and thoughts, as well as the reasons behind them. Freire describes this awareness as 'consciousness of consciousness,' and I was beginning the eternal process of a problem-posing method of education . . ." What Anna was "beginning to become aware of" was that good grades didn't necessarily mean good education: "My grades said that I was learning in school . . . [but] I realize[d] that I wasn't being educated.

Even though students in this particular class had a free choice of topic for their biweekly papers after the initial case study I asked them to do, Anna was surprised to discover that her essays often revealed the continuation of a strand of thinking that had first emerged in a reading response or earlier paper. It is only when Anna examines all her papers together, however, that she discovers she has been involved in an ongoing quest for a new definition of education. In hindsight, Anna sees that each response and paper she has written seems to have further contributed to an enlarged understanding of what education means to her.

In her first reading response of the term (to Richard Rodriguez's autobiographical chapter on his schooling) she tentatively begins to piece together a new sense of education. She writes in her reflection:

> After reading Rodriguez's essay I felt unsettled. I did not agree with the general concept of this style of education, but I was not sure what I thought was the correct style of education . . . . I came to the conclusion that Rodriguez learned while he was in school, but he was not becoming educated. Education must not only be logic and reason, but must include feelings and heritage as well.

It's interesting to me that here again we see a student discovering that education is both subjective and objective. Anna's conclusion is similar to the realization Chad comes to in his essay, "Head and Heart," and that Kay makes in her response to Freire's text. However, Anna's realization is only intellectual at this stage; she has not yet tested it on herself. As Anna continues to examine her work from her perspective at the end of the semester, she sees that "this [response] was not the end to my process of defining education." She next looks at her response to Joyce Carol Oates' fictional excerpt,"Theft," about Marya, a young woman obsessed with her grades, and she notices how her own idea about education has undergone further complication. Here is Anna's reading of Anna reading:

> After identifying Marya's education (or lack of), I looked at myself. I identified with Marya through my beliefs that school is the main priority . . . and my personal development is addressed only when time permits. I felt while reading about Marya I was a walking Marya brought to life . . . As I read my voice into Marya's words, we asked together what significance grades held.

Anna writes that the essay she wrote following her response to Oates' text illustrated how "I write to sort things out that exist in a jumbled state in my mind. . . .The essay addressed my concerns about whether or not I am working for an education and how I could determine the answer to my question." She finds that this essay yields the new thought that perhaps education is (or should be) a "lifelong process" that "extends past the formal structure of school systems." Anna now uses her newly formulated "theory" to look at her own educational experience: "My essay forced me to evaluate my education and the time I have spent in college."

Anna writes in her reflection that although "Rodriguez sparked my interest in determining what an education was [and] Oates helped me decide what some of the criteria were," it was Paulo Freire's chapter that "enabled me to identify the different aspects of education posed by Oates and Rodriguez. By connecting the ideas presented by each, I can synthesize . . . and evaluate my education thus far." Each piece of writing that she examines seems to have built on and subsumed (rather than replaced) her previous understanding. She realizes she has been involved in a kind of learning that, in James Britton's words, "consists of a process of making finer and finer distinctions" (qtd. in Graham 1991, 77). Anna's reflection has uncovered a Deweyian truth: Each definition of education results in a temporary "consummation" of her thinking, not a "cessation" of her inquiry. She explains that the "essays that I have written and read in the past will help me read and write essays in the future. I am becoming actively aware and involved in my thinking process." Thus, her encounters with the ideas of others have invited her to do more than simply "acknowledge that I have an opinion about a subject." *She has also become reflexive:* "I now look for the reasons that shape my opinions and my ideas about the subject."

I believe that students can learn a great deal about themselves as readers, writers, thinkers, and learners when they have an opportunity to reexamine the written texts they have produced throughout the composition course. After covering the curriculum of the course, they now have an opportunity to uncover the significance of their transaction with it. What students discover about their earlier papers won't necessarily change the grades they received on those papers, but what they learn will prove more valuable in the long run. For Anna, the notion of lifelong learning is no longer a hand-me-down idea. She has claimed it for herself. She has thus earned her insight that "I will never be fully educated because I will always be in the process of education." Her papers and responses reveal how her own understanding has been modified gradually over time.

Just as my retrospective reading of my own work in Chapter One results in a unique, personal understanding, so does Anna's reading of her texts. We have each composed a coherence of how we got *here*—where *here* is but a temporary resting spot in the journey we both are still making to *there*. The understandings Anna, Chad, Rob, Kay, and I have reached are partial (in both senses of the word), provisional, and approximate. Graham Good (1988) describes the essayistic transaction as a moment of temporary illumination: "Self and object define each other, but momentarily. The self will go on to other definitions through other objects; the objects, whether places, works of art, or issues, will find other definitions in other selves" (5).

Teachers and Essayistic Reading

Students seem to be well aware that their texts are likely "to find other definitions in other selves," especially when those definitions are manifested in the selves who determine and distribute grades. The sheer number of students who admit to the practice of "giving the teacher what she wants" suggests that they believe teachers' readings of their texts are for the most part purely subjective. Therefore, it seems vital that teachers be aware of and be able to explain how they arrived at their readings and evaluations of student texts. Teachers are in positions of power (in relation to their students) and, if they are to resist superimposing their "ideal" versions of what a text should say (and how it should say it) onto what a student's text actually does say, they need to be conscious of the prejudices they carry (Knoblauch and Brannon 1984). As Brenda Deen Schildgen suggests, teachers, "must be conscious of their own convictions about writing, able to scrutinize the limits and possibilities of these attitudes, and willing to concede that these convictions are open to question, correction, and adaptation . . . " (1993, 36). To read students' texts well—that is, sensitively, fairly, fully—I believe it is helpful for teachers to read them reflexively, both for what the texts say and for how they are written.

When teachers read student texts and encounter words that don't quite fit, sentence patterns we don't recognize, or ideas that have not been fully fleshed out, it might be helpful for us to recall our own memories of schools and ourselves as novice writers and new learners. For instance, I would say that it is Mike Rose's ability to read his students' texts and lives through the lens of his own experience, that is, dialogically and reflexively, that makes *Lives On the Boundary* such compelling work. In his book (which I might argue is really an extended essay itself), Rose not only gains a more complicated insight into students' struggles on the margins of academic life, he also seems to reap a fuller understanding of the nature of his own literacy development. I suspect that it is because he sees a connection between the kinds of academic problems his students face and his own history of failure as a student that he is able to read their work so sensitively and carefully. Lisa Delpit (1988) reminds us that teachers, as persons with power, have a responsibility to try to understand their students' perspectives. Essayistic reading offers one way for us to do so. To illustrate, I return to my reading of Ralph's paper, "Who Wears the Pants?" that I discussed in Chapter Two. In doing so, I hope to demonstrate the slippery, but, I believe, necessary role the teacher's subjectivity plays in our interpretation and evaluation of student texts.

Reading "Who Wears the Pants": Take Two

When anthropologist Alan Peshkin (1988a) talks about the need for researchers to identify and monitor their "subjective Is" during the research process, he is talking about the researcher's preconceptions or prejudices. Teachers also need to be aware of how their "subjective Is" come into play during their reading of student texts.

My role as a teacher affects the degree to which I was or am able to open to Ralph's text. In other words, this engagement is not a free or chance encounter between equals (as few encounters between teachers and students are). I bring certain assumptions and expectations about the conventions of writing (style, length, language, diction, grammar, etc.) to this text that I am not likely to be easily persuaded to modify. These are conscious preconceptions. For the most part, I know what they are before I begin to read Ralph's paper.

However, my preconceptions also come into play when I am responding to the content of Ralph's paper, and these "subjective Is"
may be more subconscious. As readers will recall, Ralph was upset
that his friend Steve had stopped spending time with the guys, and
he believed that Sheila, Steve's girlfriend, was to blame for this situation. According to Ralph, she had taken to "wearing the pants" in
the relationship, leaving Steve defenseless, emasculated.

To read Ralph's paper essayistically, I have to be willing to put
my own concerns on hold (at least temporarily), seek common
ground, and open myself to the "otherness" of his text. In this case,
the otherness in Ralph's text goes beyond simple student otherness
(e.g., naive, underdeveloped, or incorrect language and content) to
an otherness that, at this time, I am eager to resist because it chafes
my sensibilities as a woman with an emerging feminist consciousness. If I attempt to engage this paper openly, tentatively, and reflexively, I know I might uncover information about my own attitudes
and prejudices toward men and the patriarchy, information that
could make me a more conscious reader and thus more effective
teacher in the long run. But why am I reluctant to open myself to
the perspective contained in this paper? To what extent is my
heightened gender sensitivity and bias operating here?

Anne Malone, a colleague of mine, presented a paper at the Conference on College Composition and Communication in Nashville
(1994) that demonstrated how the meaning of a story (as well as the
story itself) changes when the sex of the characters is changed. How
would I have read Ralph's paper if the narrator had been a female
writing about her female friend's relationship with a male? Lorraine
Code (1991; 1993) asks if the sex of the knower is epistemologically
significant. While I am not exactly answering that question here, I
think it will be evident to readers that changing the sex of the people
in this paper changes the meaning of the paper and the readers' responses to it. And for teachers, that is *pedagogically significant*. Here
are excerpts from Ralph's essay with Steve and Sheila's sex reversed:

- Those men, as nice as they are, just won't let my friends breathe.
  I mean what's so bad about the girls having a night to ourselves
  at the ballpark? Don't guys like nights to themselves once in
  awhile? I've heard them say they do but rarely does it happen.
  They're simply too busy hounding us . . . .

- Sheila couldn't do this, Sheila couldn't do that. She couldn't go
  here; She couldn't go there; and it's all because he said so. How
  does he think he can control her like that . . . .

- Instead of confronting Steve when they have a conflict of inter-

est, she keeps her mouth shut, and as a result we never see her
. . . God knows we begged her to confront him. She is so reluctant that I would say she's scared . . . Why Steve can't see that
he's crowding her absolutely mystifies me. Perhaps that is just
the way some men are, but that certainly doesn't justify it . . . .

- Sheila simply seems to have lost her confidence, assertiveness
  and the ability to tactfully stand up for herself . . . Sheila feels
  as though she must act responsible and proper in front of him
  because there have been times when she hasn't, and he was fu-
  rious . . . .

- When Sheila does confront him about something, one of two
  things happen. One, he gets his way (normally the case) and
  Sheila is once again reduced to nothing, and the other is that
  she gets her way, but the two end up mad at each other . . . .

- It may sound like we're sticking our noses in where they don't
  belong, but Sheila is a good friend, so we have all the right to
  involve ourselves to a certain extent. All we want is to help
  Sheila assert herself so she can have a little bit more space.
  She's told us several times that she'd love to have a little bit
  more room to do what she wants and not have to worry about
  the consequences . . . .

The stance represented in this version of the paper is no more
essayistic than the original. The imaginary female writer does not
probe her own perspectives or acknowledge how her own frame of
reference works to shape her interpretation. The female writer also
seems unable or unwilling to move beyond her already formulated
thesis. It would seem that this writer's inability or refusal to reflexively examine her own assumptions and how she came to hold
these assumptions prevents her from viewing the situation from
multiple perspectives, and therefore limits her ability to engage essayistically with the subject. Just like Ralph. But no, something has
definitely changed.

By reversing the positions of the key players, we have got a very
different story. To me, this new story speaks of silencing, of fear, of
overwhelming control, oppression, and possibly violence. As a female reader, I am more sympathetic to this story because this is a
tale that affirms an understanding I already have about many relationships between males and females. Without much effort, I not
only comprehend why this writer is upset, I believe she is justified
in feeling this way.

I was not sympathetic to Ralph's position; nor did I feel he was
justified in his complaints. In Ralph's paper, Steve is made to seem

the poor, henpecked male, victim of an overbearing, unreasonable woman. In the hypothetical female writer's paper, Sheila appears to be a real victim of male dominance and control. My concern, as a teacher, that this writer open herself to understanding the other (in this case the "oppressor's" perspective) is overshadowed by my concern for the writer and the woman she's writing about. In both versions of these papers, then, my subjectivity directs my reading. It determines what I focus on, what it means, and how I will respond. Reader subjectivity is, of course, a given in reader response theories of reading literary texts; however, a reader's subjectivity is more complicated when the reader is a teacher reading a student text.

Regardless of my sympathies, however, my usual pedagogical response as the teacher-reader of student papers, as I explained in Chapter Two, is to introduce some kind of counterdiscourse. However, I realize the counterdiscourse I would propose is different for each version of this essay. In the last chapter, I mentioned that after I received a draft of Ralph's paper, I urged him to make use of some of the readings we had been examining in class. I hoped that the literature we had read theorizing the differences between male and female relational needs and desires might enable him to reconsider Steve and Sheila's relationship from a broader perspective, one that would enable him to see Sheila (and Steve) more sympathetically. What happened was that Ralph interpreted these texts so as to maintain agreement with his own view. He read relationship to simply denote male-female relationship and, thus, was able to adhere to his original position.

For the female version of this paper, my (hypothetical) response would also be to introduce another view. Here, however, I don't think I would urge the writer to seek "common ground" with Steve, the other, or suggest she attempt to understand Steve's view from a broader perspective. I would not push her to examine and write about how she has come to the conclusions she has; nor would I suggest that she question the validity of her conclusions. Whereas Ralph's stance toward his subject appears myopic and prematurely certain to me, the certainty expressed in the female writer's stance that the situation between Sheila and Steve is a real problem seems like a perceptive observation. Thus, I would not ask her to interrogate her own perspective; I would try to get her to complicate her understanding about Sheila, who is portrayed as a real victim in this version of the story. I would suggest that the writer examine Sheila's reluctance to speak up for herself in her relationship with Steve. My counterdiscourse, then, might include other readings about women who stay in relationships in which they are silenced or abused.

In each case, the writers of both versions of this paper appear no closer to understanding the actions of their friends by the end of their papers. Writing has not enabled them to see their situations more clearly. As the teacher, I want to help them become unstuck, but not by having them latch on to some simplistic answer ("that's just the way women/men are"), but by inviting them to use reading and writing as methods for reflexive inquiry. I want them to earn their insights about the various ways men and women are positioned in this culture. And yet, the ways I devise to do this are different for each paper because of my different responses to the situations they describe. The question I must now ask myself is this: Is my subjectivity interfering with my ability to read these texts fairly (or at least in a way that is helpful to the students)?

Timothy Crusius suggests that once individuals have identified their preconceptions, the next step in hermeneutic inquiry is to "distinguish . . . between enabling and disabling prejudices" (1991, 89). I believe it is our unconscious prejudices that have the most potential to become "disabling." That is why my reading of these texts needs to be reflexive; I need to identify and interrogate the assumptions and beliefs I bring to my reading, especially to texts like Ralph's which have a tendency to elicit a strong response from me. Looking at my reactions to these two papers, I see that my response is influenced by my beliefs about the power relations between males and females. And I may be privileging the female perspective because I still see women at a disadvantage in both these encounters.

In each version of the paper, I focus on Sheila as the other. Sheila, however, occupies different positions in each paper. In the first paper, Sheila is the woman, whom Steve, Ralph's friend, elects to spend time with instead of Ralph. In the second version, Sheila is the female narrator's friend who was being controlled by Steve. I use active and passive verbs deliberately here, because I think they are indicative of my take on the situation in terms of who is in a position of power, who has agency, and who does not. In each case, my sympathies lie with the person I perceive to be the underdog, and in this situation, that person is always the woman.

I didn't focus on Steve as an other in the original paper because, unlike Ralph, I perceived Steve, a male, to be a person with agency; I believed that his decision to spend time with Sheila must be a conscious decision, one that he and Sheila have probably mutually agreed to, despite what Steve may say to Ralph when they are alone. However, for Ralph, Steve, the once familiar, has now become strange. Steve has become an other that Ralph no longer recognizes or identifies with *because Steve seems to have lost his agency* (that

which previously defined him as male?). Even though Ralph sometimes gets angry with his friend for not standing up for himself, he
places most of the blame for Steve's loss of agency on Sheila. He
seems to think that Sheila is a being more capable of agency than
Steve (although it's a type of agency he does not really comprehend).
And in the hypothetical female's essay, I did not focus on Steve, who
now occupies the Sheila position from the original essay, as an other
because from the female narrator's point of view, he may be an other,
but he is an other *with agency.* In this case, he is the oppressor.

Neither version of this paper is essayistic. But neither is essayistic for different reasons that are related to questions of agency. Earlier in this chapter, I suggested that two different stances were
antithetical to the spirit of essayism: uncritical acceptance and hypercritical attack. In one approach, the self surrenders to the *other;*
in the second approach, the self overrides the *other.* Ralph seems to
be moving toward the latter stance in his judgmental objectification
of Sheila. My response was directed toward helping him to examine
his own position, rather than privilege it or impose it on his subjects. The hypothetical female writer, upset as she appears to be,
still seems in danger of submitting to the situation and simply accepting her own and Sheila's powerlessness to change it. Thus, my
response is directed toward enlarging her understanding of why
some women might behave as Sheila does. My reading of these papers is not simply based on my bias for the female perspective (although I can't deny that is part of it); rather, it is informed by my
diagnosis of each writer's failure to essay.

Reading "Who Wears the Pants": Take Three

My response and Ralph's response to the situation between Steve
and Sheila were different because our readings of the world at that
time were very different. As the teacher, I attempted to make another
reading possible—not so Ralph would immediately embrace it, but
so he would reflect on his current situation from a new vantage
point. While I don't think I purposely tried to *impose* my reading of
the world onto Ralph's text, I do wonder how hard I worked to understand Ralph's perspective.

In a thoughtful and courageous essay entitled "Teaching and
Learning as a Man," Robert Connors cautions, "There is a great danger of stereotyping students . . . but it is easier to casually assume
stereotypes about young men than almost any other group" (1996,
149). Recently, when I shared Ralph's paper as part of a conference
presentation on reflexivity, I noticed the audience (both male and

female) chuckle (or snicker), shake their heads, and roll their eyes. Thinking about their reactions made me want to reconsider my own. As Connors notes, the tendency to stereotype means that

> [o]ur readings of male students are often too simple; . . . Although it is understandable why male attitudes, fears, and psychological structures have been either ignored or subjected to offhand dismissal in the discourse of contemporary composition, the result *has not been a more effective understanding of our students* (my emphasis, 156).

When I first received Ralph's paper in class, I did not really read it essayistically. I read it critically. My own agenda as a teacher concerned with finding ways to help students develop an essayistic stance took precedence over my attempts to understand and learn from the perspective reflected in his paper. And while these two positions are not unrelated—I need to understand Ralph's point of view in order to help him become a more effective essay writer—my purpose in this textual encounter is not first and foremost to deepen my *own* understanding. But should it be? And can it be?

Donald Murray, Donald Graves, and other proponents of writing process and response theories of teaching have argued that to be effective teachers, teachers themselves need to be learners. They suggest that the teacher's job is to help her or his students teach the teacher what they have to say. If teachers only read as learners, might not their own learning and understanding take precedence over the learning and understanding of their students? On the other hand, if teachers want to become more reflective and effective teachers, don't they have to try to remain open to the lessons their students have to teach?

Perhaps I read Ralph's paper more critically than if it had been the first writing I had seen from Ralph. "Who Wears the Pants" was the second paper Ralph had written in my course. Even though I wasn't consciously aware of doing so at the time, I realize I probably carried my experience of reading the first text into my reading of his paper about Steve. It's only much later, when I found this abandoned draft in his file, that I discovered the similarities between the two papers. In his first paper, he wrote about an incident in high school in which the coach of the previously all-male soccer team had allowed a woman to try out for the team. Ralph used this incident to argue that women should not be allowed to play men's sports. Rosy, the sister of one of his best friends, was a fine athlete and a "real sweetheart," and Ralph writes how he tried to comfort her after the guys on the team had given her a rough time. He says

I felt caught in the middle because I didn't feel she should be trying out for the men's team in the first place. I didn't want to tell her
that men and women don't belong on the same field because Rosy
was already upset and I knew we just would've gotten into an argument.

Once again, we see Ralph, the loyal friend, offering his advice
about a situation that makes him uncomfortable. As with Steve, he
seems to want to "talk some sense" into Rosy, but he is worried
about confrontation, or getting into an argument. It's easy for me to
read this behavior as patronizing, especially in lieu of the reason
Ralph does not think women should play on the same field as men.
As Ralph explains, not "too many men would be turned on to the
fact that this woman is out on the field sweating, hitting, rolling
around in the mud, and doing things that girls supposedly don't
do." To me, it seems Ralph really doesn't appear to be concerned
about how Rosy would feel, but rather about how the men would
feel. Maybe that's the point that I have been missing all along.
Ralph *is* writing about how men feel in both these essays. Did I dis-
miss Ralph's feelings as irrelevant or unimportant because of my
perception of him as male occupying a position of power?

As it turns out, Rosy doesn't make the team, and interestingly,
Ralph praises her: "She held her head high . . . she realized the courage it took to even step out on the field." Ralph concludes his paper
by opting for a relativistic nonconclusion, saying that "everyone's entitled to their opinion" of whether or not women should "break into
the male sports world." But almost as an aside, he adds: "but *I don't
think it's such a crime if things remain as they are at least for the time
being . . .*" (my emphasis). In both these essays, I can now see a young
man desperately clinging to an understanding of the world that seems
to be rapidly changing. Here is longing and loss that I think many
adults (male or female) might be able to understand. If I construct Ralph with agency, I find myself less sympathetic. However, if I hear this
swagger as the false bravado of the growing pains of youth caught in
the whirlpool of developmental and cultural reconfiguration, I am
more apt to look beyond the mask of masculinity. Connors makes the
point that our male students often make it difficult for us to get beyond
our stereotypes and negative reactions: "We are often not invited to go
deeper, especially not by the young men themselves . . . [but] we must
strive to get beyond our own reactiveness" (149).

In order to help me get beyond my own reactiveness, I need a
counterdiscourse. Let me return for a moment to Chad's essay in response to Alice Walker. Chad, I believe, allows me to peer beyond

the mask and glimpse some of the burden of masculinity associated with being a white male in this culture. Toward the end of his paper, Chad writes:

> I'm lost without knowing how to be found. I'm dead. I'm black and female in a white male's world. But I'm really white and male. No one calls me nigger so I'm supposed to know who and where I am. I'm supposed to take jobs of power and know I desire them. I'm not supposed to question my own right to exist. But I do. . . .

Chad acknowledges the privilege afforded him by his race and sex; at the same time, he makes it possible for me to begin to grasp the implication of being "black and female in a white man's world" or black and female in a white man's body. Chad's essayistic, exploratory stance toward his subject helps me to get beyond the stereotypes. I have to work much harder to overcome my reactiveness in papers like Ralph's.

Reflexive reading can help both teachers and students get beyond their initial reactiveness. Unfortunately, I did not have students in Ralph's class reread the writing they produced during the course to look for patterns and insights, as I did with Anna's class. Perhaps doing so would have enabled Ralph to begin to theorize about his experience. I do think teachers can learn to identify their reactiveness by developing the habit of attending to it. I don't want to sound like I am placing an additional pedagogical burden on overworked teachers when I suggest that they need to continually monitor the assumptions they bring to their readings of student texts. By periodically paying attention to our responses to student texts, especially the ones that elicit strong reactions, negative or positive, I believe we can change the way we read all of our student work. I originally chose to reread Ralph's paper because it evoked such a strong reaction from me. By identifying and looking closely at the ways my "subjective Is" were operating and continue to operate in my response to this text, I am now more likely to be aware of their influence on my reading of other student texts. In some cases, a single, significant reflexive encounter has the capacity to alter the way we see ourselves and our worlds.

As teachers, every time we teach a text—whether it be written by an established author, professional critic, or student—we have an opportunity to enlarge our own understanding of what that text means. When I turn my reading of student texts into a reflexive inquiry, I find that I not only deepen and complicate my own understanding of my pedagogy, but I am more responsive to my students.

Because I am consciously seeking to identify and examine my own preconceptions and prejudices, I am more likely to remain open to papers like Ralph's. These papers have the potential to turn me into a reluctant or resisting reader, a stance I don't think teachers can afford to unconsciously assume. As I have revealed, my prejudices are not fixed assumptions. They evolve, deepen, recede, and even disappear (although new ones take their place). As Herbert Spiegelberg notes, "the only cure for subjectivity is reflexivity, which is 'more and better subjectivity, more discriminating, and more self-critical subjectivity . . . '" (qtd. in Babcock 1980, 11). It is often difficult to turn my critical gaze inward and open myself to self-scrutiny, questioning my authority and leaving myself vulnerable to doubt. I have, however, come to realize that unless the teacher is at risk, perhaps she is not really teaching.

Notes

1. All of these essays except the one by Richard Wright were from David Bartholomae and Anthony Petrosky's *Ways of Reading* (2d ed.) Boston: St. Martins, 1990: They included Jane Tompkins, "Indians: Textualism, Morality and the Problem of History"; Richard Rodriguez, "The Achievement of Desire"; Walker Percy, "The Loss of the Creature"; Joyce Carol Oates, "Theft" (From *Marya, A Life*). Richard Wright's excerpt was from his autobiographical novel, *Black Boy: Record of Childhood and Youth*. I use the Bartholomae and Petrosky anthology, but not their sequencing or assignments.

2. Davidson, according to Reed Way Dasenbrock, takes issue with Fish's point that, as members of different interpretive communities, we can not know what someone else means, only what we take them to mean. (We can only know the text that we read, not the one the writer has written.) On the contrary, Davidson, Dasenbrock says, assumes that we in fact do know what the other means:

> To say that someone's beliefs are unknowably different from our own is to imply that we know what these beliefs are and therefore know them to be different . . . . once we grant that we can mean different things by the same words . . . [we must also grant that] we can also mean the same thing by different words . . . What it means is that the world contains different speakers and interpreters, who sometimes use the same words, and sometimes not, who sometimes hold the same beliefs, and sometimes not (Dasenbrock 1991, 10–11).

The point, as Dasenbrock notes, is that it's not our membership in different interpretive communities that makes understanding difficult, but our different interpretations. For one thing, we belong to many interpretive communities simultaneously, any one or some which may exert a stronger influence on our reading or interpretation at any given time. For instance, when I went back to review some of Fish's work that I first read in 1985, I found that I had drawn from Walter Kintsch's theories of macrostructures, work that I was trying to understand at the time, to help me understand Fish's text. I realize that I tend to use my newest (often not yet fully formulated) thinking in my efforts to make sense of new ideas. Another way of saying this is that I foreground those interpretive communities in which I am currently trying to become a part (or in which I am trying to determine if I want to or should become a member).

3. For a description of the ways I get students to read and reflect on their own developing drafts, see my essay, "Using Reading in the Writing Classroom," in *Nuts and Bolts: A Practical Guide to Teaching College Composition* (1993), edited by Thomas Newkirk.

Chapter Four

Collaborative Inquiry
and Reflexivity

*In taking seriously the interpretive insights of the other
. . . we can begin to develop our own. Our own understanding can become richer and more differentiated to
the extent that we try to understand the point of other interpretations, come to understand our own in relation to
them, try to accommodate within our own interpretations
the insights we think those other interpretations may possess, and work to preserve our own interpretations from
the lacunae we find in others.*

—Georgia Warnke,
Feminism and Hermeneutics

In the last two chapters, I examined essayistic writing and essayistic reading as a dialogic and reflexive approach to texts, an approach that could enlarge, challenge, or transform students'
understandings of their subjects and themselves. In this chapter, I
want to further illustrate how reflexivity can lead to the development of more complex and complicated perspectives, by describing
a collaborative inquiry project that uses and builds on these essayistic approaches to texts. The essayistic stance that I have been considering thus far has focused on a single transaction between a
writer or a reader and a text. Collaborative inquiry increases the
number of transactions, as students attempt to negotiate several
multiple (and often conflicting) perspectives at once. They must be
open to and engage various experts and authorities on their topic as

well as each member of the group's evolving perspectives. Collaborative inquiry entails genuine dialogic encounters with flesh-and-blood beings who are capable of talking back.

The collaborative inquiry project I describe typically occurs in the last four and a half weeks of a fifteen-week-long composition course, and requires groups of two or three students to work closely together investigating, discussing, reading, and writing about an issue, problem, or concern of their choice. These self-selected groups decide on a subject for inquiry, conduct research and interviews, and spend a great deal of time in and out of class thinking, talking, and writing about their information. Individually, students keep a personal journal to reflect on their topic and their group's processes of collaboration. Twice a week they draw from their journals to write "reflective memos" to other members of the group. These memos become the basis for further dialogue within the group. Students use their conversations with others to arrive at their own (hopefully more complicated, but not necessarily resolved) understanding of their topic, an understanding which shares some aspects of the group's perspective, but which has been individually and subjectively processed and "claimed." Eventually, students produce separate research essays on their common topic. They read each other's essays and coauthor an introduction to their collection of papers. The introduction discusses why the group chose their topic and examines the similarities and differences in their positions. Students submit their journals, memos, papers, and introduction for evaluation. Half of their grade is based on the "density" of their journals and memos, and the other half is based on their paper and foreword. Thus, the actual essay counts for only about 40 percent of their total grade.

These projects are not designed to produce consensus (although they can); my aim is for students to uncover both similarities and differences in their ways of thinking and writing about their topics. Collaborative inquiry often makes manifest the largely invisible and unconscious processes of thinking and inquiry. By working closely with others for an extended period of time, students can actually see how their ideas develop and change. For example, in the following journal entry, Carrie not only notices the different perspectives that emerge in her group, but more importantly, we see how she has come to understand and value these differences:

> We all had our own ideas and conceptions coming into our talk, yet as we talked, they seemed to bend, stretch, and grow under the weight of the other's words [as well as] our thoughts about these words. At first I noticed this in listening to Liz and, in truth, was

annoyed. I thought, How can she change her mind like that? Didn't she just say . . . That's where I stopped. I realized that it was not a fault as I had wanted to believe, but that it was someone trying to amalgamate all of her present thoughts, and she was merely trying to articulate them . . . I think through having to learn to communicate your ideas and feelings that you can't help but come to appreciate the person more . . . . Unless there is some great gulf (so great that people cannot, or shall I say will not, consider the thoughts of others), you can't help but come to . . . respect a person for the fact she stands for something and is basically a thinking person with ideas and feelings.

Carrie's first reaction to Liz's changing her mind is that it is a "fault"; only when she grants Liz her own subjecthood can she then begin to see Liz's actions as intelligible and intelligent. Parker Palmer says that when we encounter the words and ideas of others, our first question should not be "How logical is that thought? [but] Whose voice is behind it? What is the personal reality from which that thought emerged? How can I enter and respond to the relation of that thinker to the world?" (1983, 64). Interestingly, this is exactly the shift that Carrie makes. Once she acknowledges that Liz is a "thinking person with ideas and feelings," and that these ideas and feelings may be different from her own (recall Gerald's realization in Chapter Two that Spanish *es diferente*), she can engage in what Maria Lugones (1987) describes as "world-travelling." To oversimplify a bit, world-travelling is a process of mentally shifting between different cultures or realities in such a way as to acknowledge and affirm the possibility of pluralist perspectives.

World-travelling is not the same as being in the state of "between" that I talk about in the first chapter. The world-traveller occupies more than one position or entertains more than one perspective. World-travelling is a both/and position. The between is more of a neither/nor position. When a person experiences the sensation of being between, she neither belongs to one world nor another. Her previous moorings loosened or disrupted, she temporarily drifts, suspended in a liminal sea between worlds. Between can be a precursory state to world-travelling, but, as I've already suggested, it can just as easily send nonreflexive individuals back to safe, familiar shores or else push them to anchor (without thinking) at the first dry port they see.

Lugones, a Latin-American woman, notes that people "outside of the mainstream . . . become 'world-travellers' as a matter of necessity and survival" (11). Because they need or desire access to the center, outsiders have "acquired flexibility" in moving from worlds where they feel at home to worlds where they may not feel at ease.

However, Lugones suggests that world-travelling can be "willfully exercised" by anyone, including those comfortably situated in the mainstream, who are genuinely interested in cross-cultural understanding. I find Lugones' metaphor of world-travelling useful for thinking about ways of engaging new ideas through writing, reading, and collaborative inquiry. World-travelling and collaborative inquiry, like essayistic reading and writing, work best when students do not try to conquer or assimilate the other, but instead, remain receptive and open to surprise and change. What prevents individuals from "going native" or losing themselves in another world is reflexivity—the backward glance and the continual monitoring of old beliefs from new positions. The process of collaborative inquiry allows Carlos, another student, the opportunity to travel to his partner's world and then to examine his own world from her position. Near the end of their self-styled project on how men and women choose mates, he offers these reflections in his journal:

> I can't get [my partner] to agree to what I think and believe; but I can get her to appreciate it. She's helped me to [also] be this way just by working with her . . . Oh Christ! I'm turning into a woman! It's a conspiracy! . . . [But] that's what collaboration means: accepting and appreciating another writer/person for what they are and what they value . . . I'm learning that my value to other people intellectually is not to put them in a position to defend themselves. I'm listening to others. I'm thinking about how my thoughts are interpreted by them . . . (Chiseri-Strater 1991, 29–30).

Carlos playfully jokes about losing his old self ("I'm turning into a woman!"), but what he has lost is his need to have other people agree with him by putting "them in a position to defend themselves." Like Carrie, he has come to see the other as a subject, one to listen to and learn from, rather than an object to master or own. Collaboration or travelling to his partner's world has afforded him the opportunity to resee his previous actions in a new, enlarged way: "[B]y travelling to someone's 'world' we can understand *what it is like to be them and what it is to be ourselves in their eyes.* Only when we have travelled to each other's 'worlds' are we fully subjects to each other" (Lugones 17). However, world-travelling and collaborative inquiry, like essayistic reading and writing, is not without its risks and difficulties.

Lugones rightly cautions that "there are some worlds we enter at our own risk . . . out of necessity and which would be foolish to enter playfully . . . " (17). She has in mind those worlds that would deny our subjecthood by trying to overpower or disempower us. This is the risk the outsider faces in trying to enter the dominant or privileged mainstream. However, world-travelling can also seem threatening and difficult to persons too comfortably and uncritically situated in their present positions. Lugones notes that people can be too much "at ease" in their own worlds to want to risk travelling to other worlds. This is the risk that the insider faces, the person already occupying a position of power, privilege, or comfort.

Jamie, another student, points to the discomfort the insider faces when he travels to other worlds. Here, he questions whether he *should* "put his beliefs on hold" (Delpit 1988, 297) in order to enter into the other's world. In his journal, he writes about the collaborative process in his group:

> The most difficult moments occurred when their thoughts seemed stupid, irrelevant or useless to me. What should I do? Reject the thoughts? Work with what I perceived to be inferior [ideas]? . . . If I see them as wrong, I have to say so, no matter who it hurts . . . . But . . . when a group member "took" my thought and changed it beyond recognition, I felt used, abused and lost . . . . A thought is your property. I didn't like having [them] take it over, change it and spurt it back to me. The biggest weakness is that collaboration requires effort, self-sacrifice and trust . . . . Do you realize what I've done? I've gone into the very minds of Phil and Chas to hear what they think. They trusted me with themselves. I don't ever want to go through this again (Qualley 1994, 38).

Jamie finds this venture in collaborative inquiry disturbing and unsettling. It is important to realize that I have not asked Jamie to travel to worlds vastly different from his own. He is in a self-selected group with two other males writing about a fairly safe topic, the university's general education requirement, that he and his group have chosen themselves. Nonetheless, Jamie exhibits an agonistic stance toward collaboration which, as Lugones points out, is "inimical to travelling across 'worlds'" (15). At this point, he is not able to entertain multiple perspectives because of his sense of rigid, moral rules that only apply one way. He is uncomfortable when group members "take" his thoughts and change them "beyond recognition." And yet, if their ideas are "wrong," he, of course, feels obliged to say so. Jamie is limited by his belief that thoughts are the privately owned "property" of individuals, and thus, for him, world-travelling probably seems a form of trespass. He is also limited by his perception that "effort, self-sacrifice and trust" are "weaknesses." For Jamie, difference seems to imply that one idea must be inferior to another. And in this case, he sees his partner's ideas as inferior, "stupid, irrelevant, useless." He has no choice but to adopt an "either/or," a "them/us," stance. There is none of the openness or "playfulness" in his stance that Lugones talks about in world-travelling. As we saw with Ralph, such a fixed and nonreflexive stance negates the possibility of the "both/and" approach characteristic of the essayistic stance and of world-travelling.

Reading or writing essayistically, collaborating, or world-travelling involves approaching a text or situation with the conscious intention of engaging in genuine dialogue, one that is initially open to all positions. As another student observed:

> You have to be willing to listen to what your partners and interviewees are saying and allow yourself to be influenced by it. If a person doesn't do this, they are not allowing themselves to re-educate themselves . . . New ideas cannot be developed and the person remains exactly where she started.

But reeducation (or what I have been calling unlearning) through these kinds of dialectical encounters with others, people, or texts, means recognizing the partial, approximate, and interpretive nature of our understanding, which of course is easy to say, but often much harder to do. Openness to the possibility of the reconstruction of our views and indeed, of ourselves, as we saw in the last two chapters, is risky. These collaborative inquiry projects reveal even more clearly just what is at stake.

In the rest of this chapter I want to take a closer look at the dynamics of one collaborative group, as the participants explore questions of racism and diversity at the university in their journals and memos to each other. The reflexive illumination that can occur from collaborating with others is what makes this kind of inquiry deeply meaningful, but it is also what makes it difficult. However, I believe these collaborative projects, which encompass the kinds of essayistic writing and reading I have discussed in the previous chapters, afford one of the few opportunities students have to engage in an educational experience at what Kurt Spellmeyer calls "the deep level of life-world politics" (1993c, 278). These projects offer students a reflexive experience that allow them to enlarge and move beyond the limits of their personal knowledge while drawing on it at the same time.

The Process of Collaborative Inquiry: Introducing the Group

Avery, Serena, and Emily are first semester students in my honors freshman English class. Emily was valedictorian of her public high school graduating class. Although she comes from a working-class community less than 15 miles from the university, she lives on campus. Avery had been a day student on scholarship and work-study to a prestigious private boarding school in the area. He continues to live at home and commutes to the university. Serena is from another northeastern state. For this project, Serena and Emily chose to work with each other, while Avery did not express a preference, saying that he would "work with anyone." Throughout the semester, Avery has been a quiet, almost shy member of class.

In order to better understand and appreciate the complexity of this group's collaboration, it is important for readers to know more about Avery, apart from how he represents himself in his journals, memos, and his research essay. Avery's writing during this project conveys a certainty of conviction, forcefulness, and assertiveness that some might associate with a more masculine voice or persona; however, this voice belies how he presents in person. Avery is a tall (6'6"), slim person with glasses and shoulder-length brown hair, which he often kept out of his face with a wide, stretchy headband. He sometimes wore (possibly homemade) chains of small, brightly colored beads around his neck that contrast with the dark colors of his loose-fitting over shirts and black pants. He speaks with a light, falsetto voice. When he found something amusing, he would often cover his mouth with his fingers as he giggled. Avery is transgendered, a fact that neither I nor his group were privy to until some weeks after the project concluded. But as we will see, Avery's gender identity is critical to understanding this group's interactions, readings, and misreadings of each other, and my own reading and misreading of the situation at times.

Avery describes transgender as being physically one sex but with a different gender construction. A transsexual, on the other hand, would be a person who has an operation and undergoes hormone treatment to make his or her sex and gender identity coincide more closely. However, transgender also operates as a kind of umbrella term that many members of the trans community use to describe themselves. Avery is biologically male with a female gender identity. However, this definition is problematic because whereas we tend to speak of *sex* as either male or female, it is more accurate to conceive of *gender* in terms of a continuum between male and female.[1] The distinction is important, but not well understood, and perhaps partially explains why sex and gender are so frequently conflated in the culture at large with sex most often being privileged over gender. At the time of this project, Avery, who has known he was different since the time he was five years old, had only just begun the process of "coming out."

As we will see, Avery often alluded to his experience of being oppressed, of having been the victim of cruel taunts and hurtful names. It was obvious (to Serena, Emily, and me) that he related to the group's topic of discrimination much more deeply and experientially than the two women, but he did not choose to share why with his partners until some months after the project concluded. When I met with him later, he told me who he was and wanted me to disclose this information to Serena and Emily. Both women in the group had known by his appearance, voice, and mannerisms that Avery was different. Emily told me she had just assumed that Avery was gay. Serena had heard from another woman in the class that Avery was neuter, without gender, but she said she didn't really know what he was.

In an earlier essay about collaborative inquiry that I wrote with Elizabeth Chiseri-Strater (1994), in which I contrasted Avery's group's collaborative style with another group's, I was concerned that readers might focus too much of their attention on Avery and miss the point I was making about collaborative inquiry. After talking with Avery, we both decided to leave his gender identity intentionally ambiguous in that piece. Avery chose the name "Avery" for that essay because it sounded gender-neutral to him. He found my use of the pronoun "he" to describe him as problematic since it described his sex and not his gender; at the time, he who had not yet come out as she could not think of an alternative. I will say more about my depiction of Avery as he in the next chapter.

I should also mention at the outset that what I say about this group is based on my *reading* of their written texts; and yet my reading has been informed by a knowledge of these students unavailable to other readers of this book. My reading is influenced by the students' previous written work, their participation in class and conferences prior to this project, and by my observations and our discussions during the four and a half weeks they worked together as a group. It is a *teacher's* reading. Drawing from the memos and journals of these students, I will show the complexity of this open, reflexive method of inquiry by highlighting specific features of the group's collaboration, and then framing these features in different ways. While no one perspective or single theory can adequately explain the group's interaction, I believe the use of multiple frameworks can enrich our understanding of this particular elephant.

The Process of Collaborative Inquiry: Choosing a Topic

In my directions for this project, I ask groups to spend as much time as they need talking with each other so they can find a topic or question that each member of the group is interested in and wants to learn more about. Since the purpose of this project is inquiry, the topic

should be one in which they do not know where they stand in relation to it. Locating such a topic can be difficult for students who have
to overcome preconceived notions of what a research topic looks like.
I have found that making interviews a requirement in the project,
however, helps to enlarge students' understanding of the kinds of
topic they might pursue. But as we shall see, the topic Emily, Serena,
and Avery finally settle on does not really meet these criteria.

Emily and Avery's initial ideas for topics immediately reveal
how far apart these students are at the start of the project. While
Emily's suggestions are reminiscent of safe, generic high school research paper topics (Are private schools better than public schools?
What purpose do guidance counselors serve? Why do reporters report what they do?), Avery, on the other hand, wants the group to
investigate topics that are more political and incendiary. He suggests they examine "various criteria which contribute to a rape culture by learning more about the work of the university's Sexual
Harassment and Rape Prevention Program or issues of diversity or
racism on campus." Avery wants to consider a topic that involves
minority populations because he feels "people learn the most from
those least like themselves." However, as we will see, people will
only learn "from those least like themselves" when they are willing
to engage in authentic dialogue, open themselves to other perspectives, and become reflexive about their own positions.

After the first group meeting, Serena and Avery are both keen to
pursue the problem of the lack of diversity on campus, but Emily is
not. Although she knows it's an "important issue," and she knows
that she "will become more involved with the more research we
do," for now, her "heart's just not into it." The topic's potential for
divisiveness leaves her feeling vulnerable. In her journal, she admits to being worried that "our differences on the subject will result
in big problems." She is "anxious" because the controversial topic
will cause "arguments and disagreements [which] will get in the
way of work." Unlike the other two members, who only use their
journal to record notes from their interviews and respond to their
readings, Emily sorts through her feelings and uncertainties in her
journal before she writes her memos to the group. At the end of the
project, she will have generated twenty-five pages of exploratory
and cathartic writing in addition to the forty-four pages of double-
column research notes. In contrast, Serena and Avery do not keep a
separate journal aside from their double-entry notes on their reading and interviews (thirty-three and thirty-five pages respectively).

In her first memo to the group, Emily explains why she is reluctant to pursue this topic and why she feels like an "oddball":

I didn't know enough to contribute anything important to the conversation. I felt so ignorant. That is not to say that I'm not aware a problem exists, it was just that I was completely lost about some of the words and names that were casually dropped. I had no clue as to what political correctness means, and when Avery mentioned the presidential candidate he voted for, I realized how sheltered I am. I had never heard of this woman! I know these are reasons I should want to do our research project on these subjects because this is how I can learn about them, but for now my ignorance only scares me away.

Because there are only about fifty African-American students out of a student body population of 12,000, it is small surprise that many students at the University of New Hampshire lack experience and knowledge of people of color.

Psychologist Beverly Tatum (1992) finds that the multiple (and often conflicting) perspectives about race that emerge among students in her psychology of racism courses can be understood as a "collision of developmental processes" (9). In an article that examines students' attitudes and resistance to race-related subject matter, Tatum suggests that knowledge of William Cross's model of black identity development and Janet Helms's white racial identity development theory can be useful for helping students understand each other's positions and their own reactions to racial issues. Since Emily, Serena, and Avery are white, I focus on the portion of Tatum's essay that discusses Janet Helms's work. Helms identifies six stages in her model of white identity development that involve "the abandonment of racism and the development of a nonracist identity" (Tatum 13). Unfortunately, I was not aware of the literature on racial identity development or Tatum's article when the students were pursuing their project, so I do not know how knowledge of this theory might have influenced their collaboration. I use these ideas now as a tool for analysis. Helms's model can help us better appreciate the difficulty these students face when they attempt to engage in dialogue (reflexive or otherwise) from vastly different knowledge and experiential positions.

When this project commences, Emily exhibits many characteristics of people who are in Helms's "contact" position. At this level, people show little "awareness of cultural and institutional racism and of one's own White privilege" (13). Because of their limited experience with people of color, many people at the "contact" level base their knowledge of other African-Americans on cultural stereotypes perpetuated by the media. Emily has enough intelligence and education not to allow herself to be easily taken in by the more obvious stereotypes, to realize that many individuals in other parts of this country are racist, and to know that her own experience with "blacks" is limited. However, she isn't as aware of the cultural and institutional forces that perpetuate racism, nor has she considered her own white privilege. In an early journal entry, she muses to herself:

> But what do I know? I'm very naive. I'm white; [I'm] from a white family; [I] live in a predominantly white state . . . I know black people—friends of our family are black . . . I never realized before that people are prejudiced in New Hampshire. I was too busy living in my own little happy world where our neighbors were black and [other] friends of the family included one black man married to a white woman with kids . . . . Maybe that's why I am not excited to do this project. I know a problem exists, but because I, myself, have no problem with blacks, I pretend it isn't as bad as it really is.

Serena's first memo also suggests that she too is situated in the "contact" position at the start of the project. While she has an awareness of some of the terms and issues surrounding the discussion of diversity, her understanding is based more on hearsay and popular opinion than the earned insight of informed experience or knowledge (she is careful to use the term African-American, for example). In her memo to the group, she writes, "Everyone is somewhat racist . . . Why should I have to pay for the mistakes my ancestors made? (I could be shot for saying this but) I believe they truly didn't think they were doing anything wrong." Although Serena doesn't want the group to think that she doesn't "comprehend the seriousness and permanent damage done to the African-American culture," she writes: "as a culture, they need a better self-image. Affirmative action just created tension between minorities and whites [and] welfare programs create dependence rather than independence." However, Serena, who has just recently asked to be moved to the international students' dorm, wants to pursue the group's topic to understand more: "I have so many questions. What can we do? What is this subliminal racism that exists in our culture and how can I identify it?" The knowledge gained through their collaborative investigation, coupled with their willingness to begin to examine their own beliefs and assumptions, will help Serena and Emily to move beyond the "contact" stage during this project.

At the start of their inquiry, Avery seems to display characteristics of Helms's "pseudoindependent" position. As Tatum describes it, in this position

> the White person often tries to disavow his or her own Whiteness through active affiliation with Blacks . . . The individual experiences a sense of alienation from other Whites who have not yet be-

gun to examine their own racism . . . Uncomfortable with his or her own Whiteness, yet unable to truly be anything else, the individual may be searching for a new, more comfortable way to be White (16).[2]

As we will see, Avery appears frequently exasperated with Serena and Emily's lack of knowledge and experience of racism. One reason might be because of how Avery is positioned at this point in his life. In saying this, I do not mean to suggest that racial identity developmental level by itself explains Avery's complicated behavior or the complexity of this group's collaboration.

While Avery does not exactly disavow his whiteness, he sometimes seems to wear it uneasily since it is a part of himself that he associates with the oppressor. He uses his first memo to the group "to sound off in general about my feelings on race, politics, and society." His three-page exposition begins with a quote from Sister Souljah that supports his idea that "racism is synonymous with white supremacy." He introduces the equation, "race (white skin) + power = racism," that will serve as a focal point for much of the group's later discussions. Avery speaks passionately and eloquently about the long history of oppression in our society, from slavery to the plight of young black men dying in the inner city to the "truth" represented by rap music. As if in answer to Serena's memo comment that the white people in the past didn't believe what they were doing was wrong, Avery writes:

> I for one feel ashamed at the masses of white people for caring so little about the injustices WE have perpetrated in the name of Christianity, "progress," and "civilized" society . . . How many more riots and how much more violence do we have to see before changes actually occur . . . . Sister Souljah is angry and radical . . . her goal is not to comfort liberal whites and tell them what a good job they are doing. . . .

Avery seems to find it easier to talk about racial discrimination rather than discrimination on the basis of gender identity or sexual orientation. Occasionally, however, he does fold in these other forms of discrimination into his discussion of racism. For example, he ends his first memo by noting that:

> racial minorities are not the only victims of violence on campus. Sexual minorities experience it as well, though it is rarely talked about due to the moral judgements which so often are visited upon these groups . . . [R]acism really stands as the standard by which to judge all discrimination . . . all other forms of institutionalized discrimination originate [from it].

From the start, these students' different kinds of experience and levels of knowledge about racism and prejudice, as well as their ways of speaking about this knowledge and experience, will affect the dynamics of the group's inquiry and complicate their abilities to engage openly with each other and reflexively with themselves.

The Process of Collaborative Inquiry:
The Complexities of Adopting an Essayistic Stance

Unlike Emily, who hopes to "learn" more, and Serena, who has "so many questions," Avery's interest in pursuing this topic is not related to his ignorance or confusion. He has specific ideas about what racism is, why it is a problem and what can be done to solve it. Most of the information the group uncovers will not be new (or "other") territory for him. Since the positions presented in the readings and interviews will affirm his own developing world view, Avery finds it harder to be critically reflexive. He may add to his knowledge, but he won't challenge his understanding of his subject or himself in this project. In saying this, I don't mean to disparage Avery's performance; what I hope to reveal are the kinds of situations and circumstances that might make reflexivity and the development of an essayistic stance more difficult or problematic.

In many ways, Avery already owns the position the women are seeking to understand. Since he is much better read and informed, his role in the group becomes one of shepherding the others, sometimes quite emphatically, toward a specific understanding of racism. He becomes a self-appointed devil's advocate within the group. However, this kind of strong, vigilant stance does not always invite shared, open, exploratory inquiry. Sometimes the women will find Avery's knowledge and observations enlightening. Serena notes that "Some of Avery's research really woke me up when it comes to subliminal racism" and Emily writes that "Avery really made me stop and think. I had never noticed how 'black' is used in our society only to describe 'bad' things. Is this a factor in our hidden prejudices?" At other times, they resent his unyielding passion. In *Community: Reflections on a Tragic Ideal,* Glenn Tinder writes that if people are "to enjoy equality" they must "be addressed and listened to in matters of the greatest moment. I am not accorded dignity by someone who feeds me but does not care what I think . . . the decisive signs of respect are serious listening and speaking" (1980, 70). At times it appears Avery is actually attempting to feed the others from his knowledge stores. His memos, often scorching diatribes that seem directed to a larger audience than this group, are thick with examples of the injustices done to minorities. After the group's second meeting, where the women had expressed their discomfort with violence as a means of solving racial discrimination, Avery responds to their concerns in his next memo to the group:

> I've been thinking about violence as a solution to the race problem in America. Theoretically, I am categorically opposed to it. I detest violence as the way to alleviate an oppressive situation. But the truth is that white people have always been violent. . . .

After detailing two pages of examples of white violence and oppression toward African-Americans from slavery to Howard's Beach and Rodney King, Avery says that he does not believe that white people are "inherently bad, but rather . . . our collective people's actions have been bad, in fact they have been egregious." Then, in a style reminiscent of the orator or evangelical preacher, he asks:

> So does it make sense for us to advocate nonviolence while we as whites have perpetuated the MOST violent history in the entire world? Both of you have said that nonviolence is the answer for change in the future. I ask you to remember the vantage point from which we speak. Try to put yourself in the shoes of a young black teenager in the inner city . . . I still want to say that I favor nonviolence and self-defense . . . but it is easy for me to say that because I am white and have not been on the receiving end of four hundred years of institutionalized racism. . . .

It might seem that Avery is encouraging an essayistic reading of the situation when he suggests that Emily and Serena attempt to open themselves to the "other's" point of view by putting themselves "in the shoes of a young black teenager." It might seem that he is being reflexive when he notes that his perspective is influenced by his own privileged position of being white. However, Avery already knows beforehand which side he is committed to. The essayistic mind does not. Moreover, his manner of delivery is not indicative of an essayistic or "learner's stance." There is nothing tentative, open, or exploratory about it. I do not mean to suggest that Avery is incapable of being open or reflexive, only that he finds it difficult to be so (as we all do) about those positions he is already so knowledgeable about and in which he is so passionately invested. As Avery sees it,

> there is NO American Dream. It, along with white, male, heterosexual superiority, are among the biggest myths to be perpetuated in the history of this violent country. It is not possible for everyone in this country to get a fair, equitable piece of the economic, political pie and never has been . . . almost all the people who have power in this country . . . have never experienced institutionalized discrimination and therefore buy into the myth of meritocracy, the idea that if you work hard enough you can make it in this country. FALSE LIES! It should be called the American nightmare.

These students' perceptions of culture and society seem directly related to their experience in it. From Avery's position on the social margins and with his history of oppression, it is evident that people are not equal and absolutely clear that no amount of hard work will change that fact. Avery's experience, however, has not been Emily and Serena's experience. While they now acknowledge that racism exists, they believe that the answers can be found within the system. Both women see education as the cure for racism: people simply need to be made aware of their "hidden prejudices." Since this project is helping them to begin to uncover some of their own assumptions, they believe all people would benefit from the kinds of experience and knowledge they have gained.

Avery suggests at one point that "the country is fucked-up beyond belief and would be better off if it all fell apart." In response, Serena writes that she was "very offended," and this view was "unfair . . . I challenge anyone to find a better and more fair justice system in the world. While our system is not perfect, I feel it is the best around." Serena responds to Avery's comment (and especially his language and tone) as a personal attack. When individuals feel threatened, coerced, or simply unheard, they oftentimes adopt a defensive posture that not only shields them from the views of others, it also closes them to their own views. Since their energy is directed toward protecting their beliefs, they resist bending back on themselves and examining them. There is an important difference, though, between Serena's defensiveness here and Avery's defensiveness during this project.

Maria Lugones might say that Serena is too much at ease in her world (of white, heterosexual, middle-class privilege) to risk travelling to the hurt and pain of Avery's world. What Serena is defending is a ready-made belief about American culture and etiquette, not an insight that she herself has earned through careful examination of experience and knowledge. On the other hand, what Avery is defending is a very fragile sense of self that is emerging out of his own experience of being "between" in a gendered world of either/or. At this point, it is not likely he would find it easy to question a position he has just reached, one he has fortified with knowledge, one he associates with strength, and one he is just now beginning to voice to others.

I don't want to convey Avery's single-mindedness as close-mindedness; such an interpretation would greatly distort the complexity of Avery's position. Avery's knowledge and conviction about discrimination and prejudice arise out of a knowledge and experiential authority these women simply do not have. However, during this project, he only alludes to the experiential source of his hurt and rage, speaking of his own oppression in the most general, vague terms in his memos to the group: "I have been on the receiving end of prejudice and discriminatory harassment more times than I care to remember and I want to get across to you that such verbal abuse hurts." He wants them to know that his knowledge of oppression is legitimated by his experience, but he is intentionally ambiguous because he is not comfortable enough to share the specifics. Although Serena and Emily know that Avery is different in some way, and although they have witnessed other people make innuendos and snide comments directly to him or within hearing distance, they do not speak about this difference to him or in their memos or journals. By ignoring or denying his difference, Serena and Emily often read his anger and pain as simply "rudeness" or "unreasonableness."

At a meeting that takes place in the study lounge of Emily's dorm about midway through the project, the group argues again about the racism equation (race (white skin) + power = racism). Avery, perhaps frustrated by his attempts to get the women to digest an understanding of racism they cannot yet (if ever) grasp asks, "How many times do I have to tell you?" And yet, that's the point. Avery can't tell them. Kurt Spellmeyer (1993c), drawing on the work of Scott Momaday, notes that words don't have a meaning until they are embodied into the life-text of a person, "until they take on the power to explain the reader's circumstances to himself" (268). As we will see shortly, Serena and Emily are gradually folding in some of these new ideas and information about racism into their own "life-texts," but perhaps not at the rate or in the manner that Avery would like. The meaning of "race (white skin) + power = racism" has not yet and may never become an earned insight for Emily or Serena in the way that it has for Avery.

In Emily's memo response, we begin to sense the complexity and difficulty involved in just trying to start an open dialogue in groups where different ways of thinking, speaking (and experiencing) exist, *but where members attempt to operate according to rules that pretend that they don't*:

> You can tell me as many times as you want, but I don't have to agree with you. I extend the courtesy of listening to what you have to say . . . [but] where does it say that your opinion is better than mine? . . . If I disagree without trying to see your point, you have the right to express your anger. There's nothing wrong with us disagreeing. We just have to respect everyone's opinions.

Since Emily is unable to use her personal knowledge to understand and gauge the "truth" of Avery's "words," she may see Avery's perspective as simply "his opinion," and from a relativist position, "everyone has a right to their opinion." Too often, however, respecting people's opinions can masquerade as an excuse for not engaging in dialogue, for not trying to understand different perspectives. If we see the other as fundamentally different, that perspective often implies (at least for our students) that nothing further can or need be said, and almost ensures their retreat into relativism. The dialogue ends before it can begin. However, thanks to Avery, the dialogue in this group does not end. "Should we respect the opinions of the KKK? The Nazis and neo-Nazis?" he asks.

In any case, genuine listening, which entails putting one's beliefs on hold and travelling to the world of the other, is not a simple, unproblematic activity. If Avery thinks that Emily and Serena don't agree with his ideas because of lack of information, he will simply try to offer them more facts. If he feels they just don't get what he is saying, then he will repeat the same points (more loudly) or in a different way. Of course neither strategy will allow the women to hear any better. If Emily feels that Avery chooses not to listen because he doesn't acknowledge her right to her opinion, she will see him as unfair at best and impolite or bullying at worst. Although Avery has a great deal of knowledge about the topic of racism, that knowledge is not getting through to Serena and Emily. My point is that all the knowledge in the world isn't going to help Emily understand any better. All the good reasons Avery provides are not going to be good reasons for Emily. Avery's delivery and manner of speaking seem unreasonable (and more importantly, discourteous) to the women. Emily writes in her journal that Avery "was downright rude! . . . The thing is, yelling doesn't get your point across. If you yell at someone it's going to make them less inclined to listen." Later, in her memo, Emily reminds the group to "keep our tempers in check and our voices at speaking level, especially when we are in a study lounge where people are trying to study." And Serena writes that the group "got entirely out of hand. Because of our yelling and arguing, we accomplished nothing . . . in the future we need to criticize less and listen more."

Avery responds to their appeals for civility by suggesting that "it is a bourgeois, elitist, intellectualist attitude to think that discussion has to always be quiet, scholarly, and rational. . . . I like things to get fiery, incendiary or controversial. If we start raising our voices, then that proves we are making strong headway." He reminds the group that their topic is a "sensitive, controversial, incendiary issue" and it is only "natural" that they will get "angry or impassioned about certain points." Since racism is "an extremely irrational institution," it is "imperative that white people start having the kind of conversation that we did to attain a consciousness of race relations . . . when people get angry, they tend to be honest about their true feelings." What is more, Avery tells the group that anger is part of his family's communication style:

> If I raise my voice or get angry or impassioned, that is not a personal indictment of you or your views. All of us have different life experiences and communication styles that affect our ways of being in the world . . . In our family, when we have a pressing concern we do not quietly talk things out; we yell and get angry. . . .

However, as both Adrienne Rich (1979) and Magda Lewis and Roger Simon (1986) have pointed out, women can feel silenced and alienated by what seems like a "discourse not intended for her." Avery may not realize that many (white, middle-class) women have been socialized to feel that anger is not natural or honest, that it is a form of personal attack, and therefore, always an emotion to be avoided or prevented. Emily and Serena cannot listen to Avery's arguments when he "gets really upset and starts yelling and swearing"; they can only hear his anger. However, later in the quiet, private space of her journal,[3] Emily momentarily becomes reflexive: as she considers what Avery has said about anger, she contemplates her own experience and begins to understand why she doesn't feel the same way:

> My parents [are] divorced. My mother, with whom I have a better relationship, always wanted to talk about problems or differences in a calm, civilized manner. Even when disciplining me, she seldom raised her voice, and I can probably count on one hand the number of times in my 18 years she actually yelled. My father, on the other hand, is the exact opposite. We have never been very close, and he loves to scream at me for stupid reasons. I guess I associate loud voices and lost tempers with all my father's negative traits. I never thought that some people would actually use screaming to communicate, and not to bully. Avery really opened my eyes.

As Emily becomes more conscious of the situated nature of these beliefs, she is poised to move beyond simple relativism. Instead of simply acknowledging that everyone is entitled to their opinion, she inquires into why she and Avery hold the particular opinions they do. By seeking to first understand where each of them "are coming from," she is in a better position to be able to defer or suspend her judgment about their differences. It is at this point that the opportunity for authentic dialogue, one that could lead to a more complex understanding of both her own and Avery's perspectives, becomes possible. However, this dialogue would require all members of the group to temporarily defer their own convictions as they explore the perspectives of the others; in a group where members perceive themselves situated unevenly, such a possibility, as we will see in the next section, is unlikely to happen.

The Process of Collaborative Inquiry: Ethical Agency

Drawing from the work of moral philosophers Nel Noddings, Edith Wyschogrod and Alasdair MacIntyre, Gregory Clark offers a conception of a reading and writing community in which the aim would be for participants to learn "how the beliefs and purposes of others can call their own into question" (1994, 73). In this kind of community, "the relational and epistemological practice of confronting differences" would take precedence over the development of the subject and technical expertise of its individual members (73). For such a community to work, it becomes necessary to redefine agency in such a way that its enactment will not deny or silence the positions and perspectives of differing others. Clark suggests that each member of the community learn to practice an attitude of "ethical deference" toward others. Ethical deference means that people agree to put their own beliefs on hold so that they can more fully consider the ideas or attempt to understand the experiences of another. For instance, in the following memo composed from Emily's earlier journal entry, Emily has temporarily put her beliefs on hold in order to try to understand Avery's position.

> Avery explained to me that in his family, they get their point across by yelling and raising their voices. That helped me to see where he was coming from. I'm not saying that I won't cringe if we start a screaming match again. Just because I now understand that loud voices don't have to be negative, doesn't mean that I'm getting used to using them to make a point.

Putting her beliefs on hold doesn't mean forsaking them, nor does understanding imply agreement. Clark is careful to note that openness to others need not and should not require that individuals permanently deny their own difference or revoke their own agency. Rather, deference and agency have to be thought of as "alternating attitudes, practiced interdependently" (67). Although Clark is not entirely clear in his discussion of these concepts, he seems to be arguing for a fuller, dynamic concept of agency, one that includes an attitude of ethical deference to others, rather than describing two separate stances. He writes, "Agency is constructed and reconstructed continually from the insights that emerge in a provisionally deferential exchange with differing others" (68). And he notes that when agency and deference are "enacted separately as absolute principles, both deny the coequality of difference" (67).

I believe Clark's notion of an agency that commences with an attitude of "ethical deference" toward others must also be a reflexive agency. In response to their open (or deferential) encounters with differing others, ethical agents need to monitor their own beliefs and assertions, identifying and examining how they came to hold these beliefs and make these assertions. Feminist philosopher Victoria Davion (1991) argues that such a process is necessary because it not only contributes to the development of integrity, it also allows for the possibility of radical change without the loss of integrity. In other words, it helps guard against unconscious "born-again" experiences or full-blown conversion. Elizabeth Minnich (1990) goes further by suggesting that "the effort to find out how and why our thinking carries the past with it is part of an ongoing philosophical critique essential to freedom, and to democracy . . ." (29). Emily begins this reflexive process when she measures the facts of the situation, Avery's response to anger, against her own subjective frame of reference, her family history. She not only learns about Avery, she discovers that she equates anger with her father, "who loves to scream at me for stupid reasons." Although she hasn't come to full consciousness of the implication of this realization, she nevertheless has made the initial connection that can lead to further insight.

I want to add a pedagogical note here. Emily's realization about her discomfort with her father's anger is just the kind of insight that leads one to essay, to explore and inquire further. Emily's realization is what Graham Good calls a "temporary illumination," rather than a conclusion or conviction. The former invites further inquiry and learning; the latter demands evidence and proof. Under ordinary classroom circumstances, I might have encouraged Emily to continue to "write to discover." I may have suggested other literature (fiction and nonfiction) that she could use to frame her experience against. Whether Emily returns to this thought at another time remains to be seen.

This concept of ethical agency then, which includes deference to others and reflexive examination of one's own position, is a characteristic of the essayistic approach to texts that I talk about in Chapters Two and Three. Both stances suggest a process of inquiry and a method for engaging others that is open, tentative, and exploratory. Lest I make this process sound easy or as simple as "just say no," let me further complicate the notion of deference by returning to Avery.

During this project, Avery seems to assert his agency by *not* deferring to others, but rather by expressing his anger and disapproval. In his final reflection on this project, he writes:

> I am struck by the anger which flares up in my writing so often. I like that part of me because I equate it with power, with successfully getting my point across to others. . . . This project has helped me to become proud of my militant edge . . . . My identity is beginning to emerge from a nebulous, pale, listless state into something with more color, shape, texture, and definition . . . In the past I have been so quiet, reserved, and passive. It truly feels liberating when I blatantly tell someone what I'm thinking and how I feel.

This project is not simply another assignment for Avery. As I mentioned earlier, it literally seems to represent a coming to voice. The voice he comes to is angry, but it is one that he initially associates with strength. It may not be the voice of an agency that bends back on itself and questions its own assumptions—yet. But I believe this voice may be a necessary precursor to it. Avery's anger is much more complex than simply being part of a family communication pattern. His anger is deeply intertwined with his own developing self-esteem and sense of self. On the one hand it represents his personal hurt; on the other it is an expression of his moral indignation.

Barbara Houston (1992) asks what kind of ethic would best serve people who are "marginalized, exploited . . . stereotyped and marked as Other . . . ?" Would it be Clark's ethic that begins with deference? Only if such an ethic also includes the expression and practice of blame. Houston argues that blaming

> can help us clarify our political and social identities . . . It functions not only instrumentally to get things done, to educate, to teach others what is wrong, to remind others of their agency . . . blaming is nothing less than a strong expression of our confidence in our moral agency, our integrity, and our sense of self-in-community (142).

Furthermore, Houston notes that to forego or withhold blame would be "to leave myself without recourse when I am wronged . . . I [would] have no way to declare my boundaries, assert my rights, or defend myself when I am treated unfairly or hurt" (133). Avery does not withhold or renounce blame. On the contrary, he casts a wide net, and his blame falls on the entire white race:

> White people have never stopped to try to put themselves in the place of racial and sexual minorities. They are so entrenched in the power structure that it is impossible for them to realize that there ARE people suffering because of their discrimination . . . things just keep on deteriorating and most white people are totally

oblivious to this and totally unwilling to admit their own PRIVI-
LEGE and RACISM.

In light of his view that white people are too "entrenched in the
power structure" to see that "people are suffering," Avery might
find Clark's notion of ethical deference as a further attempt by those
in power to continue to silence him and the topic of racism of
which he speaks. Why should he defer to their views? Why should
he continue to listen to "false lies"? His self-designated purpose in
this project is to get the mainstream to listen to the part of the story
that has not been told, the part he feels those in power have not
been willing to listen to, much less understand, the part that "continues to go largely unspoken and unchallenged."

Perhaps ethical agency involves knowing when to defer and
when to express disapproval. At one point during the meeting in
Emily's study lounge, another student present calls one of his pro-
fessors "a homo," and Avery is offended that Emily, their "host,"
does not speak up or cast blame where blame is due. He writes in
his memo:

> That's exactly the kind of homophobic hatred that needs to be
> reckoned with. Your responses that you did not know him well,
> and that you cannot control what he says, are feeble, weak, and
> pitiful excuses. Maybe you don't realize how painful it is to be
> singled out and attacked again and again for being different, and
> how that cuts away at your self-esteem.

For the most part, Emily and Serena are not consciously aware
of what it might feel like to be "attacked again and again," and so,
of course, they cannot imagine "what it's like." And yet, I am re-
minded by Barbara Houston (personal communication) that both
Emily and Serena, as women may have, in fact, been attacked, de-
valued, and silenced many times in their lives, but may not have
obtained full consciousness of their situation yet. They experience
Avery's anger as a kind of attack, and yet they explain it away as
simple rudeness. Furthermore, Emily and Serena have probably
been socialized (more than they realize) to defer (politely) to males.
Even though Avery's gender is in question, they respond to him as
male. Nonetheless, both these women would probably see themselves as agents. Emily (the former valedictorian) has been educated to believe (perhaps falsely) that, female or not, she does have
"the right to her opinion." She is confident and sure of her ability
to engage in rational discussion and argument with others, as long
as everyone plays by the rules and the talk doesn't get out of hand.
It is easy for her to defer, and perhaps too easy to yield the floor to

others without feeling threatened herself or without feeling the need to express disapproval. Regarding the student in the study lounge, Emily writes in her journal that she didn't say anything to the student "because even though the word [homo] made me cringe and feel uncomfortable . . . I knew by saying something in front of the others it would make Roy defensive and I didn't even know him, so I didn't want someone I don't know to feel that they can't speak in front of me." Emily writes that if Roy had been a person "I was friendly with, I would have said something right away." She does however talk to Roy after the rest of the group leaves. She politely and calmly tells him: "Roy, my friends and I were uncomfortable when you used the term 'homo'." Now, is Emily deferring to a male? Is she expressing blame in the only way she knows how?

In response to Avery's memo about speaking up against homophobic hatred, Emily writes in her journal that "it's great that Avery's against racism and prejudice, but I think he takes things we say a little too personally. He becomes indignant and shuts his mind off (which is when he turns his voice on full blast) . . ." But again, this situation is personal for Avery. After not being heard for so long, "full-blast" may be the only way Avery feels he can make his point:

> The sexual minority liberation movement has a slogan: "Silence = Death." Words are a potent force against hateful and offensive speech. That's why neither you nor I should remain silent when something is said that unjustly denigrates an individual or group.

All three students would agree that words are a potent force, but they would disagree about the method people should use to deliver their words. For Avery, quiet, calm rationality is not sufficient to communicate the depth and scope of the injustices done to minorities. It is time to blame by shouting "out loud from every mountain." Toward the end of the project, he writes,

> I don't think these painful events should be silenced. I think they need to be shouted out loud from every mountain . . . If you want to get something done you need to let the world know in no uncertain terms, that you are a force to be RECKONED with . . . We, meaning all people, cannot let racist, sexist, homophobic comments and behavior go unchallenged. It is imperative that we let the perpetrators know loud and clear that what they are saying is offensive and will not be tolerated. It is no longer a free exchange of protected speech.

If the discourse is no longer open or free, the hermeneutic circle is ruptured, and dialogue based on a "deferential exchange with differing others" (Clark 68) is no longer possible. In this situation, people do not have a right to their opinion if that opinion expresses racist, sexist or homophobic beliefs, which means that Avery feels he is under no obligation to defer to these others—even temporarily—or to attempt to understand their attitudes.

According to the equation, "race (white skin) + power = racism," people without power (presumably people of color) cannot be racist, no matter what they say (something that Emily and Serena find difficult to accept). However, what happens when a person of color makes a classist or homophobic comment? When Avery and Serena visit a meeting of the African-American Student Organization, Serena writes that some of the male students in attendance made "blatantly rude and caustic remarks directed toward Avery. I don't know if it hurt his feelings, but it certainly offended me. It often seems to me that Avery thinks of the black race as infallible. I hope this told him that everyone has the potential to be rude." Avery, however, does not speak up or let the "perpetrators" of these comments "know that what they are saying is offensive and will not be tolerated." Nor does he write about this incident in his memos to the group. Here, it might seem that Avery does defer to "differing others," others who are as marginalized on campus as he is. It is possible that he is very much aware of the privilege afforded by his skin color, and being involved in his own identity struggles may have made him sensitive to the needs of these students to assert themselves. We might also recall that Avery seems to have much in common with whites who are at the "pseudoindependent stage" of the racial identity model. As Tatum notes, the person at this level has not yet become reconciled to his own whiteness, and may accept the suspicion or criticism of blacks without argument. On the other hand, it is just as likely that Avery's silence is not the deference of ethical agency, but rather the silence that comes from a lack of agency. Since the African-American students do not seem to be responding to his whiteness, but to his gender identity, Avery's silence may represent the traditional female victim's response to a group of taunting males.

At any rate, this incident and the one in the study lounge serve to complicate the notion of ethical agency. On what basis do we defer? On what basis do we express disapproval or outrage? It may be that the ability and desire to open oneself to another's ideas or to question or express disapproval of another's ideas, as well as the ability to interrogate one's own beliefs and actions, is greatly affected by how one is positioned to begin with. What all of these students seemed to have overlooked, though, is that people do not occupy the same location all the time. Sometimes they inhabit more than one position at once. People constantly shift location in response to others and themselves.

The Process of Collaborative Inquiry:
Understanding Difference Through Connection

In his final reflection on the project (unfortunately not written to and shared with the other group members), Avery identifies the kinds of experiences that have given rise to his beliefs and actions during this project. Although he is not yet ready to critically examine these attitudes, beliefs, and assumptions, we can see how Avery draws on his own experience of oppression to try to understand the experience of other minorities. His "anger, frustration, and rage," along with his own "social isolation" are "tools" that he can use to empathize with the pain and isolation other minorities feel:

> From the first grade on, I was the object of ridicule, offensive taunts, and cruel "jokes." It was during these incidents that I first began to truly contemplate the ramifications of being "different." Later on, this awareness became more politically based, and I learned about the power of self-respect, speaking out, and kinship with others who are oppressed and have the ability to empathize ... The ironic point is that I want to remember the severity of this pain. Not because I enjoyed it or because I want to play the victim or martyr, but because I need to carry the pain so I will never lose the feelings that accompany it—anger, frustration, even rage.[4] The social isolation I experienced and continue to experience is a powerful tool I can use to understand and empathize with a number of groups ... being different also ... keeps the issue of diversity and being sensitive to people who don't fit into the "mainstream" on the front burner.

However, "being different," as we have seen, does not always help Avery be sensitive to Emily and Serena. Although Avery says that "being different . . . keeps the issue of diversity alive," the reason Avery may find it easier to be sensitive to minorities seems to be because they are the people he feels to be *most* like himself, not *least* like himself. Because he identifies with their experience, he may be more open to trying to understand their situation than he is the mainstream white population, who he discounts as "different" in another way: they are the oppressors, "thick," and "oblivious," and incapable of understanding the situations minorities face. Although Emily and Serena have demonstrated their willingness to listen whenever he shares the circumstances that have given rise to his beliefs (e.g., his family's conversational style), Avery has learned to be cautious, and rightly so, about revealing the personal details of his life.

Emily and Serena also apply a similar strategy to the one Avery employs in that they use their own experience (as women, children, etc.) to try to comprehend and empathize with the lives of others.

Drawing from Wyschogrod's discussion of empathy, Clark cautions that empathy—trying to understand an other on one's own terms—is "an interpretation that eclipses, at least partially, the full reality of another's difference" (66).[5] I would argue, however, that as long as students acknowledge that "full mutual understanding is impossible" (Clark 66), the strategy of trying to understand the other on their own terms is necessary in helping them begin the process of making sense. Educator Deborah Meier argues that "[t]he capacity to see the world as others might is central to unsentimental compassion and at the root of both intellectual skepticism and empathy" and are "precisely the habits of mind that require cultivation" in our schools (1995, 63).

When Emily and Serena make connections between their lives and the lives of minorities, they are quick to note that although their experience may be similar, it is never the same. Here Emily offers a rationale for why, and an example of how she uses her own experience as a way to begin to understand the other:

> We discussed how we can try to understand what blacks and other minorities go through by looking at situations in our lives when we've been judged . . . How can I even attempt to compare my experiences with those of people who are oppressed? They've been through so much more than I have! Then I thought: Hey, maybe that's the whole point. If you can think of an experience that was difficult or hard for you, and you know you can't begin to compare it to what a black person must experience, then it gives you a better understanding of what he or she did go through, and it makes you realize how terrible it must be. One experience I thought of was how store clerks always watched my teenaged friends and I like a hawk when we entered their store; because [we were] adolescents, they expected us to shoplift. This always offended me. I've never stolen anything in my life. Then I thought of the stories I've heard of blacks who experienced the same attitudes. The difference is people were suspicious of me because of my age. People are suspicious of blacks because of their skin color. I will grow up but blacks will never grow out of their skin.

As we saw with Kay's reading of Freire's text and Chad's reading of Alice Walker's essay in Chapter Three, once Emily has established a connection, she can then note the differences between her experience and the experience of minorities, such as the important distinction that the discrimination she experienced in her youth was isolated and temporary. Seeking connections and then noting differences is a two-step process. The second part of the process is necessary to ensure that the other (in this case, the experience of minorities) is not erased (overpowered) or assimilated (disempowered). *Making connections opens the dialogue. Noting differences makes the dialogue reflexive,* as we examine our own experience in light of the other's. I believe that difference can only be discovered through connection. If students are unable or unwilling to first find a connection between their lifeworlds and the lifeworlds of others, they are not likely to concern themselves with trying to understand the differences between them, and the reasons that have given rise to the differences.

In contrast to Avery, however, neither Serena or Emily began the project from a position in which they were heavily invested. Generally, they find it easier during this project to look at their own assumptions about racial minorities because their assumptions are mostly composed of hand-me-down notions and ready-made ideas rather than knowledge they, themselves, have invested time and energy constructing. In their journals (written in double-entry format with notes from their sources in one column and their thoughts on that information in the adjacent column), we can further see how the women use their own experience to attempt to understand the situations minorities encounter. In this entry from Emily's journal, Emily first looks for an experience in her own life that will give her a sense of "subtle" or indirect racism. Once she has come up with an example, she then notes the differences:

Source	Emily's Response
Ann Lima says "it's called subtle racism . . . It's not acceptable to lynch people anymore. I'm not afraid for my physical safety, but the more subtle type is worse. I'd rather be slapped in the face. I'd rather know the person is prejudiced than to have them say they are not when they really are."	I can apply this to my own life—of course it's not the same because I am white. I hate when I meet people and I can't read their actions. They're nice to you but in the back of their mind, you're sure they'll talk about you as soon as you're out of earshot . . . Being white, I know a lot of other people who I feel comfortable with, so as soon as I leave the person I don't really care if they are two-faced . . . but minorities on campus may not have this option [of finding other people they are comfortable with].

Although Emily has identified a difference between her experience and the experience of minorities, she has not really begun to examine what this difference might mean for herself. It's important to note that reflexivity is a process that we engage in by degrees, like peeling the layers from an onion.

Serena is able to peel away more layers from her onion. At times, she goes beyond merely identifying difference. To really be able to understand and make sense of a sensitive and complex subject like racism, a reader has to be willing to examine her own assumptions as well as the subject itself. By examining her own racism, Serena is in a much better position to identify the racism in the society at large, as well as how she, herself, may unconsciously be contributing to it. She is also more likely to begin to grasp the complexity of racism. (In other words, she comes to see that racism is not a black and white issue.)

Source	Serena's response
College Republican poster: "Smash Apartheid on Campus. Resist special privileges based on race." This was an effort to compare special privileges for black students on campus with special privileges afforded whites in South Africa.	I thought to myself, "This makes a good point. There really is no difference." Then I realized they are like night and day. The whites in South Africa have oppressed the blacks for many, many years. The blacks in this country have never had this kind of power . . . I don't know why I sided with the racist point of view at first. Maybe it was easier to see my race as the oppressed in this situation instead of as the oppressor.
(From the *New York Times*) "National figures like Mike Tyson, Marion Barry, and Dr. Leonard Jeffries are disgraceful and cannot be excused, and as role models, their behavior can bring shame to their race."	I definitely take notice when a black person or minority messes up because oftentimes people (myself included) apply it to the whole race and therefore think less of the race. Why is this? Why am I able to separate Jeffrey Dahmer from the rest of the white race and not Mike Tyson from the rest of his?

As the project progresses, Serena continues to question her assumptions. After the group's interview with the head of Affirmative Action, she writes "I thought I knew everything about affirmative action . . . [but] I found myself embarrassed by my lack of understanding." After meeting with Ms. Fuentes, the assistant director of the Office of Multicultural Affairs, Serena writes that "I was ashamed for not knowing more about his [Malcolm X's] life . . . I was embarrassed for not having more of an interest to begin with. Once again I caught a glimpse of the racist side of myself."

When Ms. Fuentes asks Serena how she defines racism, Serena explains why she disagrees with the idea that blacks cannot be racist because they have no power. Serena argues that "blacks possess physical power. Walking alone at night in the city, I do not have control." However, Serena reexamines her position when Ms. Fuentes offers a counterargument that Serena says "really made sense":

> If I am attacked by a group of black men because they are more powerful than me, that is not racism. This is because, after [being] caught, they will be arrested, tried, convicted and sentenced by whites (most likely) and be subject to their prejudices. Whereas, if I am attacked by a group of white men, they will not receive the same degree of punishment (most likely). I never saw it in this light before. I have since thought a lot about the equation and now I wonder how anything gets done for blacks in this country. How can bills, legislation, and programs get enacted when no one in power can truly relate to the problems of minorities (because they have never been a minority)?

Serena seems quite willing to reconsider her previous assertions in light of Ms. Fuentes' example, delivered calmly and rationally. Also in this memo, we can detect what may be the spark of a new, more politicized consciousness emerging as Serena delves deeper into her understanding of the relationship between racism and power.

Not all of Serena's encounters with others take place in such a supportive environment. When Serena and Avery attend the meeting of the African-American Student Organization, both are immediately aware of their "outsider" status. For Avery, however, feeling like an outsider is more or less a fact of life; for Serena, the experience is new and extremely uncomfortable. As the only white woman in the group of twenty-five (mostly male) black students, Serena says in her memo that:

> No one spoke to us, and we were pretty much ignored . . . I learned a lot about the kind of person I am. I am a product of white culture. I like "white" music. I like the "white" English form of speaking. I

don't know whether this is right or wrong . . . When a representative of the Greek Council came to answer some quick questions, the [African-American] group spoke in perfect "white" English to the white woman. When she left, they went back to "Yo, home boy, what's up." Is that good or bad? Why can't I speak two languages like they can? Why don't I want to?

The kinds of questions Serena raises here are complex and not ones that she will be able to answer during the course of this project. But for me, the teacher, this is one of the purposes of reflexive inquiry: to encourage students to pose "hard questions" that defy ready-made or simple solutions. It is the questions—not the answers—that continue to complicate and deepen our understanding of our subjects and ourselves.

While Serena attempted to examine her own hidden racial prejudices at the African-American Student meeting, she cannot open herself and, therefore, think reflexively about "bad" language (swearing), which chafes her class notions of "decency" and "etiquette." When Avery gives Serena a copy of the video, *Jungle Fever,* we begin to see that limits of reflexive inquiry are different for different individuals. Serena writes that "this video was one of the worst movies I have ever seen in my life. This [reaction] seemed to upset Avery, but I don't care. I really didn't like the movie (and I don't think I disliked it for racist reasons either)." Like so many white Americans, class is still very much an invisible concept for her:

> Every other word was fuck. Avery seems to think that this is a true representation of the black culture and Italian culture that make up the main characters. I agree the language was appropriate in the scenes with drugs and uneducated white people . . . but not for the main characters. The black couple were educated and spoke like that. What is Spike Lee trying to say? It seems (and I could be wrong) that he is putting down his own race.

Although Serena has observed that the African-American students at the meeting she and Avery attended know "two languages"—she witnessed them slipping in and out of black vernacular and standard American English with ease—she is, nonetheless, not prepared to even consider the possibility that "educated" people might also use "bad" or improper language. Serena finds it much harder to be reflexive when race and class issues are intertwined, probably because she does not yet acknowledge that class differences exist.

Serena also complains about a conversation between black women in the movie that "ripped apart the morals and values of white women. I don't appreciate the assumption that all white women are after sex with black men just because they are curious. If the reverse were said about black women in a predominantly white movie there would be an awful uproar." Serena bristles at this negative representation (which in her mind, is no less discriminatory as the reverse situation), but she sees it as a purely racial issue and misses the class implications completely. Had she been able to bend back on herself and examine her anger and defensiveness, she might have come to a deeper understanding of the kinds of unfair accusations minorities frequently experience (but certainly don't "appreciate"), but more importantly, she might have complicated her understanding by seeing how race and class are intertwined. This, however, would have been a huge step, and perhaps not one Serena—or most students for that matter—are prepared to make. Educator Lisa Delpit, however, makes it poignantly clear how difficult and threatening it is to engage in this kind of reflexivity, which involves "turning yourself inside out, giving up your own sense of who you are and being willing to see yourself in the unflattering light of another's angry gaze" (1988, 297).

The Product of Collaborative Inquiry: Enlarged and Complicated Understanding

By the end of the project, Serena, Emily, and Avery have learned a great deal about racism on campus from their interviews, reading, and discussions. Each of these students gain knowledge, but they do not gain the same understanding of what that knowledge means. Serena and Emily, for instance, come to realize that they are themselves "prejudiced." Serena writes that "when I began, I had a somewhat righteous attitude regarding prejudice and racism . . . I discovered that I am not as perfect as I had originally thought . . . This project has begun the process of positive change . . . I can see a transformation occurring."

Whereas Serena is energized by her enhanced awareness, Emily remains more cautious and unsure. Emily's thinking is still in flux; she is unclear about what it is that she has learned, although she knows that learning has occurred. She is unsure what it is that she can now say that she knows. Yes, she has absorbed a lot of information about the plight of minority students on campus, but she is uncertain what it means for her. What makes reflexive inquiry different from an ordinary research assignment, as these excerpts from Emily's final reflections suggest, is that the understanding that emerges is seldom simple, clear, or complete. But what is also different about reflexive inquiry is that the inquiry is not likely to end when the project does. Emily writes:

- Every time I read something or every time we discussed something, I learned more facts, but I became confused as to where I personally stood on the issues . . .
- Saying that I believed everyone holds hidden prejudices included me, but did not single me out. When I wrote my essay, I finally stated that I am prejudiced. But I am still not comfortable admitting this . . .
- Realizing how and why I am prejudiced is a big step in my emotional and mental development, and I was not prepared to take that step. I was already preoccupied with adjusting to college life, and trying to sort out my prejudiced feelings only complicated my adjustment . . .
- I am not ready to evaluate where I stand in my own life. In a way, my inability to examine my own feelings on our topic allowed me to understand how important it is for people to recognize their prejudices . . .
- I know I learned a lot—not just about political correctness or racial tensions on the UNH campus—but about my own beliefs and ideals. I think this project would have been a waste of time if it had not made me think about things I already thought I knew. . . .

Although Avery does not really use this project to understand the topic of racism, he does begin to see his methods of communication with others in a more complicated way:

> I seem to veer toward the militant ends of various movements. Maybe it's because of the unusual situation I find myself living in. Often extreme conditions demand extreme solutions. But I also realize some of the dangers involved in these kinds of absolutist politics. Sometimes the oppressed can become so enraged and dictatorial that they begin to resemble their oppressor. . . .

I have suggested that learning always involves some modification to what we know and believe as a result of our encounters with others. At its simplest level, learning may simply involve adding to what we know and believe. But learning can also mean complicating, deepening, and transforming the way we see others and the way we see ourselves. For this latter kind of learning to occur, I believe learners must become reflexive—that is, in response to their encounters with others, they must identify and examine their own assumptions. These collaborative inquiry projects reveal how reading and writing, especially essayistic reading and writing, can assist this reflexive process. As I said earlier, essayism refers not so much to the form, but to the stance and approach a writer or reader adopts toward her subject and/or audience. The essayist measures the objective facts of the situation against some subjective frame of reference. When Emily says that she learned more "facts," but became "confused" as to where she "personally stood on the issues," she reveals that she is involved in a reflexive (and messy) process of interrogating and reinterpreting her own frames of reference. In the collaboratively written foreword to their three essays, the students write that they "have wrestled with the definitions of racism and diversity [and] . . . are still not in agreement . . . But we do have a clearer understanding of the life experiences that have shaped our individual attitudes."

I have tried to show throughout this book that the "understanding" of one's own life experiences—and that includes personal as well as cultural—should be an important aim of education in general and composition and literacy studies in particular.

The Written Products of Collaborative Inquiry

In the papers they write for this project, both Emily and Serena combine their own insights about themselves with their research findings and write what may be considered "personal" research essays. Drawing from their research and their own experience, they reveal how they have arrived at their current understandings on their topic.

Serena's paper, entitled "Minorities at the University of New Hampshire," focuses on her own changing awareness of the kinds of "subtle" and "symbolic" racism minority students face. In her lead, she frames the problem in terms of her own experience:

> When I came to the University of New Hampshire I often thought about the lack of minority students on campus. Until recently, I never gave thought to the minority students already here. I never considered what they must go through.

In the next three paragraphs, she defines the two forms of racism and then goes on to illustrate these forms of racism with further examples from her own experience. She writes about how she first considered a group of African-American men who frequently sat together in the dining hall with suspicion. Then after reading several articles she realized, "They have found an escape from the isolation of 'subtle racism'. They have united and seized one of the few opportunities they have to truly let go and act as they want." As further evidence, she describes her feelings as the only white woman at the African-American Students Organization meeting, and makes a connection between her feelings of being the outsider with how the men in the dining hall must feel:

> I have never felt more awkward in my life. I felt very alone and self-conscious the minute I walked in . . . The difference between my uncomfortable situation and the daily life of the black men at [the dining hall] is similar but also very different. While my feelings of "not fitting in" lasted a little more than an hour, the black men are only able to *escape* these feelings for an hour.

Next, she offers another example, of passing a Native American woman on her way to class. She writes, "Afraid of overcompensating, afraid of whatever, I usually look at my shoes as we pass." After framing her actions once again with her research, she notes, "I have decided this [behavior] is a classic example of subtle racism. Now when I pass I say 'hello', but I still feel awkward." Reflecting on her actions, she then raises one of those "hard questions" that further complicates the situation: "How is it possible at the University of New Hampshire to get enough interaction so that the awkwardness is no longer present?" The last half of the paper details the difficulties facing the university in its attempts to create more diversity on campus and at the same time to provide for the needs of minority students. Serena closes her five-page essay with herself again:

> Since starting this project I have learned much about my attitude regarding racism. I found that I do have a prejudiced side and have begun the process of questioning it. While I still have a lot to learn about the hardships minorities face and how I can change things, I now have a base to work with. Everyone deserves the kind of enlightenment that this project has afforded me.

Serena's paper is the most essayistic of the three papers. It is not more essayistic simply because she uses more personal examples; rather it is essayistic because she has shown us how she came to her own understanding. We have witnessed her struggle to make sense and have been privy to her process of making sense of racism and prejudice at "the 'deep' level of life-world experience" (Spellmeyer 1993c, 278). Her paper suggests, more clearly than will Emily's or Avery's, that her new understanding is tentative. She reminds us that her knowledge is not complete when she writes, "I still have a lot to learn . . . " In the coauthored foreword to their essays, when the students introduce their different perspectives on the racism equation, Serena's response is again tentative: "Serena is still questioning this theory and has come to no surefire conclusions; however, she does have a better understanding of how difficult it is for any minority to succeed in the infrastructure without representation from their race." Here too, Serena explains how she moved from her initial position of certainty ("Serena firmly believed it was possible for anyone to be racist . . .") to her current position of "still questioning" by describing her discussion with Ms. Fuentes.

Emily's paper entitled "But I'm Not Prejudiced!" contains moments of essayistic writing as she reveals how her research has changed her own thinking. Like Serena, she begins the paper with her arrival on campus:

> If I dropped my tray in the middle of the lunch line, few people would know, and more importantly no one would care. I was just another face in the crowd; nothing drew attention to me. I never imagined what it would be like for the small number of minority students attending UNH . . . With freshmen naivete, I believed because I had not heard of any racial incidents or hate crimes on campus that meant that racial tension did not exist at UNH. If people aren't hostile toward minorities here, I reasoned, UNH must provide minorities with an excellent learning environment. I was wrong. . . .

Unlike Serena, however, Emily's focus in her paper is not specifically on her own understanding. The "I" in the title is not meant to simply be a singular "I." After citing evidence that the campus community offers a "chilly climate" for minority students because of ignorance and white students' own hidden beliefs, she introduces the idea that everyone is prejudiced. She begins by using herself as an example, but then quickly moves to talking about prejudice in more general terms. As she mentioned in her reflection, it is less threatening for her to talk in terms of "all" rather than "I."

> When I first began to learn about the problem of racism on campus, it was easy for me to pretend I was not involved. "I'm not prejudiced," I would tell myself . . . But I am prejudiced, just as *all people* are. *We* all carry preconceived notions about minorities within ourselves; the question is whether *we* realize they are there. It's those people who recognize their prejudices, confront them, and try to understand them that help to make the campus a better place (my emphasis).

In the rest of the essay, Emily will use her own experience without referring to it directly. Whereas Serena illustrates specific concepts with examples from her own life, Emily will draw from the wellspring of her epiphanies during the project to form generalizations or "personal truths" about the nature of prejudice—but she does not specifically focus on the revelations themselves. For instance, having read her journal and memos, we can see how the following insight has emerged from her examination of her experience and her own realizations about herself: "People are not born with prejudices. Prejudices are attitudes that are learned as the individual grows and develops, and may manifest themselves in subtle ways, so that the person who claims 'But I'm not prejudiced', actually is and just hasn't recognized the fact." To illustrate these hidden prejudices, Emily constructs a hypothetical example instead of using a real incident that she wrote about in her journal. In her journal, she talked about an experience in which a man kept asking her to dance. She told him she wasn't interested because she already had a boyfriend. When she relayed this story to her friends later, she writes in her journal that "I found myself always mentioning that the man was black. Why should it have mattered? . . . I must have subconsciously felt it was important. I guess that just shows that I do carry hidden prejudices." However, in her essay, Emily does not write about this incident. Instead, she writes:

> The strongest example I have found to show people how prejudices emerge is when white people label minorities when they speak of them. Instead of saying, "A man at the office," people tend to say, "A *black* man at my office." If a white person wanted to speak about another white person whom they knew, they would not say, "You know Lisa, my *white* friend."

The points Emily offers to support her contention that everyone harbors hidden prejudices are supported by her research, but arise from her own discoveries about herself during this project. For example, it comes as no surprise that Emily is "convinced that education is a key factor in alleviating racial tension on campus," since she has just witnessed how her own education about the plight of minorities on campus during this project has revealed her own hidden assumptions. Interestingly, she ends her paper with an argument that seems to contradict her own experience of working on this project. Emily concludes that college *is* the ideal time for students to examine assumptions and beliefs they have previously taken for granted:

> People who are freshmen in college are separating themselves from their parents and community . . . They are beginning to develop their own ideals and their own philosophies about life . . . If their university educates them about the racial problems on campus, they might be able to recognize their own prejudices and examine them . . . It is far better to admit "Yes, I'm prejudiced," and

work at understanding how the prejudiced feeling developed and evolved than to insist that you are not prejudiced. Ignoring the problem will not make it go away. . . .

She makes this argument despite the fact that she originally balked at pursuing a potentially contentious topic where "feelings would get in the way of work"; she makes this argument even though she complains her own realizations have come at a bad time ("I was already preoccupied with adjusting to college life and trying to sort out my prejudiced feelings only complicated my adjustment"); she makes this argument knowing that her own realizations of being prejudiced were difficult for her to admit ("I was not prepared to examine and discard the ideals I had formed while growing up"); and she makes this argument knowing that these realizations were painful to acknowledge (at one point, she wonders if she is on "a moral level comparable to that of bigots and KKK members"). While Emily's apparent change of position may represent memory's capacity for melioration or the student's penchant for upbeat and tidy conclusions, this new perspective may simply reflect the tentative nature of essayistic insights. These insights are not fixed perspectives. It is not unusual for students who immerse themselves in a project for an extended period of time to flip-flop their perspectives many times. And with further reflection and knowledge, individuals continue to understand things differently.

Emily concludes by saying that "it's far better to admit 'Yes, I am prejudiced,' and work at understanding how the prejudiced feeling developed and evolved than to insist that you are not prejudiced." Her closing position as presented in her paper appears much less tentative than Serena's. Emily writes that she "is *convinced* that education is a key factor . . ." (emphasis added), and she details just what she thinks the university needs to do and why. Although Emily projects a more certain voice in her paper, her memos and journal suggest that she, more than any member in the group, has ended this project somewhere in "the between."

Whereas Emily's and Serena's papers focus on what can be done to identify and correct prejudice at the individual level, Avery, noting that racism is institutionalized discrimination, concentrates on the educational institution itself. His paper, entitled "The Quest for Diversity at UNH: Ways to Combat Bigotry and Discrimination," offers statistical evidence to contradict the idea that colleges and universities today are "great, liberal, open-minded institutions where students receive a well-rounded education. . . ."

Emily and Serena are a visible presence in their writing. When we read their papers, we immediately know that what we are reading is a perspective; it is the view from a very specific somewhere. Avery, however, writes a more traditional research paper, one that marshals evidence from a variety of other sources to support an already established thesis. Unlike Emily and Serena, Avery does not refer to his own experience at all in his essay. Since Emily and Serena see racism as a problem of individuals, their inclusion of their own personal experience of being prejudiced not only helps explain and illustrate their points, it also counts as valid evidence. Avery, however, sees racism as a problem of institutions, and he may see his own personal experience as less relevant to his argument. However, since he, the writer, is less visible in the writing, the fact that he is presenting a position is less apparent. Avery opens his paper with a string of incidents cited from various reputable publications that depict discrimination and racial hatred on college campuses. His next paragraph then begins:

> You may think the preceding examples of racial hatred on college campuses happened twenty or thirty years ago. In fact, all of them took place during the last few years . . . Some form of racial discrimination and racist incidents have been reported at more than 300 colleges in the last five years . . . These numbers are disturbing and speak to the mind-set prevalent in many embittered white students . . .

When Avery says "these numbers are disturbing" he is telling the reader how he or she should respond to the evidence he is presenting. In contrast, an essayistic approach might note that he, the writer, is disturbed by these numbers and explain why. It would then be up to readers to decide for themselves how they should interpret the information. In presenting his ideas in this way, Avery has simply replaced one master narrative with another. Regardless of the veracity of this new narrative, its packaging is the problem. (Avery's paper is not essayistic, but at the same time, I need to make it very clear that Avery's paper is an excellent piece of writing, much more sophisticated than Emily or Serena's papers. As a teacher, I certainly do not penalize him for not writing a more essayistic paper. He receives a well-deserved A.)

Part of the reason for the tone and style of Avery's paper may have to do with the fact that this project involved research, and even though I emphasize that a research *essay* is not like the traditional ("I-less") high school term paper, many students still feel bound by this tradition. However, it is important to remember, that unlike Emily and Serena, this project has not been a voyage of discovery for Avery. If we recall what I suggested earlier—that Avery's purpose in this project is overtly political, to make (white) people aware of the injustices done to African-Americans and other minorities—then we can see why he might desire to represent his perspective as objective and unmediated truth.

This topic is not one he is the least bit tentative about. As he said in his earlier memo, "if you want to get something done you need to let the world know in no *uncertain* terms." For the most part, even the emotion-laden language of his memos disappear in his paper. Just as he did not talk specifically about his own history with Serena and Emily, he may not want to "bias" his case in the paper by opening himself to criticism that he is *only* talking from personal experience or that his view is simply "his opinion." He may want readers to see that (regardless of his own experience on these matters), the facts are there, and people need to know what they are. At times, however, his interpretation of the facts gets intermingled with the hard evidence he presents. For example, at one point he offers the following opinion as clear fact (no evidence required): "The Eurocentric point of view is a major contributing factor to the racist brainwashing and conditioning which whites experience in American society." While such a claim may be warranted, it is not fact.

It is difficult to adopt an essayistic stance toward your subject if you believe you already know what the truth of that subject is. It is difficult to adopt an essayistic stance toward your audience if you believe it is your obligation to inform or persuade others about your truth. While informing and persuading are legitimate reasons for writing, they are not the reasons one chooses to pursue inquiry. Inquiry is best served by an open and tentative essayistic stance. As I mentioned before, my pedagogical purpose for this assignment was for students to select a topic *for inquiry* and to use reading and writing *to inquire*. The fact that Avery began this project from an extremely knowledgeable position made it difficult for him to adopt this essayistic approach. In his reflection on the project, he emphasizes that people have a moral responsibility to make the "truth" known:

> White people have a *duty* to remind other white people, particularly those in "high" places, that the American dream is a myth being perpetuated to oppress people of color, and to remind them that not one shred of equality has ever existed in this troubled land. Maybe if we are consistent enough in our *aiming* of words, we will *hit* a target. Hopefully this hit will break off the protective shield of someone and cause them [sic] to finally stop and THINK (my emphasis).

When truth is aimed like a weapon, it will not set people free. Avery has chosen to "hit" the audience for his paper with information

designed to "cause them to finally stop and THINK" about race relations, by accepting his conclusions rather than inquiring into the
evidence themselves. Avery presents an argument that makes it difficult (although not impossible) for readers to adopt an essayistic
stance in response. Carlos Fuentes believes the kind of text determines what stance the reader will take. In a *Harpers* excerpt (1989)
written in response to the death decree laid on Salmon Rushdie by
the Ayatollah, he distinguishes between sacred and secular texts.
The sacred text is supposed to represent The Truth; the secular text
(in this case, the novel) represents the search for truth. Fuentes
writes, "The sacred text is, by definition, a completed and exclusive
text. You can add nothing to it. It does not converse with anyone. It
is its own loud speaker" (17). In contrast, Fuentes believes the novel is a text that "indicates we are always becoming. There is no final solution. No last word" (17). Avery's stance toward his topic and
what kind of paper he writes is closed. Although in contrast to Fuentes, I think it's possible for the reader to learn to adopt an essayistic response to a "sacred" text; it's much easier, however, to adopt
this stance when the text represents a "search for truth" and depicts
how the writer came to hold his or her beliefs.

Victoria Davion notes that "one can tell as least as much about
a person's character by looking at how she arrived at her beliefs as
by looking at which beliefs or values she views as unconditional at
any particular moment" (1991, 183). The arguments and evidence
Avery presents are not used to show readers how he came to hold
his beliefs, but rather to persuade readers why they should adopt
his position. I need to emphasize that I am talking about persuasion
from a rhetorical perspective and not on epistemological grounds.
My concerns are more about his stance toward his audience than
his actual arguments. For the most part, Avery offers many good reasons, which I for one find particularly persuasive. However, his
stance does not always invite assent; at times, it seems to coerce it.
What is more, Avery's paper masks the complex, messy, and at
times, elusive nature of truth and understanding that we have seen
emerge in the group's collaboration. Instead, Avery has adopted a
method that embodies an objectivist view of the world, one that
Avery himself would probably be the first person to criticize as being false! Drawing on James Berlin's notions of different rhetorics,
Paul Heilker notes the kind of epistemological perspectives represented by the linear thesis/support paper and the essay:

> It seems clear that the thesis/support form (in its attempt to fix truth
> in certainty and to declare a definite and singular reality, one that
> is knowable from a single, immobile point-of-view and completely

representable in correctly used language forms) embodies a positiv-
istic epistemology and rhetoric that runs counter to the . . . view that
sees truth and reality as, at best, multiple, provisional, and tentative
(1996, 5).

In order to be effectively convincing to others, Avery seems to think
he must sound certain himself—or must he? Is Avery's certainty
more convincing than Serena's tentativeness?

Another difference that I see between the standard unified and
coherent thesis/support paper that Avery has elected to write and
the essay of inquiry is that in the thesis/support paper the writer has
already done all the thinking and all the reasoning and often leaves
little work for the reader to do, other than to simply agree or disagree. The essay has been called an "egalitarian" form (Zeiger 1989;
McQuade 1992) because it presents information in such a way that
the reader can participate in the reasoning process and can come to
her own conclusions. She takes what the writer has provided and
then combines this information with her own subjectivity to earn
her own insights. Elizabeth Minnich reminds us that "to achieve a
truly egalitarian pluralism, conceptually and politically, it is necessary for all groups to achieve self-knowledge, developed from within rather than imposed from without" (179). I understand her to
mean that individuals need to use their subjectivity to interpret the
objective facts and arrive at their own understanding. How we come
to know something matters, as do the methods we use for communicating that knowledge. Students will learn to use the methods that
are used with them. In using these methods, they are likely to (unconsciously) adopt the particular epistemology the methods represent. If we want students to learn to wrestle with the hard questions,
education can not be about efficient delivery of ready-made information, no matter how accurate or truthful that information may be.

I have emphasized the importance of adopting a tentative, exploratory stance toward one's subject of inquiry as well as one's audience. However, I am not saying that the goal of all educational
inquiry should be the loss of certainty so that students end up
"dazed and confused" somewhere in the "between." Although I
would have liked Avery to originally have pursued a subject in
which his position was less well formulated or certain, so that he
could experience writing and reading as methods for inquiry, he did
not. Instead, he used this project as an opportunity to finally articulate ideas that were vitally important to him. Nonetheless, given
his motives and the strength of his conviction, by presenting his
ideas in a less seamless, mono-voiced paper and a more disjunctive,
polyphonic essay, he might have found a more politically effective

and less politically coercive method for "representing, engaging, and altering social and political realities [and] challenging both cultural hierarchies and the notion of a fixed and unified subjectivity" (Faery 1996, 62).

For many students, after four weeks of intense research and discussion the writing of the essay is anticlimactic in terms of the students' actual learning. But perhaps not for Avery. Looking back on this project now with the clarity of teacher hindsight, I realize that Avery had been writing more disjunctive kinds of essays prior to this project. I am wondering if Avery's paper is less the product of his own certainty than an indication of his uncertainty; but perhaps it's simply the result of a pedagogy that didn't follow all the way through.

In contrast to the strident and divisive discourse that sometimes occurred during the group's collaboration and writing, interestingly, Avery ends his paper with an uplifting, conciliatory but no less certain appeal for everyone to work hard to unite around their differences:

> Often facing something as enormous as institutionalized and socialized discrimination seems insurmountable. To combat this, we must all remember the indomitable spirit and strength which is present in every human soul, and we must constantly strive to cherish all of the unique, beautiful gifts that the diverse members of the human family bring into the world. If we remember and respect these tenets, there is no limit to the depth of our power.

No matter how right or moral our position seems, as Kurt Spellmeyer notes, "any knowledge which might be useful must give people something 'deeper' than one gospel or another" (1993c, 281). And while Avery's knowledge is impressive, his arguments persuasive, his stance pushes me away. Although he helps me to understand how we could find ourselves in such a potentially unrelenting, unreflexive position, I fear such a position dooms us to repeat what we are trying to overcome. And yet, I do not know how to quell the tide of (nondeferent) certainty that threatens to sweep me and others along in its wake, unless it be with what I hope by now is a warranted belief in an ongoing, reflexive dialogue.

If we want our students to seriously engage with other perspectives, we need to provide them with a method of inquiry and the time and opportunity to use it. None of these students in this collaborative project simply hitched a ride on the back of a ready-made idea; all three of them earned their insights, either during the project or long before. But even so, we can see how much work we still have to do if we are to ensure that our students' close encounters with others are dialogic and reflexive.

Notes

1. Avery now finds the categories male and female problematic. He is seeking a metaphor for gender that doesn't depend on the male-female binary, a difficult task given the constraints of our language.

2. It is interesting to note that Avery's best friend was an African-American woman who actually attended one of the group's conferences with me. After the group interviewed Isabella Fuentes, a Latina woman who was the assistant director of the Office of Multicultural Affairs, Avery began working in the office. The semester following freshman English he enrolled in a special introductory section of Women's Studies that focused on African-American women.

3. In her reflection on the project, Emily notes how important her journal was for allowing her to examine her thoughts and feelings. During the groups' meetings she says "I was often too busy defending myself and my ideals to try to understand why I felt the way I did. My journal . . . was the only place I felt safe and comfortable voicing my opinions."

4. When the group met with the assistant director of the Multicultural Students Organization, a Latina woman, Avery asked her how she handled "the rage." Emily writes in her journal that she assumed Avery meant "the rage of having people treat you different as a minority." As reported by Emily, the woman said rage was the only response: "there was no other way; it made her a stronger person, and she saw it as a challenge." Avery may have been influenced by her response.

5. I'm not sure how Clark (through Wyschogrod) is interpreting Noddings' concept of empathy. Clark describes Noddings' concept of empathy as "an attempt to receive another's reality as one's own" (66). And yet, he then criticizes it from Wyschogrod's position as an interpretation "that directs me to understand the other in my own terms" (66). The latter assumption does not follow from—in fact it seems to contradict—the initial description of empathy. I don't see "an attempt to receive" as an attempt to interpret, but rather as an attempt not to interpret, to defer interpretation.

Chapter Five

Some Tentatives for a Reflexive Pedagogy

Anyone with an active mind lives on tentatives rather than tenets.
— Robert Frost

We must try harder to understand than explain.
— Vaclav Havel

William Zeiger notes that the essay's "egalitarian nature comes from its intention not to attempt to constrain its subject matter or to subdue its audience, but to render as truly as possible the confluence of impressions and reflections which shape one's thought" (1989, 244). In the previous four chapters I have sought to gradually build an understanding of reflexivity and its relation to essayistic writing and reading without fixing it to a single, precise definition. I have not attempted "to constrain my subject matter." I have constructed it broadly and suggestively, allowing my thinking to spill over at will into the margins of my topic, to momentarily meld with contingent ideas, and inviting my readers to do the same. In this final chapter, I focus on some of the practical, epistemological, and ethical implications of a reflexive pedagogy that uses reading and writing as vehicles for constructing, deepening, and challenging students' and teachers' understandings of their subjects and themselves.

137

Practical Features of a Reflexive Pedagogy

Reflexivity describes the feeling of heightened self-awareness or consciousness that can occur in response to a dialectical encounter with an other. Interest in reflexivity seems to have emerged most strongly in fields with real, visible others: anthropology (cultural other), feminist theory (gendered other) and philosophical hermeneutics (textual other). In contrast, reflection has dominated discussions of problem solving in the cognitive and developmental sciences. Composition studies have borrowed from all these disciplines; it is no surprise that a conflation of these terms frequently occurs. More confusion arises because reflection and reflexivity, as I noted earlier, are not entirely separate processes, but rather different aspects of the same process that can work separately or together.

My focus in this inquiry differs from many cognitive researchers in composition who are looking at how reflection—defined as anything from the writers' backward scanning of written text to their deliberation and evaluation of knowledge and rhetorical strategies during planning and drafting—improves the actual written text. However, Cynthia Onore (1989) argues that if we are going to think of writing as a form of inquiry, we can not measure improvement by the written text alone. I have suggested throughout this book that writing and reading can lead to gains in learning, and the generation of new meanings. And yet, sometimes this more sophisticated exploration of subject matter leads to a temporary loss of rhetorical control. At any rate, my focus in this book is more on the writer and reader's exploration of subject matter, rather than technical control of text.

Mariolina Salvatori (1996) has recently pointed out a bitter irony of our educational system. She notes that students are "so often expected to demonstrate but so seldom given an opportunity to learn" the critical, analytical, and reflexive habits of mind they need to carry out their work in the university. Our methods of education have "consistently and repeatedly skirted the responsibility of nurturing one of the most fundamental of human activities—critical self-reflexivity" (452). But what would a pedagogy look like that emphasized and encouraged critical reflexivity? I think such a pedagogy would include and emphasize the following features.

The Other

As Harriet Malinowitz observes, "[a] composition class is a particularly fit site in which to discover that the word of the other subtly colludes with, melds with—indeed, is embedded within—one's

own" (1995, 43). The encounter with the other initiates the reflexive turn to the self, and the continual interplay between self and
other is what prevents self-consciousness from slipping into nar-
cism or solipsism. I have mostly characterized the other in its extreme, "not us" form: e.g., my Australia; the peace corps volunteers'
Dominican Republic; Mindy's Lucille; Ralph's Sheila; Kay and
Rob's difficult, abstract text; Chad's African-American women; and
Avery, Emily, and Serena's inquiry into the topic of racism and the
treatment of minority students at the university. Each of these encounters with others contains the ingredients for individuals to undergo "the stranger experience," where they discover that their
customary ways of making sense may not be sufficient for understanding their subjects or themselves.

As we saw with Anna's examination of her papers and reading
responses from a semester's composition course, the other may also
be a text written by an earlier self. When that text is viewed from
the perspective of a more experienced or knowledgeable self, what
was once familiar can become strange. The other may also be the
other within. A single mind can embody many perspectives. Hannah
Arendt (1971), for example, talks about the "two-in-one" of Plato's
"soundless dialogue . . . between me and myself" (185). However, I
believe this internal dialectic is made possible because of previous
interaction with others outside of ourselves. As Vygotsky notes in
his discussion of internal thought, "an interpersonal process is transformed into an interpersonal one" (1978, 57). Likewise, Karen Burke
LeFevre has suggested that in order to create or invent, we require
"the presence of the other. This 'other' may at times be another part
of the rhetor herself—an internalized construct that she makes from
social experience—or it may be a perceived audience of actual others"
(1987, 38). Thus, Donald Murray's description of writing as a conversation between two selves carries the trace and residue of many
external conversations:

> The act of writing might be described as a conversation between
> two workmen muttering to each other at the workbench. The self
> speaks, the other self listens and responds. The self proposes, the
> other self considers. The self makes, the other self evaluates. The
> two selves collaborate: a problem is spotted, discussed, defined;
> solutions are proposed, rejected, suggested, attempted, tested, dis-
> carded, accepted (1982, 165).

Writers and artists have long talked about the necessity of having
their internal others present for the execution of their creative work.
Sometimes these others are friendly, supportive muses; at other
times they are critics, devils, "watchers."[1] Whether the other ap-

pears externally or is manifested internally, it is the dialectical engagement between self and other that triggers the reflexive response.

We will not respond reflexively to every other we meet. But in each encounter, the conditions for a reflexive response are present. As Emily, Serena, and Avery reveal in Chapter Four, the context and timing of the encounter are important. Emily writes in her journal that as a student new to the university, already experiencing many changes and adjustments, she is not ready or prepared to call up and examine all her long-held beliefs. Avery, boldly emerging from the silence, is not likely to want to turn back to interrogate the sound of his voice. And Serena, who has begun to peel away the layers of her "racist self," balks when confronted with others who appear rude or use impolite language.

In terms of a specific pedagogy, certainly new or complex texts and genres of writing can serve as others for students, and provide them with the opportunity for engaging in the stranger experience. For example, many readers will find that their customary, unconscious habits of reading do not help them to make sense of a book like Gloria Anzaldua's *Borderlands/La Frontera: The New Mestiza* (1987) with its continual shifting and blurring of genre, language, and mode of writing. Anzaldua's mix of poetry and prose, Spanish and English, and personal, mythic, and historical content pose a challenge for readers on this side of the border. Only as readers begin to grasp the dynamic and plural nature of the other—La Mestiza—do they begin to make sense of the text, and their own ways of reading (and being in the world) are disclosed and held open for inspection. Mariolina Salvatori (1996) describes a number of other ways that encourage students to "self-monitor" their engagement with difficult texts, thereby "making what is imperceptible—thinking—at least dimly perceptible" (449).

Teachers can also create assignments that require students to go into the field to observe or interview others. For example, we might ask students to pay a number of visits to a site or place they wouldn't normally frequent and examine their own changing reactions over time. Or we might have students conduct multiple interviews with someone whose positions they don't already understand or ascribe to. Such interviews often produce reflexive encounters that lead to the discovery of the interviewer's own "inner-views." As Parker Palmer notes, interviews can offer "a way of looking into other people's behaviors and attitudes that opens our own lives to view" (1983, 62). Assignments like the collaborative inquiry project I describe in Chapter Four, which allow for close and long-term engagement with many others, also provide the conditions for a reflexive encounter.

Teachers can also assume the role of an other by introducing a counterdiscourse or alternative interpretation or perspective. By counterdiscourse, I do not mean the teacher becomes a devil's advocate. Instead, the teacher makes available alternative positions on topics that students are reading or writing about, or poses questions that may complicate students' thinking. The purpose of the counterdiscourse is to make the familiar strange. It is a heuristic for inquiry. For instance, hindsight tells me that I could have pointed Rob to other passages in Freire's text and asked him to consider these passages in light of his contention that his fraternity was an example of Freire's philosophy. When I asked Mark, who was writing about the positive relationship between hard work and success, if he could imagine any situation in which more hard work might have negative effects, I was nudging him to find his own counterdiscourse.

I want to caution that simply introducing an other in the form of a text is not enough for students to automatically enlarge their understanding. There seems to be a presumption among some educators that if we simply introduce or add multicultural texts and experiences into the curriculum, we will have done our bit for diversity. Providing access to other texts and ways of looking at the world is a start, but unless we also teach students methods for engaging with these others, the other will remain just that—other.

An Open Stance

We need an approach, a method for engaging the other that is receptive, deferent, exploratory, tentative. Learning to adopt this stance takes conscious effort, as many of us have discovered when we tried to do as Peter Elbow suggests and believe *before* we doubt. It can be difficult for academics to relinquish the tendency to rush to judgment. In fact, a study reported by Daniel Goleman in the science section of the *New York Times* in the summer of 1995 suggested that it is impossible for human beings to be completely impartial because our "seemingly neutral" first impressions are already biased. It seems that human beings form an evaluation upon perception, during that "first moment of contact between the world and the mind." These instantaneous and unconscious judgments predispose us to think positively or negatively, even about things that we have never encountered before. Through "conscious thought," however, researchers believe people can become aware of their own biases and assumptions, and eventually override or flesh out these initial, automatic judgments. The essayistic stance is sophisticated, one that few of us can adopt all the time, and one that few of our students will have learned to adopt at all, especially in academic settings. But that's the point. On both intellectual and ethical grounds, I believe we should begin to teach students how to adopt this open, tentative approach toward others. As Palmer writes, "To be inhospitable to strangers or strange ideas, however unsettling they may be, is to be hostile to the possibility of truth; hospitality is not only an ethical virtue, but an epistemological one as well" (1983, 74).

I have found that it is easier to teach students to adopt an essayistic stance when the subjects they are writing about are complex, strange, or difficult to assess. Once students learn to approach a complex situation essayistically, they are more likely to complicate subjects of seeming simplicity. For example, I encourage students to write about situations that confuse them or subjects where they haven't already figured out where they stand. I use difficult, academic texts (texts, that are obviously other) to teach essayistic reading. Once students learn to adopt an essayistic approach to understanding these kinds of texts, they begin to look deeper into texts they might have previously seen as easily accessible or seemingly simple, like a Raymond Carver short story.

I also believe that teachers should practice and model this stance for their students. Teachers are sometimes told that their job is to present the facts in a neutral and objective way. They are not supposed to indicate where they stand in relation to the subject at hand because that might unfairly bias or pressure students. Such a concern is understandable if all teachers are doing is presenting the conclusions and products of their own thinking. However, if as teachers, we also share how we came to formulate our positions or how we came to hold the beliefs we do, we can model a way of approaching and thinking about ideas for students to emulate. Such an approach has something in common with Gerald Graff's suggestion that we "teach the conflicts"; (1992) however, he seems more focused on helping students understand the actual content and issues of particular conflicts; my focus is on modeling a process of approaching and engaging these complicated ideas. This is what I tried to do with Leah, the graduate student who was concerned that my Grandmother Qualley was a "colonizer." I responded to Leah's criticism of my grandmother by using it as an opportunity for me to inquire further and reexamine my own assumptions. When teachers make a point to share their processes of thinking about ideas, they set up the conditions for students to learn their methods of inquiry as well as the subject under discussion.

When people are told what to think or which stance to adopt, they may respond defensively rather than reflexively. Instead of opening themselves to the view of the other, they may seek ways to preserve their own view (often without examining what it actually is they are trying to safeguard). For example, when Avery tries to persuade Serena and Emily that whites are responsible for past injustices done to African-Americans, the women emphatically resist this idea. Serena argues that "people back then didn't really realize the atrocities they were committing. As wrong as it was, it was considered acceptable." To support her assertion, she reminds the group that "in the essay, the Indians were invisible." Here, Serena is referring to an essay by Jane Tompkins that the class had read earlier in the semester.[2] This essay chronicles Tompkins' attempts to understand the conflicting historical interpretations and first-hand accounts of what happened between Europeans and Native Americans in the seventeenth century. Tompkins shows how the various accounts can be explained by examining how their authors were situated. What the writers notice, and what counts as epistemologically significant for each of them, varies according to their social, cultural, and historical situation. And in many of these accounts, the Indians did not appear to count as "human beings," or as a significant part of the wilderness. They were "invisible." In making a connection between Tompkins' essay and the treatment of African-Americans during slavery, Serena, to her credit, is attempting to make a sophisticated argument on the grounds of cultural and historical relativism; however, she could have just as easily used this piece to examine her own situatedness.

Emily also insists that whites should not be held accountable for the past, but she justifies her position in a different way. After discovering that she is only the fourth generation to be born on United States soil, she writes that since her ancestors couldn't have owned slaves, and were in fact treated harshly themselves, that she certainly cannot be held responsible for the atrocities committed in the past:

> My father's great-great-grandmother was 100 percent full blooded Algonquin Indian from Canada . . . my mother's great-grandmother worked in the mill . . . as did my father's great-grandmother. I will be the first to admit that they weren't half as oppressed as the slaves, or blacks since, but as Franco-Americans in New England, my ancestors weren't always treated with respect, especially in the mills. To my knowledge, my ancestors had nothing to do with the slaves . . . If either of you have heard stories of the Franco-Americans oppressing blacks, please let me know, because it might give me a different outlook on this topic.

Emily's response can be seen in part as a defensive maneuver against what she and Serena feel is an unjust attack on all white people. Had Avery introduced his argument by sharing why he found it persuasive, Emily and Serena may still not have agreed with him, but perhaps they would have tried to understand his position, instead of seeking ways to refute it and justify their own. This closed stance on the part of all three students prevents the possibility of dialogue on this topic.

The other extreme occurs when individuals uncritically assume the perspective of the other. For example, after I had lived in Australia for a couple of years, my initial defensiveness about the United States disappeared as I opened myself more and more to Australian culture; however, it took me a while to become fully reflexive about the culture in which I was born. I noted in a letter home that "I was a book and Australia was writing all over me, revising pages and pages from the earlier chapters of my life." Rather than examining one set of beliefs from the position of the other, I simply replaced them. When I returned home for my first visit, I was no longer the proud advocate of the work ethic. I came back to the States for a month's stay with a mind filled with the words, habits, and perspectives that I had gradually, but unconsciously, assimilated down under. And true to the spirit of my Grandmother Qualley, I felt obligated to immediately enlighten my family about their American shortcomings, which included: too much faith in authority, big business, and polyester, and too little regard for labor unions and socialized medicine. I thought my family needed to know what was wrong with their lives and what they could do to fix them. Not only was I not yet reflexive, I certainly had not adopted an essayistic approach toward my American audience. It is important to note that many people come to adopt an essayistic stance and approach to texts and situations gradually. In the process, they may resist the other by seeking to fortify and protect their own positions, or alternatively, they may renounce their beliefs, don the garb of the other, and go native. However, continual dialogue between self and other can help prevent either of these practices from becoming permanent conditions.

Agency

It is difficult to be open and receptive toward others without a strong sense of our own agency. If we have too little sense of agency, we can be disempowered, subsumed by the other; with too much sense of our own agency, we may overpower or oppress the other. We also need to have enough autonomy, self-trust and self-esteem to withstand our own rigorous self-scrutiny. When we have no sense of our own agency—I'm thinking, for instance, of abused wives, children or my hypothetical female writer of Ralph's paper—we can't, and probably shouldn't, try to be reflexive about the oppressor's position. In doing so, we might contribute to our own oppression, thereby further diminishing the possibility for agency. What Trudy Govier (1993) says about the importance of self-trust for women, also applies to teachers and students:

> [a] person who has no resources to preserve her ideas, values, and goals against criticism and attack from others will be too malleable to preserve her sense that she is a person in her own right . . . In order to reflect on and appraise one's options and beliefs, and implement decisions based on the reflecting judgments, one must trust oneself. . . . Without self-trust a person cannot think and decide for himself or herself and therefore cannot function as an autonomous human being (111–112).

Interestingly, even though Avery tells Serena and Emily that he has been oppressed for being different, and even though Serena and Emily are witness to this oppression by others on several occasions, they do not see Avery as a person without agency because of Avery's intelligence, knowledge, and conviction about their topic of racism. However, Avery's strong, uncompromising stance during the project suggests that he sees deference and agency as separate stances rather than one inclusive position. I have suggested that an ethical agency requires that we monitor and continually examine our words and actions, lest we (un)wittingly impose our beliefs on others, thereby contributing to their objectification and/or victimization. A good example of a person with a strong sense of ethical agency—way beyond most of us—is the nun in the film *Dead Man Walking*, who is able to open herself to the other, the convicted killer, without losing herself in the process.

All too frequently, though, our methods in the teaching of composition seem to encourage false or premature agency or an illusion of power. As Sherrie Meyer (1993) notes, learning to write in the university can often mean learning to play the "confidence game." When students assume an authority in their written texts before they have had an opportunity to earn it through inquiry, they "participate in an illusion of mastery" that belies an inadequacy they often still feel about themselves as writers. Their stance toward their subject and their audience is often more "cocksure" than "confident" (47). I see this false confidence most frequently when students are encouraged to focus on the surface features of rhetorical style or technique before they have done the necessary foundational inquiry. For example, many of my students have been told to avoid "I" in "formal writing" by their high-school teachers, and so they frequently attempt to adopt a more authoritative stance by writing from a "we" perspective. Unfortunately, the models for such a voice are frequently drawn from what they are most familiar with in popular culture: the glorious sounding but empty rhetoric of politicians or the comforting homilies of writers like Robert Fulgrum. (As I listen to political conventions during this presidential-election year, I realize all too well the extent that our culture rewards glibness over thoughtfulness. All the more reason, I think to myself, why methods of education need to act as a counterdiscourse to culture!)

Dialogue

As I have tried to make clear, individuals need a way to mediate between self and other so that neither is disempowered or overpowered. Since reflexivity is a response to a *dialectical* encounter with an other, dialogue is essential to this transaction. Parker Palmer observes that dialogue is necessary to resist the tyranny of objectivism: "Genuine dialogue is possible only as I acknowledge an integrity in the other that cannot be reduced to my perceptions and needs" (1983, 56). Genuine dialogue also presupposes that participants are not isolated in their own subjectivism and are open to considering other positions. As Palmer notes, "if my private perceptions are the measure of truth, if my truth cannot be challenged or enlarged by another, I have merely found one more way to objectify and hold the other at arm's length, to avoid again the challenge of personal transformation" (55). The kind of dialogue I have in mind is not the finite dialogue that necessarily leads to consensus and agreement, but the dialogue that leads to a deepened or more complicated understanding. This is the kind of dialogue envisioned by hermeneutics. It is also the kind of dialogue that Maria Lugones equates with world-travelling, and that I seek from students engaged in collaborative inquiry. Georgia Warnke notes that once we recognize the interpretive nature of our own understanding, we begin to "acknowledge not only the possible existence of other interpretations, but also the importance of considering them and even of trying to learn from them" (1993, 92). Even though we may not adopt another's interpretation in the end, we may find that dialogue with other perspectives can help us to illuminate or rethink our own. Engaging in this kind of dialogue enables Susan to discover why she is willing to change her name; it allows Mindy to see how people like Lucille, the hardened, disagreeable nursing assistant, are at least partially constructed by the situations in which they live and work; dialogue with Freire's text enables Kay to complicate her understanding of the homeless, and as Chad (literally) talks to the African-American women in Alice Walker's text, he begins to gain a much fuller sense of the oppression that both links and separates them. And it is this kind of dialogue that eventually allows Avery, Serena, and Emily to develop a more complex understanding of racism on campus, an understanding which shares some features of each others' perspectives, but which has been individually processed and individually claimed.

Dialogue begins when students make connections with others. Thus, as a teacher, I first attempt to help students find ways to make connections with the texts we read, write, and talk about. Once a connection has been established, the channels are open for exploratory and, eventually, more critical dialogue. One way to begin to make a connection and begin a conversation with a text is to make a mark in the margin. When Kay writes in the margins of Paulo Freire's text, "I sometimes see the world as separate from me" she opens the possibility for productive dialogue. Salvatori, Bartholomae and Petrosky, and others emphasize the importance of teaching students to mark their texts as a way to encourage them to become reflexive and reexamine their initial reactions. Such marks can "yield a dramatic visualization of how much a text's argument can be erased because of preestablished conclusions or inattentiveness to the construction of the argument" (Salvatori 1996, 449). Although making a mark is important, examining the implications of those marks is essential. When I have used portfolios in my composition classes, I use them as a tool for examining the written "marks," the marginalia, notes, informal written responses, and papers students have made during the course. Anna's reading of her semester's work is an example of the kind of critical and reflexive dialogue portfolios can generate.

As we have seen, if students do not know how, or are unwilling or unable to find a way to connect with other perspectives, dialogue, and thus, learning (where learning is defined as the modification of what's in our heads as a result of our dialogic encounters with the world) is unlikely to occur. Elizabeth Minnich says that we have not done a very effective job teaching students how to engage in the kinds of dialogue needed to engage differing others in authentic conversation. I quote her at length:

> Over and over I have found [students] retreating to a position of relativism when they fear that there is about to be a conflict over moral positions. . . . I have come to believe that such retreats from

discussion of moral difference are "caused" not by the relativism students are so often charged, but by moral absolutism. The dominant tradition has not helped young people learn how to converse together about the most important values they hold; it has taught them that these values must be absolutely right or they are not values at all. So when students encounter serious differences, they are startled, troubled, frightened. And rather than fight with their friends over who is absolutely right, they prefer to say, in effect, I hold my absolute values, you hold yours. *Both* absolutism *and* radical relativism make it possible, even necessary, to avoid serious engagement with differences. If we want people to cease being absolutists or relativists, we need to open to them the challenge of exploring the rich complexity of differences understood from the beginning as being in transactional relation to each other. We will not get past the problem of relativism by retreating to the good old established certainties; when we do that, we simply ensure that those who want to get along with people who are not already just like them will have nowhere to go but relativism (1990, 167).

The dominant tradition has not helped Ralph know how to talk to Steve about Sheila because he's afraid he'll "get Steve mad." He is reluctant to engage in a dialogue with Rosy about playing on the male soccer team because he doesn't want to "get into an argument." In the beginning of the collaborative project, we see Emily's concern about investigating a topic that is likely to cause conflict among group members. Instead of seeing the group's different views as an opportunity to enlarge her own understanding, she worries these views will "result in big problems" and cause "arguments and disagreements that will get in the way of work." Both Ralph and Emily, if they want "to get along with people who are not already just like them will have nowhere to go but relativism." According to Palmer, relativism, the idea that everyone sees things differently, simply "concedes diversity," and conceding diversity is as problematic as suppressing it (61). Time and again our students, lacking a method that could help them learn from difference, avoid it either by forcing their views on others or retreating from any engagement at all by waving the white flag of relativism: "everyone's entitled to their own opinion." Serena responds to Avery's statement that the country "is fucked," not by seeking to discover what has led him to this conclusion, but challenging "anyone to find a better and more fair justice system in the world." Thus, she avoids dialogic engagement by falling back upon a cultural myth, a "good old [ready-made] established certainty." But Avery also avoids dialogue when he tries to forge ahead into new certainties about racism. Productive conversations, notes Lorraine Code, "have to be open, moving, and hesitant to arbitrary closure; sensitive to revisions of judgment; prepared to leave gaps where no obvious consensus is possible" (1991, 308).

Bakhtin tells us that dialogue is the force that drives intellectual and moral development (Tappen 1991). Ongoing dialogue with others (and ourselves) works to prevent premature closure and affirms the possibility of pluralist perspectives. However, students will need to be taught how to hold productive conversations. The aim of the collaborative inquiry project is to provide students with multiple opportunities over an extended period of time to engage in the kind of dialogue that allows them to come to a more complicated understanding of their subjects and themselves. Students engage in dialogue with "experts" through interviews and in their double-entry journals. They carry on both face-to-face and written dialogue with each other in their group meetings, and through their written memos. And they dialogue with themselves in their personal journals and individual reflections. The written dialogue is important because students have radically different ways of speaking that can prevent them from hearing each other. Emily seems to think that discussion simply means "respecting everyone's opinion," by quietly listening while each member of the group has her say. Avery believes that "raising our voices means that we are making strong headway." The memos act as both a rehearsal for and a reflection of their face-to-face conversations. In addition, Emily also uses her journal as rehearsal and reflection for her memos. It provides her with a quiet and safe place to process the sometimes fiery conversations of the group.

Reflexivity is not possible without dialogue. But we should not assume that the conditions for dialogue automatically exist or are always capable of being realized in our classrooms. That is why Australian educators Jane Kenway and Helen Modra suggest that "perhaps we would do better to see dialogue as the goal of pedagogy, not the condition for it" (1992, 163).

Recursiveness

I make an effort to build recursiveness into my composition courses because the insights we (my students and I) gain when we revisit earlier work can be so illuminating. Throughout this volume, I have tried to reveal the value of a bidirectional process of education, one that allows us to continually reexamine our thinking from the perspective of our present encounters.

If we construct our courses in spirals or circles rather than lines, we can build in recursiveness. We can sequence readings and assignments in such a way that students must not only draw on their earlier work to help them make sense of their current work, they must also use the perspectives gained from their current reading and writing to uncover subjects they have already covered. Following the example of *Ways of Reading* (Bartholomae and Petrosky 1987), a number of composition anthologies are realizing the importance of an intertextual approach to writing and reading. However, rather than following a textbook's ready-made sequences, I would encourage teachers to make their own connections and construct (and reconstruct) their own sequences of texts (print and nonprint). I usually construct the first sequence of readings in my composition course so that I can teach my students how to use one text to read another. But later, I like to demonstrate the "proximity factor" by showing students how different sequences of readings can cause readers to focus on different ideas and come to different understandings. What I am calling the proximity factor refers to people's tendency to form connections with new ideas by first drawing on what is currently foremost in their minds. As we saw in Chapter Three, Kay uses her recent encounter with the homeless, and Rob draws on his current interest with his fraternity to connect with Paulo Freire's text. Teachers, however, can create the conditions for different kinds of intertextual experiences themselves. For example, after everyone in my class reads "The Achievement of Desire" by Richard Rodriguez, I sometimes ask half the class to read "Theft" by Joyce Carol Oates and the other half to read "The Loss of the Creature" by Walker Percy. I then ask each group to use the understanding they have gained from reading these texts to revisit the Rodriguez chapter. Invariably, each group reconnects with the Rodriguez text in different ways. Or, at the end of the course, I might ask students to each select a text of their choice to revisit.

By travelling back to the texts that we have already read, as well as the texts we have already written, we deepen our understanding of our subjects as well as ourselves as writers, readers, thinkers, and learners. Such a process helps students to experience revision as a creative and intellectual process. It also nurtures an important, intellectual, and ethical habit of mind in both students *and teachers*. In Chapter Three, I revealed how my experience of reading Ralph's first paper about Rosy, the soccer player, probably affected my reading of his second paper about Steve and Sheila. Although this realization came after the fact, it has made me more conscious of the ways in which my students' papers flavor my responses to their later work. My ready-made knowledge of intertextuality has become earned-insight.

Epistemological Features of a Reflexive Pedagogy

A reflexive pedagogy emphasizes understanding. Understanding represents both the process and product of the transaction between knower and known. I suppose that occasionally we might experience understanding as a sudden flash of insight, the eureka moment. More frequently, however, I believe the realization that we understand emerges gradually, and we only become aware of it when we make a reflexive turn. (For instance, at what point in this inquiry did you first become aware that you *understood* reflexivity?) As I have tried to demonstrate throughout this book, understanding occurs by degree and is always subject to change with additional knowledge and experience. Our understanding can deepen and develop in complexity, or we may later refute an earlier understanding altogether. The students' essays and responses that appear in the previous chapters, along with my different readings of their work, reveal how understanding is always partial, provisional, incomplete. I do not believe there is such a thing as nonpositional understanding. We understand an other by continual reference to our own perspective, although we may not always be aware of doing so.

Lorraine Code reminds us that evaluating and constructing complex knowledge claims always requires taking subjectivity into account. Once we take subjectivity into account, we begin to recognize the interpretive nature of our understanding. When we find ourselves in familiar situations that we can easily comprehend, we may not pay much attention to this instrument of interpretation. When faced with a new or strange situation or a difficult text, we may be forced to attend to our subjectivity if we wish to make sense. We search for some familiar frame that will enable us to understand. As we attempt to measure the facts at hand against our frame of reference, the frame itself becomes discernible and open for examination. We become reflexive if and when we momentarily turn our attention from the text or situation back to these subjective frames, beliefs, assumptions, and theories that have now come into relief.

Donald Murray offers a good example of a writer, teacher, and learner who has made a reputation for himself by paying attention to his subjectivity, keeping a constant check on his understanding, and encouraging others to do the same. He tells readers of *A Writer Teaches Writing* (1985) to use their subjectivity as they read his book. He hopes they "will become, through the experience of writing and teaching, the writer in the title; that each of us individually and differently will use the book and depart from it as we learn from our own pages and our own students" (5). In *Shoptalk: Learning to Write With*

Writers (1990), a collection of quotes by practicing writers but filled with the (subjective) idiosyncrasies of Murray's life, Murray encourages readers to "make my book your book" (xii). Since "each writer brings an individual history to the writing task," Murray tells his audience that it is their "challenge to read these quotations in light of [their] own experience writing, learning, teaching writing, observing writing, [and] reading writing" (xv). He even provides blank pages for readers to add their own quotes and comments. Even though Murray's ideas have been stolen, embraced, and modified by thousands of teachers and students, Murray has never claimed that his "speculations" about writing and teaching speak for anyone but himself. In a recent essay entitled "Knowing Not Knowing" (1994), he writes,

> From the beginning it was clear that my answers were speculations—guesses. Informed guesses, but not TRUTHS. And I tried to make my idiosyncratic subjectivity clear to my students and my readers. What I had to say was based on my evolving understanding of how I wrote at the moment, how published writers I knew or studied wrote, how my current students wrote and my personal interpretations of this information (61–62).

Murray writes that at one point he hoped that composition research would "replace" his "subjective speculations with more objective knowing." Although Murray sometimes seems to devalue the importance of what he calls his "subjective speculations" ("I was after all, a practitioner" (60)), I have tried to suggest that we can't develop a complex understanding of our subjects or ourselves without taking subjectivity into account. Thomas Newkirk (1991) makes a similar point:

> Teachers need to recognize that the source of their authority comes from their intimate knowledge of the classroom and students, and from intuitions honed by making thousands of judgments and observations of student work. It does not come through deference to expert opinion or through suppressing intuitive resources in favor of more distanced—and academically respectable—means of observation (133).

Taking subjectivity into account does not mean ignoring objectivity. And objective research need not replace subjective understanding. Both are needed to balance the excesses of the other. As Palmer notes, "objectivism tells the world what it is rather than listening to what it says about itself. Subjectivism is the decision to listen to no one except ourselves" (67).

The impetus for this book, like most inquiries conducted by teachers, arises out of my desire to understand *better,* a desire that we inquirers do not expect to assuage fully or completely with any single "been-there-tried-that" effort. For many years, Donald Murray's "subjective speculations" have been propelled by his need to understand (better, differently) how and why writers write. Murray seeks to use his "knowing" to continually push himself into the realm of "not knowing." As he says in *A Writer Teaches Writing*: "I have learned from writing it, and having written it, I will learn to depart from it" (1985, 5). Both Murray and I each seek to deepen our understanding of our respective elephants. But our philosophy and our methods for gaining and evaluating this understanding—as well as communicating it to others—are very different than those employed by the six blind men of Indostan.

The kind of approach to understanding and learning that I am privileging here has much in common with recent work in feminist theory. According to Lisa Heldke, "philosophy is valuable not because it can uncover The Real, but because it can create alternative ways to think about whatever reality it is we've inherited/discovered/created" (1988, 16). Too much emphasis on uncovering the real (and trying to persuade others to our conclusions), as we saw with our six blind men of Indostan, can "hobble efforts to inquire into, and theorize about, our experiences" (16). For Heldke, the ongoing debates over foundationalism and relativism in philosophy prevents feminists from constructing and using theories that are "respectful and representative of the differences in women's experiences without being glib, unreflective or uncritical about these differences" (17). For me, it's the debilitating (and rarely productive) either-or discussions that so frequently occur between composition departments and the rest of the university about personal (subjective) writing versus academic (objective) writing. Perhaps composition should be involved in showing other disciplines how subjectivity and objectivity work together to create a more complex understanding of subject matter. I think Irene Papoulis (1993) is correct when she suggests that composition studies is positioned to play an important role in discussions about teaching and learning throughout the university because "our knowledge about the interaction between intuitive insights and theoretical ideas can help us find ways to allow subjectivity to be part of the academic writing of both women and men" (135). Understanding of self and other, as I have tried to suggest here, translates into better *learning,* learning that is bidirectional and ongoing, learning that enables all of us to develop an ethical agency.

Ethical Features of a Reflexive Pedagogy

Throughout this work, I have intimated that the process of understanding others and ourselves has ethical overtones. I now want to attempt to explain more fully what has led me to this belief by first returning to what Gadamer says about the relationship between understanding and application.

Gadamer's account of understanding borrows from Aristotle's discussion of ethical knowledge as a form of practical knowledge, a kind of knowledge that also includes technical expertise. In her discussion of Gadamer, however, Georgia Warnke points out that ethical knowledge should not be confused with technical knowledge. She notes that it is possible to apply technical expertise unconsciously as a means to an end, in which both means and end are known or predetermined. It is not necessary for individuals to subject their technical skill or knowledge to reflexive questioning—indeed, such a move may forestall or prevent the desired outcome. On the other hand, ethical knowledge is always situation specific and requires conscious interpretation and application. It is a matter of weighing various options against a normative framework that is itself modified or clarified by the options one chooses through a process of ongoing, reflexive dialogue. For this reason, ethical knowledge "never involve[s] simply the application of a formula . . . nor can the desired results be determined in advance of the situation" (Warnke 1987, 94).

Much of the public and many of our students, however, see (and have always seen) reading and writing as *only* a form of technical knowledge, that once learned can be used in any situation in which writing and reading are called for. With the continued growth of computer technology and the increase in the number of technical writing courses, there seems to be an even greater push toward making writing and the teaching of writing—not necessarily more thoughtful—but certainly more technically precise. Given the current intellectual (anti-intellectual?) climate, fueled by the public's growing suspicion and dissatisfaction with institutions of higher learning and the exorbitant cost of education, it's not surprising that we are hearing more demands for efficiency and accountability. Nonetheless in *Teaching Writing as Reflective Practice* (1995), George Hillocks cautions that our emphasis on technical solutions to complex problems is "precisely the wrong move to deal with change" because such solutions suggest that clear answers exist (211). And Mariolina Salvatori observes that "the educational system has consistently opted for simplifying solutions every time it has been confronted with the inherent and inescapable complexity of educational issues" (1996, 452). Technical knowledge is the kind of knowledge that my student Mark is most comfortable with. As we saw in Chapter Two, Mark submitted a computer program as an example of the kind of thinker he was: "you input data into the computer and the computer will give you the answer . . . " But as I have tried to make clear, writing and reading involve more than applying a ready-made knowledge of conventions, rules, and formulas.

When Mindy simply applies a preconceived standard to Lucille, she is not only prevented from understanding the other, her own code of ethics remains tacit and immune to examination or critique. Mindy's difficulty is not with her technical expertise as a writer or reader. She knows how to produce a ready-made thesis. It's already very clear to her: People like Lucille should not work at the nursing home; people like Lucille should leave; society needs to find ways to prevent people like Lucille from ever obtaining the job in the first place. She knows how to construct a coherent paper using her thesis. In writing her early drafts, Mindy applies the means to writing an acceptable paper that have always worked for her in the past (and that will no doubt continue to work for her in many of her other courses). However, I have asked her to use reading and writing not to *solve* the problem of Lucille, but to *find* the problem, to explore it, examine it, complicate it. I have asked her to examine the implications of her composition.

In *Fragments of Rationality* (1992), Lester Faigley draws from the work of Jean-Francois Lyotard's to suggest why the practical knowledge base of composition studies cannot simply be technical expertise. For Lyotard, the phrase is "the basic unit of discourse." The rules for linking various phrases together (I assume for the purpose of making sense) are determined by genre. For any set of phrases, "many genres of linkage are possible . . ." (236). But how do we choose a genre to use if there is no single, external, objective "discourse we can use to validate this choice[?]" (237). The genre we select to link our ideas cannot simply be a technical choice but "requires a momentary delay of those linkages and a questioning of their ethical implications" (239).

Certainly, as Rosemary Gates (1993) reminds us, composition studies, with its emphasis on composing, always entails a process of "putting together." Indeed, most composition texts focus on teaching students how to link their ideas effectively (and *correctly*) according to a predetermined external standard. Even such thoughtful texts as Ann Berthoff's *Forming, Thinking, Writing: The Composing Imagination* (1982) (one of the better composition texts in my opinion because it attempts to provide a philosophical rationale for what it says) only conceives of composition as "a matter of seeing and naming relationships, of putting the relationships together, ordering them" (71). It does not say anything about the importance of examining the relationships themselves.

But now, as Faigley suggests, simply knowing how to compose, how to make connections by forging "new rational relations" between ideas is not enough. There are ethical implications in our linkages that we need to attempt to account for. The ways in which we make sense of the words, ideas, and situations we encounter matter. Rob links Paulo Freire's problem posing theory with the philosophy of his fraternity, while Kay links one of Freire's key ideas to her perception of the homeless. I link Australian work habits to bad business practice and laziness. Emily links Avery's anger to rudeness. What are the implications of these linkages?

As I have emphasized throughout this inquiry, making connections is an important first step in opening a conversation with an other, but it cannot be the last. Our linkages must remain tentative, open to further inquiry. When there is no external, validating discourse that we can agree upon to measure the truth of our linkages (and I would argue even when we think such a discourse exists), then we need to pause again (and again) to examine our connections. Reflexivity enables us to look at the implications of our linkages and to take responsibility for our judgments. In the postmodern world, composition has a dual responsibility: to help students compose an understanding and to assist them in examining the implications of their compositions. As Faigley notes, "Lyotard insists that ethics is also the obligation of rhetoric. It is accepting the responsibility for judgment. It is pausing to reflect on the limits of understanding. It is respect for diversity and unassimilated otherness. It is finding spaces to listen" (239).

At different points in this book, I have paused to examine the implications of my linkages. Now, I want to return to my text and once again attempt to stretch "the limits of my understanding."

Turns of Thought and Provisional Insights

Earlier I showed how my reading of Ralph's paper, "Who Wears the Pants?", changed when I changed the sex of the narrator and the subjects of the paper, Steve and Sheila. Changing the sex changed the way I interpreted the story because of my perception of gender and agency. Such a slick rhetorical move becomes possible when gender is represented as dual, either/or male and female positions.

But the transgendered person occupies the liminal space between and outside of duality. This is a space that is hard for most of us to conceive, let alone represent.[3] Even if I could break conceptually free of gender dichotomies, I would still be imprisoned by a language that offers no easy way out of the binary. My use of "he" to describe Avery is not only inaccurate, it actively distorts the very reality I am trying to understand. At the time of the collaborative inquiry project, Avery was still in the process of publically (pro)claiming her sheness. And, yet, simply reversing the pronouns does not work here, since my prejudices are complicated by my construction of the gender binary itself as well as other factors. In the following exchanges, for example, the speakers' genders seems less significant than their class and culture:

Avery: "How many times do I have to tell you?"

Emily: "[Avery] was downright rude . . . The thing is, yelling doesn't get your point across. If you yell at someone, it's going to make them less inclined to listen . . . [We must] keep our tempers in check and our voices at speaking level, especially when we are in a study lounge and people are trying to study."

Avery: "It is a bourgeois, elitist, intellectualist attitude to think that discussion has to always be quiet, scholarly and rational . . . when people get angry, they tend to be honest about their true feelings. . . ."

Avery: "The country is fucked up beyond belief and would be better off it all fell apart."

Serena: "[I was] very offended . . . I challenge anyone to find a better and more fair justice system in the world."

Even though I noted earlier that anger is often an uncomfortable emotion for women, Emily's reading of Avery's anger and yelling as "rudeness" and Avery's response that Emily's cry for rationality is "bourgeois" seem to be more class inspired than gender specific. In the second exchange, Serena's response to Avery's language and criticism of America seems less the result of her perceiving Avery as male than it is the product of her own middle class ideology. The question I still need to ask myself, though, is if constructing Avery as "she" would have changed the way I read Avery's angry, unyielding stance. If the speaker of the following words is female, does that fact alter my perception of the writer's ethos and, thus, my reception of what she is saying?

> I am struck by the anger which flares up in my writing so often. I like that part of me because I equate it with power, with successfully getting my point across to others . . . This project has helped

me to become proud of my militant edge . . . If you want to get
something done you need to let the world know in no uncertain
terms, that you are a force to be reckoned with. . . .

My reading of Avery's position in the group's collaboration does not
hinge on a preconception of gender in the same way that my reading of Ralph's paper did, since I acknowledge Avery's history of oppression. If I had used "she" to talk about Avery, I don't think I
would have constructed her with less agency than I did. Perhaps the
feminine pronoun might have indicated a slightly less unified self
(since we know Avery's sex is male), and thus moved me closer to a
more accurate representation. But no matter what pronoun I choose,
I am still limited by the language itself which suggests a person
with a *coherent* gender construction.

Now, several years after the collaborative inquiry project, Avery
expresses herself through her gender identification rather than her
sex, but in truth, she is not female: she is *trans;* she is neither/nor;
she is both/and. She resides permanently in the space between.
Unlike some members of the trans community, who seek a way out
of the between by bringing gender and sex in closer alignment via
hormones or surgery, Avery has opted to stay in the space between
(or beyond) gender. As Avery now sees it, the "problem" resides not
with her but with a culture that insists on a male-female binary. Refusing the binary allows her "maximum navigation" for *travelling
between (and beyond) worlds.*

When I first introduced the concept of the between, I noted that
the liminal space of between is sometimes conceived as a frightening
place of nothingness and sensory deprivation, or to use Victor Turner's
ironic and bittersweet characterization, a "no-man's-land." However,
throughout this book I have tried to show why I think the between can
become a potentially positive space, a place of possibility, where the
mood is one of "maybe, might be, as if, hypothesis, fantasy, conjecture,
desire" (Turner 1986, 42). Although it is often challenging to negotiate,
the stranger experience of the between invites reflexivity and offers
the possibility of learning and enlightenment by calling into question
the absolute nature of our understanding. Earlier, I suggested that the
neither/nor experience of the between might operate as a precursory
condition to the both/and perspective of Maria Lugones' concept of
world-travelling; however, I implied these were separate positions.
Avery has now complicated and clarified my understanding of the between. I think it might be more accurate to suggest that "no-man's-
land" and "world-travelling" are not different locations but represent
different *responses* to the same place.

I have depicted the *between* as temporary, a transitional moment, somewhere *between* here and there, *between* self and other. I wrote, "When a person experiences the sensation of being between, she neither belongs to one world or the other. Her previous moorings loosened or disrupted, she temporarily drifts in a liminal sea between worlds." But for Avery (unlike myself and most of the students I have described in this book), there are no previous moorings; the between is not a state Avery is merely passing through on her way to somewhere else; she lives there and has always lived there. Although Avery's location in the between is fixed, her experience of that location is not. Avery shows us both the risk and the generativeness of living in the "fructile chaos" of between.

In Chapter One, I suggested that as a teacher, one of my roles is to provide students with a counterdiscourse. For students who are already comfortably, but uncritically situated in a ready-made and coherent perspective, my job is to nudge them off their perch. For students who are struggling to make sense of their subjects and themselves, my job is to help them restore their center of gravity and come to a new balance. As I have shown, reflexivity usually serves to knock us temporarily off balance. It pushes us into the stranger experience of between. But if we are already in the between, too many nudges may simply induce a state of nonproductive hyperreflexivity. Reflexivity has a positive effect when it pushes us out of stasis, causing us to reorient ourselves, reexamine our position from another perspective, and learn. We see the positive effects of reflexivity for Serena, who writes in her final essay, "Everyone deserves the kind of enlightenment that this project has afforded me." However, Avery is positioned very differently than Serena or Emily. Avery is not comfortably or uncritically perched in the sleep of the cultural mainstream. Her identity is in flux; she is already in motion. I realize now that my wanting her to turn back and examine the position she has only just begun to reach is exactly the wrong response because it is premature. It does not allow Avery enough time to live in this new perspective. Instead of encouraging further learning, I might be preventing it.

Still, my concern, as I noted at the end of Chapter Four, is that by adopting the traditional thesis-driven paper, Avery has chosen a method that doesn't return her to a "new center," but simply takes her back to the illusion of false coherence, the very place she finds so problematic and seeks to critque. A more polyphonic essay could expose the contradictions between the prevailing master narrative and her own lived experience, and put Avery is in a much better position to to both explore and challenge "cultural hierarchies and the notion of a fixed and unified subjecitivity" (Faery 1996, 62).

According to Faigley and Lyotard, the choice of genre matters on both ethical and ideological grounds. I have tried to show why I find the essayistic stance a desirable method and the essay a useful genre for enacting composition's dual purpose. By my definition, the links established by the essay are always open to further inquiry. When readers and writers adopt an essayistic stance and approach to texts, they open rather than fill the space for learning. They can step into this open but bounded space created by the texts they are writing or reading, and discover how these texts might be understood and how they might understand themselves in relation to them, *again and again*. Insights are provisional because truth, notes Adrienne Rich, is a matter of "increasing complexity" (1979, 187).

Although my emphasis in this book is on learning, such a focus should not imply political muteness. Understanding always involves application, and application enlarges understanding. Thomas Harrison suggests that the habit of essayism offers "a paradigm for both thinking and *acting*" (my emphasis, 1992, 4). Adopting this open, dialogic stance does not negate the possibility of taking critical action any more than Peter Elbow's believing stance precludes serious critical doubting. William Zeiger, Paul Heilker, and others have argued that an emphasis on inquiry will lead to stronger critique. I have tried to show why this inquiry needs to be reflexive. The act of turning back on ourselves to examine our own assumptions, to my way of thinking, *is* a political act, as well as an ethical one. To reiterate Elizabeth Minnich once again, "the effort to find out how and why our thinking carries the past with it is part of an ongoing philosophical critique essential to freedom, and to democracy . . . " (1990, 29). Even though I write in the Introduction that my intention "is not to argue for a particular version of reality, but rather to model it and reveal how I came to construct it," in making this claim, I *am arguing* for a particular version of reality.

Notes

1. It would be interesting to explore this notion of the "other within" more thoroughly from a range of perspectives. I am thinking of James Britton's concept of the spectator, for example, George Herbert Meade's idea of the internalized other, Freud's triumvirate of ego, superego, and id, or even through such beliefs as spiritual possession.

2. Tompkins' essay, "'Indians': Textualism, Morality and the Problem of History," originally appeared in *Critical Inquiry* but was anthologized in

our text, *Ways of Reading,* 2nd ed. (1990), edited by David Bartholomae and Anthony Petrosky.

3. Avery shared some of the ways members of the trans community are described: gender-conflicted, gender-variant, gender-disturbed, gender-confused, gender-atypical, gender-outlaw, gender-ambiguous, gender minority, gender-euphoric, gender-dysphoric, gender bender, gender blender, gender transender, gender-neutral, cross-gender, bigender, transgender, gender chameleon, gender identity crisis . . . to name just a few.

References

Alcoff, Linda, and Elizabeth Potter, eds. 1993. *Feminist epistemologies.* New York: Routledge.

Anderson, Chris. 1989. *Literary nonfiction: Theory, criticism, pedagogy.* Carbondale, IL: Southern Illinois University Press.

Anson, Chris. 1989. Response styles and ways of knowing. In *Writing and response: Theory, practice, and research.* Edited by Chris Anson. Urbana, IL: National Council of Teachers of English.

Anzaldua, Gloria. 1987. *Borderlands/la Frontera: The new mestiza.* San Francisco: Aunt Lute Books.

Arendt, Hannah. 1971. *The life of the mind: Thinking.* New York: Harcourt, Brace, and Jovanovich.

Babcock, Barbara. 1980. Reflexivity: Definitions and discriminations. *Semiotica* 30:1–14.

Bakhtin, Mikhail. 1981. *The dialogic imagination.* Edited by Michael Holquist. Austin: University of Texas Press.

Barnes, Douglas. 1975. *From communication to curriculum.* New York: Penguin.

Bartholomae, David, and Anthony Petrosky. 1986. *Facts, artifacts, and counterfacts: Theory and method for a reading and writing course.* Portsmouth, NH: Boynton/Cook.

———. 1993. *Ways of reading: An anthology for writers.* Third ed. Boston: St. Martins.

Bartky, Sandra Lee. 1975. Toward a phenomenology of feminist consciousness. *Social Theory and Practice* 3(4):425–440.

Belenkey, Mary Kay, Blythe McVicker Clinchy, Nancy Rule Goldberger, and Jill Mattuck Tarule. 1986. *Women's ways of knowing: The development of self, voice, and mind.* New York: Basic Books.

Benjamin, Jessica. 1988. *The bonds of love: Psychoanalysis, feminism, and the problem of domination.* New York: Pantheon.

Berlin, James. 1982. Contemporary composition: The major pedagogical theories. *College English* 44:765–777.

————. 1988. Rhetoric and ideology in writing class. *College English* 50: 477–494.

Berthoff, Ann. 1981. *The making of meaning: Metaphors, models, and maxims for writing teachers.* Portsmouth, NH: Boynton/Cook.

————. 1982. *Forming, thinking, writing: The composing imagination.* Portsmouth, NH: Boynton/Cook.

Bleich, David. 1978. *Subjective criticism.* Baltimore. Johns Hopkins University Press.

Brodkey, Harold. 1985. Reading, the most dangerous game. *The New York Times Book Review* 24 November, 1/44–45.

Butrym, Alexander J., ed. 1989. *Essays on the essay: Redefining the genre.* Athens, GA: University of Georgia Press.

Chiseri-Strater, Elizabeth. 1991. *Academic literacies: The public and private discourse of university students.* Portsmouth, NH: Boynton/Cook.

Clark, Gregory. 1994. Rescuing the discourse of community. *College Composition and Communication* 45(1):61–74.

Clifford, John. 1990. Enacting critical literacy. In *The right to literacy.* Edited by Andrea A. Lunsford, Helen Moglen, and James Slevin. New York: Modern Language Association. 255–261.

Code, Lorraine. 1991. *What can she know? Feminist theory and the construction of knowledge.* Ithaca, NY: Cornell University Press.

————. 1993. Taking subjectivity into account. In *Feminist epistemologies.* Edited by Linda Alcoff and Elizabeth Potter. New York: Routledge. 15–48.

Connolly, Paul H. 1981. *On essays: A reader for writers.* Cambridge, MA: Harper and Row.

Connors, Robert J. 1996. Teaching and learning as a man. *College English* 58(2):137–157.

Crusius. Timothy W. 1991. *A teacher's introduction to philosophical hermeneutics.* Urbana, IL: National Council of Teachers of English.

Danto, Arthur. 1990. Are we cracking under the strain? Review of *Modernity on trial,* by Leszek Kolakowski. *The New York Times Book Review* 23 December, 1/22.

Dasenbrock, Reed Way. 1991. Do we write the text we read? *College English* 53:7–18.

————. 1993. A response to 'Language philosophy, writing, and reading: A conversation with Donald Davidson'. *Journal of Advanced Composition* 13:523–528.

Davion, Victoria M. 1991. Integrity and radical change. In *Feminist ethics: Problems, projects, prospects.* Edited by Claudia Card. Lawrence, KA: University Press of Kansas. 180–192.

Delpit, Lisa. 1988. The silenced dialogue: Power and pedagogy in educating other people's children. *Harvard Educational Review* 58:280–298.

Dewey, John. 1929. *The quest for certainty: A study of the relation of knowledge and action.* New York: Minton Balch and Company.

——. 1938. *Experience and education.* New York: Macmillan.

——. 1991. *How we think.* New York: Prometheus Books.

Dewey, John, and Arthur F. Bentley. 1949/1973. Knowing and the known. In *Useful procedures of inquiry.* Edited by Rollo Handy and E. C. Harwood. Great Barrington, MA: Behavioral Research Council. 89–192.

DiCenso, James. 1990. *Hermeneutics and the disclosure of truth: A study in the work of Heidegger, Gadamer, and Ricoeur.* Charlottesville, VA: University Press of Virginia.

Dively, Rhonda Leathers. 1993. Religious discourse in the academy: Creating a space by means of poststructural theories of subjectivity. *Composition Studies/Freshman English News* 21:91–101.

Ede, Lisa, and Andrea Lunsford. 1990. *Singular texts/plural authors: perspectives on collaborative writing.* Carbondale, IL: Southern Illinois University Press.

Elbow, Peter. 1973. *Writing without teachers.* New York: Oxford University Press.

——. 1981. *Writing with power: Techniques for mastering the writing process.* New York: Oxford University Press.

——. 1986. *Embracing Contraries: Explorations in learning and teaching.* New York: Oxford University Press.

Faery, Rebecca Blevins. 1996. Text and context: The essay and the politics of the disjunctive form. In *What do I know? Reading, writing and teaching the essay.* Edited by Janis Forman. Portsmouth NH: Boynton/Cook. 55–68.

Faigley, Lester. 1992. *Fragments of rationality: Postmodernity and the Subject of Composition.* Pittsburgh: University of Pittsburgh Press.

Fish, Stanley. 1980. *Is there a text in this class? The authority of interpretive communities.* Cambridge, MA: Harvard University Press.

Fleischer, Cathy. 1995. *Composing Teacher Research: A Prosaic History.* Albany: State University of New York Press.

Flower, Linda, David L. Wallace, Linda Norris, and Rebecca E. Burnett, eds. 1994. *Making thinking visible: Writing, collaborative planning and classroom inquiry.* Urbana, IL: National Council of Teachers of English.

Freire, Paulo. 1970. *Pedagogy of the Oppressed.* New York: Continuum.

Fuentes, Carlos. 1989. "Sacred truths, novelistic truths." *Harpers* May, 17–18.

Gadamer, Hans Georg. 1989. *Truth and method.* Rev. and trans. by Joel Weinsheimer and Donald G. Marhsall. New York: Continuuum.

Gage, John T. 1986. Why write? In *The teaching of writing: Eighty-fifth yearbook of the National Society for Education.* Edited by Anthony R. Petrosky and David Bartholomae. Chicago: University of Chicago Press. 8–29.

Gannett, Cynthia. 1992. *Gender and the journal: Diaries and academic discourse.* Albany: State University of New York Press.

Gardiner, Judith Kegan. 1993. Toward a feminist theory of self: Repressive dereification and the 'subject-in-process'. *NWSA Journal* 5:303–324.

Gates, Rosemary. 1993. Creativity and insight: Toward a poetics of composition. In *Into the field: Sites of composition studies.* Edited by Anne Ruggles Gere. New York: Modern Language Association.147–158.

Gere, Anne Ruggles, ed. 1993. *Into the field: Sites of composition studies.* New York: Modern Language Association.

Goleman, Daniel. 1995. Brain may tag a value to every perception. *The New York Times* (August 8) B5+.

Good, Graham, ed. 1988. *The observing self: Rediscovering the essay.* New York: Routledge.

Govier, Trudy. 1993. "Self-trust, autonomy and self-esteem." *Hypatia* 8:99–120.

Graff, Gerald. 1992. *Beyond the culture wars: How teaching the conflicts can revitalize American education.* New York: Norton.

Graham, Robert J. 1991. *Reading and writing the self: Autobiography in education and curriculum.* New York: Teachers College Press.

Griffiths, Morwenna, and Margaret Whitford, eds. 1988. *Feminist perspectives in philosophy.* Bloomington, IN: Indiana University Press.

Hairston, Maxine. 1982. The winds of change: Thomas Kuhn and the revolution in the teaching of writing. *College Composition and Communication* 33:76–88.

Hardwick, Elizabeth. 1986. Its only defense: Intelligence and sparkle. *The New York Times Book Review,* 14 September, 1/44–45.

Harrison, Thomas. 1992. *Essayism: Conrad Musil and Pirandello.* Baltimore: Johns Hopkins University Press.

Haskell, Molly. 1989. Review of *Travels with Alice,* by Calvin Trillon. *The New York Times Book Review,* October 22, 10.

Heath, Shirley Brice. 1987. The literate essay: Using ethnography to explode myths. In *Language, literacy and culture: Issues of society and schooling.* Edited by Judith A. Langer. Norwood, NJ: Ablex. 89–107.

———. 1990. The essay and the routines of everyday discourse. Paper presented at the Conference on College Composition and Communication, March, Chicago.

Heilker, Paul. 1996. *The essay: Theory and pedagogy for an active form.* Urbana, IL: National Council of Teachers of English.

Heldke, Lisa. 1988. Recipes for theory making. *Hypatia* 3:15–29.

Higgins, Lorraine, Linda Flower, and Joseph Petraglia. 1992. Planning text together: The role of critical reflection in student collaboration. *Written Communication* 9(1):48–84.

Hillocks, George. 1995. *Teaching writing as reflective practice.* New York: Teachers College Press.

Hirsch, E. D. 1987. *Cultural literacy: What every American needs to know.* Boston: Houghton Mifflin.

Hirsch, Kathleen. 1995. "The return of the essay: A profile of Robert Atwan." *Poets and Writers Magazine* (November/December):31–37.

Holt, John. 1964. *How children fail.* New York: Dell.

Holzman, Michael. 1993. Some thoughts on ethnography as a method for evaluation in education. Paper presented at the Fourteenth Annual Ethnography in Education Research Forum. February, Philadelphia.

Houston, Barbara. 1992. In praise of blame. *Hypatia.* 7:128–147.

Hugo, Richard. 1979. *The triggering town: Lectures and essays on poetry and writing.* New York: Norton.

Hunt, Douglas, ed. 1990. Introduction. *The Dolphin Reader,* 2d ed. Boston: Houghton Mifflin.

Kauffmann, R. Lane. 1989. The skewed path: Essaying as unmethodical method. In *Essays on the essay: Redefining the genre.* Edited by Alexander J. Butrym. Athens, GA: University of Georgia Press. 221–240.

Kegan, Robert. 1982. *The evolving self: Problem and process in human development.* Cambridge, MA: Harvard University Press.

Kent, Thomas. 1993. Language philosophy, writing, and reading: A conversation with Donald Davidson. *Journal of Advanced Composition* 13:1–20.

Kenway, Jane, and Helen Modra. 1992. Feminist pedagogy and emancipatory possibilities. In *Feminisms and critical pedagogy,* edited by Carmen Luke and Jennifer Gore. New York: Routledge. 138–166.

Kintsch, Walter. 1980. Learning from text, levels of comprehension, or: Why anyone would read a story anyway. *Poetics* 9:87–98.

Kitchner, Karen S. 1983. Educational goals and reflective thinking. *Educational Forum.* 75–95.

Knoblauch, C. H., and Lil Brannon. 1984. *Rhetorical traditions and the teaching of writing.* Portsmouth, NH: Boynton/Cook.

Langer, Judith A., and Arthur N. Applebee. 1987. *How writing shapes thinking: A study of teaching and learning.* Urbana, IL: National Council of Teachers of English.

LeFevre, Karen Burke. 1987. *Invention as a social act.* Carbondale, IL: Southern Illinois University Press.

Lewis, Magda, and Roger I. Simon. 1986. A discourse not intended for her: Learning and teaching within the patriarchy. *Harvard Educational Review* 58:457–472.

Lugones, Maria. 1987. Playfulness, 'world'-travelling, and loving perception. *Hypatia* 2:3–19.

MacIntyre, Alasdair. 1984. *After virtue: A study in moral theory,* 2d. ed. Notre Dame: Notre Dame University Press.

McCaffrey, Anne. 1978. *The dragonriders of Pern.* Garden City, NY: Nelson Doubleday.

McCarthy, John A. 1989. *Crossing boundaries: The theory and history of essay writing in German, 1680–1815.* Philadelphia: University of Pennsylvania Press.

McQuade, Donald. 1992. Composition and literary studies. In *Redrawing the boundaries: The transformation of English and American literary studies.* New York: Modern Language Association. 482–529.

Malinowitz, Harriet. 1995. *Textual orientations: Lesbian and gay students and the making of discourse communities.* Portsmouth, NH: Boynton/Cook.

Meier, Deborah. 1995. *The power of their ideas: Lessons for America from a small school in Harlem.* Boston: Beacon Press.

Meyer, Sheree L. 1993. Refusing to play the confidence game: The illusion of mastery in the reading/writing of texts. *College English* 55(1): 46–63.

Minnich, Elizabeth. 1990. *Transforming knowledge.* Philadelphia: Temple University Press.

Montaigne. 1958. *The complete essays of Montaigne,* translated by Donald Frame. Stanford: Stanford University Press. (Original work published 1580–1588.)

Murray, Donald. 1982. The interior view: One writer's philosophy of composition. In *Learning by teaching: Selected articles on writing and teaching.* Edited by Donald M. Murray. Portsmouth, NH: Boynton/Cook. 7–14.

———. 1982. Internal revision: A process of discovery. In *Learning by teaching: Selected articles on writing and teaching,* edited by Donald M. Murray. Portsmouth, NH: Boynton/Cook. 72–87.

———. 1982. The listening eye: Reflections on the writing conference. In *Learning by teaching: Selected articles on writing and teaching.* Edited by Donald M. Murray. Portsmouth, NH: Boynton/Cook.157–163.

———. 1985. *A writer teaches writing.* 2d ed. Boston: Houghton Mifflin.

———. 1990. *Shoptalk: Learning To Write With Writers.* Portsmouth, NH: Heinemann.

———. 1994. Knowing Not Knowing. In *Taking Stock.* Edited by Lad Tobin and Thomas Newkirk. Portsmouth, NH: Boynton/Cook. 57–65.

———. 1995. *The craft of revision.* 2d ed. Fort Worth, TX: Harcourt Brace.

Myerhoff, Barbara, and Deena Metzger. 1980. The journal of activity and genre: Or listening to the silent laughter of Mozart. *Semiotica* 30(1–2):97–114.

Myerhoff, Barbara, and Jay Ruby. 1982. Introduction. In *A crack in the mirror: Reflexive perspectives in anthropology.* Edited by Jay Ruby. Philadelphia: University of Pennsylvania Press. 1–35.

Newkirk, Thomas. 1989. *Critical thinking and writing: Reclaiming the essay.* Urbana, IL: National Council of Teachers of English.

—. 1991. The politics of composition research: The conspiracy against experience. In *The politics of writing instruction: Postsecondary.* Edited by Richard Bullock and John Trimbur. Portsmouth, NH: Boynton/Cook. 119–136.

—., ed. 1993. *Nuts and bolts: A practical guide to teaching college composition.* Portsmouth, NH: Boynton/Cook.

Noddings, Nel. 1984. *Caring: A feminine approach to ethics and moral education.* Berkeley: University of California Press.

Norris, Linda, and Linda Flower. 1994. Creating a context for collaboration: A thumbnail history of the Making Thinking Visible Project. In *Making thinking visible: Writing, collaborative planning, and classroom inquiry.* edited by Linda Flower, David L. Wallace, Linda Norris, and Rebecca E. Burnett. Urbana, IL: National Council of Teachers of English. 23–36.

Oates, Joyce Carol. 1993. Theft. In *Ways of reading: An anthology for writers and readers.* Edited by David Bartholomae and Anthony Petrosky. New York: St. Martins. 381–419.

Onore, Cynthia. 1989. The student, the teacher, and the text: Negotiating meanings through research and revision. In *Writing and response: Theory, practice, and research.* Edited by Chris Anson. Urbana, IL: National Council of Teachers of English. 231–260.

Palmer, Parker. 1983. *To know as we are known: A spirituality of education.* San Francisco: Harper and Row.

Papoulis, Irene. 1993. Subjectivity and its role in "constructed" knowledge: Composition, feminist theory, and psychoanalysis. In *Into the field: Sites of composition studies.* Edited by Anne Ruggles Gere. New York: Modern Language Association. 133–146.

Parker, Robert. 1982. Writing courses for teachers: From practice to theory. *College Composition and Communication* (33)4:411–419.

Percy, Walker. 1993. The loss of the creature. In *Ways of reading: An anthology for writers and readers.* Edited by David Bartholomae and Anthony Petrosky. New York: St. Martins. 423–436.

Peshkin, Alan. 1985. From tide to tide: The evolution of perspective in naturalistic inquiry. *Anthropology and Education Quarterly* 16(3):215–224.

—. 1988a. In search of subjectivity—one's own. *Educational Researcher* 17:17–21.

—. 1988b. Virtuous subjectivity: In the participant-observer's I's. In *The self in social inquiry: Researching methods.* Edited by David N. Berg and Kenwyn K. Smith. Newbury Park, CA: Sage. 267–281.

Peterson-Gonzalez, Meg Joanna. 1991. Vivenicias: Writing as a way into a new language and culture. Ph.D. diss., University of New Hampshire.

Phelps, Louise Wetherbee. 1988. *Composition as a human science:*

Contributions to the self-understanding of a discipline. New York: Oxford University Press.

——. 1989. Images of student writing: The deep structure of teacher response. In *Writing and response: Theory, practice, and research.* Edited by Chris Anson. Urbana, IL: National Council of Teachers of English. 37–67.

——. 1991. Practical wisdom and the geography of knowledge in composition. *College English* 53(8):863–885.

Polanyi, Michael. 1962. *Personal knowledge: Toward a postcritical philosophy.* Chicago: University of Chicago Press.

Qualley, Donna. 1993. Using reading in the writing classroom. In *Nuts and bolts: A practical guide to teaching college composition.* Edited by Thomas Newkirk. Portsmouth, NH: Boynton/Cook. 101–128.

——. 1994. Being in two places at once: Feminism and the development of both/and perspectives. In *Writing and reading (in) the academy: Pedagogy in the age of politics.* Edited by Patricia A. Sullivan and Donna J. Qualley. Urbana, IL: National Council of Teachers of English.

Qualley, Donna, and Elizabeth Chiseri-Strater. 1994. Collaboration as reflexive dialogue: A knowing "deeper than reason." *Journal of Advanced Composition* 14(1):111–130.

Recchio, Thomas E. 1989. A dialogic approach to the essay. In *Essays on the essay: Redefining the genre.* Edited by Alexander J. Butrym. Athens, GA: University of Georgia Press. 271–288.

Rich, Adrienne. 1979. Women and honor: Some notes on lying. In *On lies, secrets, and silences: Selected prose 1966–1978.* New York: Norton.

Rodriguez, Richard. 1993. The achievement of desire. In *Ways of reading: An anthology for writers and readers.* Edited by David Bartholomae and Anthony Petrosky. New York: St. Martins. 481–500.

Rose, Mike. 1989. *Lives on the boundary: The struggles and achievements of America's underprepared.* New York: Free Press.

Rosenblatt, Louise. 1978. *The reader, the text, the poem: Transactional theory of the literary work.* Carbondale, IL: Southern Illinois University Press.

——. 1983. *Literature as exploration,* 4th ed. New York: Modern Language Association.

Ruby, Jay, ed. 1982. *A Crack in the mirror: Reflexive perspectives in anthropology.* Philadelphia: University of Pennsylvania Press.

Salvatori, Mariolina. 1986. The dialogical nature of basic reading and writing. In *Facts, artifacts, and counterfacts: Theory and method for a reading and writing course.* Edited by David Bartholomae and Anthony Petrosky. Portsmouth, NH: Boynton/Cook. 137–166.

——. 1996. Conversations with texts: Reading in the teaching of composition. *College English* 58(4):440–454.

Schildgen, Brenda Deen. 1993. Reconnecting rhetoric and philosophy in the composition classroom. In *Into the field: Sites of composition studies*. Edited by Anne Ruggles Gere. New York: Modern Language Association. 30–43.

Schön, Donald. 1983. The reflective practitioner: How professionals think in action. New York: Basic Books.

Schutz, Alfred. 1971. The stranger: An essay in social psychology. In *School and society: A sociological reader*. London: Routledge and Kegan Paul.

Seller, Ann. 1988. Realism versus relativism: Toward a politically adequate epistemology. In *Feminist perspectives in philosophy*. Edited by Morwenna Griffiths and Margaret Whitford. Bloomington, IN: Indiana University Press. 169–186.

Shekerjian, Denise. 1990. *Uncommon genius: How great ideas are born.* New York: Viking.

Smith, Frank. 1978. *Understanding reading: A psycholinguistic analysis of reading and learning to read.* 2d ed. New York: Holt, Rinehart and Winston.

———. 1990. *To think.* New York: Teachers College Press.

Smith, John K. 1992. Interpretive Inquiry: A Practical and Moral Activity. *Theory Into Practice* 31(2):101–106.

Spellmeyer, Kurt. 1989. A common ground: The essay in the academy. *College English* 51(3):262–276.

———. 1990. Kurt Spellmeyer responds to Charles Bazerman and Susan Miller. *College English* 52(3):334–338.

———. 1993a. A comment on "Democracy, pedagogy, and the personal essay." *College English* 5(1):89–92.

———. 1993b. Being philosophical about composition: Hermeneutics and the teaching of writing. In *Into the field: Sites of composition studies*. Edited by Anne Ruggles Gere. New York: Modern Language Association. 9–29.

———. 1993c. Too little care: Language, politics and embodiment in the life-world. *College English* 55(3):265–283.

Tappen, Mark B. 1991. Narrative, authorship, and the development of moral authority. *New Directions for Child Development* 54:5–25.

Tatum, Beverly Daniel. 1992. Talking about race, learning about racism: The application of racial identity development theory in the classroom. *Harvard Educational Review* 62(1):1–22.

Tetel, Marcel. 1990. *Montaigne.* Updated ed. Boston: Twayne.

Tinder, Glenn. 1980. *Community: Reflections on a Tragic Ideal.* Baton Rouge: Louisiana State University Press.

Tompkins, Jane. 1993. Indians: Textualism, morality, and the problem of history. In *Ways of reading: An anthology for writers and readers*. Edited by David Bartholomae and Anthony Petrosky. New York: St. Martins. 548–602.

Trebilcot, Joyce. 1988. Dyke Methods. *Hypatia* 3(2). 1–13.

Tremmel, Robert. 1993. Zen and the art of reflective practice in teacher education. *Harvard Educational Review* 63(4):434–458.

———. 1994. Beyond self-criticism: Reflecting on teacher research and TA education. *Composition Studies* 22:44–64.

Turner, Victor W. 1985. *On the edge of the bush: Anthropology as experience.* Edited by Edith L. B. Turner. Tuscon: University of Arizona Press.

———. 1986. Dewey, Dilthey, and drama: An essay in the anthropology of experience. In *The anthropology of experience.* Edited by Victor W. Turner and Edward M. Bruner. Urbana, IL: University of Chicago Press. 33–44.

Turner, Victor W., and Edward M. Bruner, eds. 1986. *The anthropology of experience.* Urbana, IL: University of Chicago Press.

Vygotsky, Lev. 1962. *Thought and language.* Edited and translated by Eugenia Hanfmann and Gertrude Vakar. Cambridge: MIT Press.

———. 1978. *Mind in society: The development of higher psychological processes.* Edited by Michael Cole, Vera John-Steiner, Sylvia Scribner, and Ellen Souberman. Cambridge: Harvard University Press.

Wallace, David L. 1994. Teaching collaborative planning: Creating a social context for writing. In *Making thinking visible: Writing, collaborative planning, and classroom inquiry.* Edited by Linda Flower, David L. Wallace, Linda Norris, and Rebecca E. Burnett. Urbana, IL: National Council of Teachers of English. 48–66.

Warnke, Georgia. 1987. *Gadamer: Hermeneutics, tradition, and reason.* Stanford: Stanford University Press.

———. 1993. Feminism and hermeneutics. *Hypatia* 8(1):81–97.

Woolf, Virginia. 1929. *A room of one's own.* New York: Harcourt Brace Jovanovich.

Wright, Richard. 1945. *Black boy: A record of childhood and youth.* New York: Harper.

Wyschogrod, Edith. 1990. *Saints and postmodernism: Reinvisioning moral philosophy.* Chicago: University of Chicago Press.

Young, Iris Marion. 1986. The ideal of community and the politics of difference. *Social Theory and Practice* 12(1):1–26.

Zeiger, William. 1985. The exploratory essay: Enfranchising the spirit of inquiry in college composition. *College English* 47(5):454–466.

———. 1989. The personal essay and egalitarian rhetoric. In *Literary nonfiction: Theory, criticism, pedagogy.* Edited by Chris Anderson. 235–244. Carbondale, IL: Southern Illinois University Press.

Index

acceptance, uncritical
    of essayistic reading, 68–69
    of ready-made beliefs, 62
    vs. reflexivity, 144–145
agency, *See also* ethical agency
    coming to voice and, 114
    ethical, in collaborative inquiry,
        112–117
    false sense of, 145
    reflexive, 113
    sense of, 145–146
    teacher subjectivity and, 87
analytic writing, learning and, 32
anger
    coming to voice and, 114
    women's attitudes toward, 111
Anzaldua, Gloria, 140
Applebee, Arthur N., 31–32
Arendt, Hannah, 139
Aristotle, 154
Atwan, Robert, 4
authentic learning, 40–41

Babcock, Barbara, 13
Bacon, Francis, 44
Bakhtin, Mikhail, 66, 149
Barnes, Douglas, 10
Bartholomae, David, 62–63, 68, 75,
    147, 150
Benjamin, Jessica, 24
Berlin, James, 3, 133
Berthoff, Ann, 156
between
    defined, 10–11
    in educational process, 22
    as potentially positive space, 158–
        159
    vs. world-travelling, 96, 160
bidirectional process
    of education, 150

essayistic reading, 70
    of personal essays, 42
blame, expressing, 114–116
Booth, Wayne, 67
*Borderlands/La Frontera: The New
    Mestiza* (Anzaldua), 140
Britton, James, 81
Brodkey, Harold, 60–61, 75

certainty, essayistic stance and, 132–
    135
change
    ease of, 19
    nature of, 21
    process theory, 20–21
Chiseri-Strater, Elizabeth, 101
Clark, Gregory, 72, 112–113, 114, 119
Code, Lorraine, 27–30, 73, 84, 149,
    151–154
collaborative inquiry
    essayistic stance, 95–96, 107–112
    ethical agency, 112–117
    group members, 99–101
    openness to dialogue and, 99
    process, 95, 99, 101–136
    reflexivity and, 94–112
    student antagonism toward, 98
    topic choice, 101–106
    understanding difference through
        connection, 118–124
    understanding as product of, 124–
        126
    value of, 95–96, 100
    world-travelling and, 96–99
    written products of, 124–136
common ground
    dialogue and, 47
    in essayistic reading, 71–72
    finding by noting differences, 76–
        79

communication, anger and, 111
Community: Reflections on a Tragic Ideal (Tinder), 106
composition as reflexive inquiry, 3
composition studies
  implications of compositions, 4–5
  process emphasis in, 156
  role of, 155
  technical knowledge and, 155–156
  traditional approach, 3–4
comprehension
  defined, 13, 62–63
  effect of writing on, 32
  vs. learning, 12, 61–63
  without reflexivity, 68, 75
conclusions, ready-made, 35, 39, 56–59
Condition of Postmodernity, The (Harvey), 21
confidence, false sense of, 145
conflicts, teaching the, 142–144
confronting differences, 112
connections, *See also* relationships
  in essayistic reading, 70–71
  ethical implications, 156–157
  with texts, 147
  understanding differences through, 118–124
Connolly, Paul, 5
Connors, Robert, 88–89
conversational reading, 65
counterdiscourse
  defined, 141
  encouraging engagement with other through, 10, 138–141, 159
  subjectivity of, 86–87
Crack in the Mirror, A (Myerhoff and Ruby), 13
critical mind, vs. essayistic mind, 67
critical reading, vs. essayistic reading, 89–92
critical thinking
  defined, 23
  as a disposition, 42
  reflexivity and, 17
critics, 17
Cross, William, 103
Crusius, Timothy, 87
cultural differences
  shifting between, 96–97
  "stranger" concept, 9–10
  transition between, writing and, 33–34
cynics, 17

Dasenbrock, Reed Way, 71–72
Davidson, Donald, 72–73, 93–94
Davion, Victoria, 41, 113, 133
Dead Man Walking, 145
defensiveness, 143–144
Delpit, Lisa, 83, 124
democratic dialogue, 74, *See also* dialogue
detachment, reflection and, 13
Dewey, John, 20, 43
dialectical encounters, 11, 146
dialogic reading, 65
dialogue, 146–150
  authentic, 74
  avoiding, 148–149
  connections and, 119
  democratic, 74
  genuine, 146–147
  internal (soundless), 139–140
  learning and, 47, 149
  openness to, 99, 107–111
  productive, 147, 150
  reflexivity and, 149–150
  relativism vs., 148–149
  teacher encouragement of, 147–150
  value of, 147, 149
  written, 149
differences
  confronting, 112
  deference to, 118
  finding common ground through, 78–79
  identifying with, 120
  understanding through connections, 118–124
disapproval, expressing, 115–116
discovery
  of relations between ideas, 58
  writing for, 33, 34–36
Dively, Rhonda Leathers, 63–64
diversity, *See also* cultural differences
  conceding, 148

earned insights, 35–37
  in reading, 63–64
  vs. ready-made conclusions, 38
  through noting differences, 78–79
  through writing, 35–40
education
  lack of critical self-reflexivity in, 138
  nature of educative experiences, 13

racism and, 129–130
reeducation, openness to dialogue
and, 99
egalitarian essay form, 134, 137
egalitarian pluralism, 134
Elbow, Peter, 35, 141, 160
empathy, understanding differences
through, 118–119
engagement
dialectical, 11
encouraging through counterdiscourse, 141, 159
with other, 11, 139–141, 159
epistemic beliefs, 12
epistemology, reflexive pedagogy features, 152–155
essayism
defined, 43–44
as discovery of relations between
ideas, 58
as process, 53–54
value of, 160
essayistic mind, vs. critical mind, 67
essayistic reading, 62–67
as bidirectional, 70
characteristics of, 64–67
vs. critical reading, 89–92
defined, 68
making connections in, 70–71
offensive attack vs., 66–67
openness to dialogue and, 99
as risky, 70
role of, 6
subjective experience and, 71
teachers and, 82–92
uncritical acceptance vs., 66–67
essayistic stance, See also open stance;
tentative stance
certainty and, 132–135
in collaborative inquiry, 94–95,
106–112
conveying in compositions, 4–5
defined, 3
ethical agency and, 114–115
lack of openness and, 107
moving toward, 58
persuasive writing and, 132–135
reader's perspective, 60
teaching, 142–144
value of, 5, 160
essayistic writing, See also essays; personal essays

openness to dialogue and, 99,
107–111
research papers vs., 131–135
role of, 5
essays, See also essayistic writing; personal essays
defined, 43
as egalitarian form, 134, 137
formal, 44
frame of reference in, 50
informal, 44
objectivity in, 45
open-ended nature of, 45
personal experience in, 131–132
preconceived theory in, 46, 52–54
products of collaborative inquiry,
126–136
research, 131–132
subjectivity in, 45
value of writing, 40
as a verb, 44
ethical agency, See also agency
in collaborative inquiry, 112–117
expressing disapproval, 115–116
importance of, 144
for marginalized people, 114–117
ethical deference
defined, 112–113
to differing others, 117
vs. expressing disapproval, 115–
116
reflexivity of, 113
ethical knowledge
defined, 154
technical knowledge vs., 154–155
understanding and, 154–157
eureka moment, 151
Evolving Self, The (Kegan), 20–21
experience
educative, 13
life-learning (lle), 33–36
personal, 132–133
stranger, 10
subjective, 71
Experience and Education (Dewey), 20

Facts, Artifacts and Counterfacts (Bartholomae and Petrosky), 63
Faigley, Lester, 18, 19, 21, 155–157, 160
feminist theory, 153–154
Fish, Stanley, 64
fixity, 29

Forming, Thinking, Writing: The Composing Imagination (Berthoff), 155
Fragments of Rationality (Faigley), 18, 155–156
frame of reference, 49
Freire, Paulo, 65, 67, 77, 79, 80, 81, 147
    student responses to, 67–75
From Communication to Curriculum (Barnes), 10
"From Dialogue to Dialectic" (Qualley), 22
Frost, Robert, 138
fructile chaos, 11, 159
Fuentes, Carlos, 133
Fulgrum, Robert, 146

Gadamar, Hans Georg, 68, 73, 154
Gage, John, 34, 42
Gardiner, Judith Kegan, 21
Gates, Rosemary, 155
gender
    expression of anger and, 111
    pedagogic issues, 157–161
    subjectivity based on, 83–88, 90
gender identity
    pedagogic issues, 158
    transgender, 100, 158
Goleman, Daniel, 141
Good, Graham, 82, 113
Gould, Steven Jay, 58
Govier, Trudy, 145
Graff, Gerald, 142–143
Graves, Donald, 89

Hairston, Maxine, 19–20
Hardwick, Elizabeth, 46
Harpers, 133
Harrison, Thomas, 53, 160
Harvey, David, 21
Haskell, Molly, 43
Havel, Vaclav, 137
Heilker, Paul, 133–134, 160
Heldke, Lisa, 153
Helm, Janet, 103, 104
hermeneutic theory, 64–65, 73, 87–88
hidden prejudices, 129
Hillocks, George, 154
Hirsch, E. D., 64
Houston, Barbara, 114, 115
How Writing Shapes Thinking (Langer and Applebee), 31–32
Hugo, Richard, 56

Hunt, Douglas, 49
hyperreflexivity, 21–22, 159

illumination, temporary, 40, 113
individuality, loss of, in education, 18
inquiry, *See also* reflexive inquiry
    defined, 3
    reading as form of, 60
    tentative stance in, 134–135
"In Search of Our Mother's Gardens" (Walker), 75–79
insights, earned. *See* earned insights. 35–37
integrity, development of, 41
internal dialogue, 139–140
internal revision, 35, 36
interpretive charity, 71–72
    unchecked, 73–75
interviews, engagement with other and, 140–141

James, William, 20
journals, vs. personal essays, 42–43
judgment
    subjectivity and, 25
    unconscious, 141–142
Jungle Fever, 123

Kegan, Robert, 20–21
Kenway, Jane, 149–150
Kitchner, Karen, 12
knowing
    objective knowledge as, 28
    vs. understanding, 27–28
"Knowing Not Knowing" (Murray), 153
knowledge
    objectivity and subjectivity in, 27–30
    of other people, acquiring, 28–29
    self-criticism and, 29
    of subjects, acquiring, 28

"labor-intensive" reading, 63
Langer, Judith A., 31–32
learner's stance, 2, 107
learning
    authentic, 40–41
    comprehension vs., 13, 61–62
    as continuing inquiry, 82
    defined, 12–13
    dialogue and, 149
    effect of writing on, 31–32

lifelong, 82
   pre-understanding and, 65–66
   by teachers, 89
   though personal essays, 40–46
LeFevre, Karen Burke, 139
Lewis, Magda, 111
life-learning experiences. *See* lles (life-learning experiences)
lifelong learning, 82
liminality, 11
linkages, *See also* connections
   ethical implications, 156–157
listening, factors involved, 110
"Listening Eye, The: Reflections on the Writing Conference" (Murray), 1–2
Lives on the Boundary (Rose), 83
lles (life-learning experiences)
   earned insights through, 35–36
   personal use of, 34
   writing, 33–34
"Loss of the Creature, The (Percy), 70
Lugones, Maria, 96–98, 108, 146, 158
Lyotard, Jean-Francois, 155–156, 160

McCaffrey, Ann, 10
McCarthy, John, 44, 61
MacIntyre, Alasdair, 112
McPeck, John, 42
McQuade, Donald, 31
Malinowitz, Harriet, 138
Malone, Anne, 84
marginalized people, ethical agency for, 114–117
marking texts, 147
meaning, discovering through writing, 34–37, 38–40
Meier, Deborah, 119
metacognition, 12
metacommentaries, student reflections on, 79–82
Metzger, Deena, 11, 43
Meyer, Sherrie, 145
Minnich, Elizabeth, 14, 23–24, 113, 134, 147, 160
Modra, Helen, 149–150
Montaigne, 42, 44
Murray, Donald, 1–2, 13, 29, 35, 89, 139, 152, 153
Myerhoff, Barbara, 11, 13, 43, 70

Newkirk, Thomas, 35, 39–40, 152–153

Noddings, Nel, 112

Oates, Joyce Carol, 71, 81, 150
objectification, 69–70
objective knowledge, *See also* knowledge
   as knowing, 27
objective reality, 22–23
objectivity
   in essays, 45
   subjectivity and, 26–27, 73–75, 153–154
   value of, 152
Onore, Cynthia, 138
open-endedness, in essays, 45
openness
   to dialogue, 99, 106–110
   ethical, 112–117
open stance, 141–145, *See also* essayistic stance; tentative stance
   consciously adopting, 141
   defensive response to, 143–143
   modeled by teachers, 142–143
   other and, 141
   in reading, 66–67
   teaching, 142
opinions, respect for, 109–110
other
   counterdiscourse and, 141
   defined, 139
   differing, deference to, 117
   educative experiences and, 13
   engagement with, 11, 139–141, 159
   ethical agency for, 115–118
   open stance and, 141
   overriding self by, 88
   reading as encounter with, 61
   reflexivity and, 139–142
   resistance to, 84
   self-monitoring engagement with, 140
   subjectivity toward, 87–88
   surrender of self to, 88
   teacher encouragement of engagement with, 140–141
   teachers as, 141

Palmer, Parker, 23, 24, 26, 96, 142, 146, 148–149
Papoulis, Irene, 25, 153
passing theories, 72

Pedagogy of the Oppressed (Freire), 65, 67
Percy, Walker, 70, 150
personal essays, *See also* essayistic writing; essays
  bidirectional focus in, 42
  defined, 42
  finding and creating meaning through, 42–43
  vs. journals, 42–43
  learning through, 40–46
  perennial dialectic in, 43
  subjectivity in, 42
personal experience, *See also* experience
  in essays, 131–132
persuasive writing, essayistic stance in, 132–134
Peshkin, Alan, 29, 83
Peterson-Gonzalez, Meg, 32–35
Petrosky, Anthony, 62, 63, 75, 147, 150
Phelps, Louise, 25
phrases, 155–156
Plato, 139
postmodern theory, 21
power, *See also* agency
  sense of agency and, 144–146
"practical wisdom," 25
preconceptions
  essaying and, 46, 51–53
  gender-based, 84–88
prejudices
  distinguishing between enabling and disabling, 87–88
  hidden, 129
  learning and, 65
  teacher subjectivity, 84–88
  understanding, 127–130
pre-understanding, learning and, 64–65
prior theories, altering with passing theories, 72
process, essayism as, 53–54
process theory, 19–24
proximity factor, 150
pseudoindependent position, 104, 117

questions, learning to ask, 123, 124

racial discrimination, 105
racial identity development, 103
racism
  choosing as topic of collaborative inquiry, 103–106

education and, 129–130
  subtle, 120, 127
  understanding connections through differences, 118–124
  writing about, as result of collaborative inquiry, 126–136
reading
  conversational, 65
  dialogic, 65
  earned insights in, 63–64
  essayistically, 62–67
  as form of inquiry, 60
  "labor-intensive," 63
  multiple, of same text, 65
  open, 66–67
  reflexivity and, 60–93
  risky, 60–61, 70
  sequences of, 150–151
  tentative, 66
"reading against the grain," 75
reading comprehension. *See* comprehension
"reading with the grain," 75
ready-made conclusions, 35
  vs. earned insights, 39
  learning to move beyond, 54–58
  uncritical acceptance of, 62
reality, seeking, 22–23, 153
reasoning process, reader participation in, 134
Recchio, Thomas E., 45
recursiveness, 149–150
reeducation, openness to dialogue and, 99
reflection
  critical self-awareness of, 13–14
  detachment and, 13
  reflexivity vs., 11–14, 17, 39
  value of, 138
reflective memos, 95
reflexive inquiry
  defined, 3
  learning to ask hard questions, 123, 124
  understanding gained from, 124–126
  value of, 5
reflexive pedagogy, 137–161
  epistemological features of, 151–154
  ethical features of, 154–157
  practical features of, 138–151

agency, 145–146
dialogue, 146–150
open stance, 141–145
other, 140–142
recursiveness, 149–150
reflexivity
collaborative inquiry and, 95–113
comprehension and, 69, 75
defined, 138
degrees of, 121
development of, 81
dialogue and, 149–150
of ethical deference, 113
ethical knowledge and, 154–157
hyperreflexivity, 21–22, 159
lack of, 68, 75, 138
learning and, 41
metacognition, 12
noting differences and, 120
process, 13–23
propensity for, 41–42
reading and, 60–93
reflection vs., 11–14, 17, 38
role of, 160–161
self-consciousness and, 13–14
stranger experience and, 10, 159
subjectivity and, 24–25, 92
threatening, 123–125
value of, 6, 91–92, 159–160
world-travelling and, 97
writing and, 31–60
relationships, *See also* connections
between ideas, 58
ethical implications, 156
relativism, 148–149
research essays, essayist papers vs.,
131–135
respect for opinions, 110–111
revision
internal, 35, 36
value of, 59
Rich, Adrienne, 111, 160
risky reading, 60–61, 70
Rodriguez, Richard, 70, 80, 81, 150
Rose, Mike, 83
Ruby, Jay, 13, 24–25, 70
Rushdie, Salmon, 133

sacred texts, 133
Salvatori, Mariolina, 138, 140, 147, 154
Saxe, John Godfrey, 22
scheme of reference, 9

Schildgen, Brenda Deen, 82–82
Schon, Donald, 3
Schutz, Alfred, 9
secular texts, 133
self-consciousness, 13–14
self-criticism, 17, 29
self-knowledge, 134
self-reflection, 11
self-trust, 145
Seller, Ann, 24
Shoptalk: Learning to Write With Writers (Murray), 151
Simon, Roger, 111
Smith, Frank, 12–13, 32, 42, 50, 61–62, 64, 75
Smith, John K., 1
soundless dialogue, 139
Spellmeyer, Kurt, 41, 44, 45, 47, 99, 109, 135
Spiegelberg, Herbert, 92
stereotyped people, ethical agency for, 114–117
"stranger" metaphor, 9–10, 159
encounter with other and, 140–141
openness to, 143
subjective Is, 83–84, 91
"subjective speculations," 152, 153
subjectivity, 24–30
essayistic reading and, 71
in essays, 42, 45
gender-based, 84–88, 90
ignoring, 29
importance of, 24
objectivity and, 26–27, 73–75, 153–155
reflexivity and, 92
self-knowledge through, 134
of students, 25–27
of teachers, 24, 82–84, 86, 91–92
understanding and, 151–153
subtle racism, 120, 127

tacit knowledge, 64
"Taking Subjectivity into Account" (Code), 27
Tatum, Beverly, 103
teachers
counterdiscourse introduced by, 86–87, 159
critical vs. essayistic reading by, 89–92

dialogue encouraged by, 147–150
engagement with other encouraged by, 141–142
essayistic reading and, 82–92
individuality and, 18
as learners, 89
open stance modeled by, 142–143
as other, 141
reading sequence selected by, 150–151
subjectivity of, 24, 82–84, 86, 91–92
"teaching the conflicts," 142–143
"Teaching and Learning as a Man" (Connors), 88–89
Teaching as Reflective Practice (Hillocks), 154
technical knowledge, ethical knowledge vs., 154–155
temporary illumination, 40, 113
tentative stance, *See also* essayistic stance; open stance
consciously adopting, 141
in inquiry, 134–135
in reading, 66
Tetel, Marcel, 31, 40
texts
making connections with, by marking, 147
reflexive reading of, 64
sacred, 133
secular, 133
vs. textbooks, 64
"Theft" (Oates), 71
thesis-support papers, 131–135
Tinder, Glenn, 106
Tompkins, Jane, 143
topics, choosing for collaborative inquiry, 101–106
Transforming Knowledge (Minnich), 23–24
transgender, 100, 161n
pedagogic issues, 157–161
transsexuals, 100
"truth," writing to convince people of, 132–134
Turner, Victor, 11, 158

uncritical acceptance
of essayistic reading, 66–67
of ready-made beliefs, 63

understanding
vs. knowing, 27–28
process of, reflexive pedagogy and, 151–154, 160
as product of collaborative inquiry, 124–126
subjectivity and, 152
unlearning, 13, 99

Vivencias: Writing as a Way into a New Language and Culture (Peterson-Gonzalez), 33
voice, coming to, agency and, 114
Vygotsky, Lev, 139

Walker, Alice, 75–79
Warnke, Georgia, 60, 73, 94, 146, 154
Ways of Reading (Bartholomae and Petrosky), 150
What Can She Know (Code), 27
"Winds of Change, The: Thomas Kuhn and the Revolution in Teaching of Writing" (Hairston), 19–20
women. *See* gender
Woolf, Virginia, 8
world-travelling, 96–99, 146, 158
openness to dialogue and, 99
Writer Teaches Writing, A (Murray), 151, 152, 153
writing
acquiring knowledge of, 29
discovery through, 34–40
earned insights through, 35–40
learning and, 31–32
practice, effects of, 37
reflexivity and, 31–60
student self-review of, 79–82
teaching of, 2–3
written dialogue, 149
written products, of collaborative inquiry, 126–136
Wyschogrod, Edith, 112, 119

Young, Iris, 72

Zeiger, William, 137, 160